PROPHETS, GURUS, AND PUNDITS

PROPHETS, GURUS, & PUNDITS

Rhetorical Styles & Public Engagement

Anna M. Young

Southern Illinois University Press
Carbondale

17 16 15 14   4 3 2 1

Library of Congress Cataloging-in-Publication Data
Young, Anna M., 1975–
Prophets, gurus, and pundits : rhetorical styles and public engagement
/ Anna M. Young.
   pages cm.
Includes bibliographical references and index.
   ISBN 978-0-8093-3294-6 (pbk.)
   ISBN 0-8093-3294-9 (pbk.)
   ISBN 978-0-8093-3295-3 (ebook)
   ISBN 0-8093-3295-7 (ebook)
1. Rhetoric. 2. Public speaking. 3. Oral communication. I. Title.
P301.Y66 2014
808.5—dc23   2013025797

Printed on recycled paper. ♻

The paper used in this publication meets the minimum requirements
of American National Standard for Information Sciences—Permanence
of Paper for Printed Library Materials, ANSI Z39.48-1992. ∞

For Calynn and Campbell, who make the world a better place

CONTENTS

ACKNOWLEDGMENTS

I am grateful to so many people for their contributions, their wisdom, and their support as I wrote this book. Like a nervous actor at the Oscars, I am afraid to miss any names. For his advice for more than a decade, I thank Barry Brummett, the White Wizard. For their editing genius, mentorship, and friendship, I thank Brad Vivian, the Rhizome, and Dan Brouwer. For inspiring much of my current scholarship, I thank the four just mentioned, as well as Dana Cloud, Rick Cherwitz, Chuck Morris, Rob Asen, and Rosa Eberly. For their work connecting scholars with communities, I thank Rick Cherwitz, Tommy Darwin, and Rob Wells. For setting the bar, for friendship, for laughs, and for unending support, I thank my friends but especially Jaime Lane Wright, Johanna Hartelius, and Jessica Moore. For being my advocate for nearly twenty years, I thank John Sloop. For taking the kids while I went down to the coffee shop to write in peace and on deadline, for believing in me, for cheering me on, I thank my husband, Tim Duggan. For a lifetime of support and encouragement, I thank my parents, Julia and Mike Young, and my sister, Laura Young.

PROPHETS, GURUS, AND PUNDITS

INTRODUCTION: RECLAIMING
ENGAGEMENT THROUGH STYLE

In a June 5, 2009, column for CNN.com titled "Don't Hold Obama to Race Agenda," Melissa Harris-Lacewell, associate professor of African American studies at Princeton University, takes her black intellectual colleagues to task about their puzzling treatment of the Obama presidency. She wonders, "One might suspect that [radio personality Tavis] Smiley would be enthusiastic about the opportunities presented by America's election of a black president. Instead, Smiley seems annoyed" (2009). Harris-Lacewell is responding, in part, to Tavis Smiley's recent documentary *Stand*, where he is joined by prominent intellectuals Cornel West and Michael Eric Dyson, both members of Smiley's Soul Patrol, on a bus sojourn through the American south. In *Stand*, these intellectuals "appropriated the legacy of Martin Luther King, Jr. to implicitly claim they, not Obama, are the authentic representatives of the political interests of African-Americans" (Don't Hold, 2009). Calling the film an enormous disappointment, Harris-Lacewell chides the false analogy between her colleagues and King: "It was not King's intellectual capacity or verbal dexterity that made him an effective advocate for racial issues; it was his own accountability to that movement" (Don't Hold, 2009). In other words, King's efficacy resided in his material involvement as a *member* of the civil rights movement, not just as one of its leaders—he was *one of them*. And, as Harris-Lacewell is quick to point out, Smiley and his Soul Patrol are largely untethered to the black constituency. The freedom-riding intellectuals in *Stand* are mostly "public personalities . . . backed by powerful corporations, like Wal-Mart and Nationwide, that have troubled relationships with these communities," while "[t]he college profs on the bus are comfortably supported by well-endowed universities" (Don't Hold, 2009). The limits of

1

this analogy between contemporary public intellectuals and King highlight the troubling nature of the relationship between intellectuals and
the broader culture—today's intellectuals often view themselves as lone
discoverers (Cherwitz, 2001) and distant observers (Dyson, 2003) rather
than as participants in the sociopolitical conditions of the public sphere.

Further proof of this worrying disconnect between intellectual and
public life can be found in the 2009 scandal involving the arrest of Harvard professor and public intellectual Henry Louis Gates Jr. outside his
Cambridge home. On July 16, 2009, Gates returned from a research trip
to China only to find he misplaced his house key. He and his driver used
physical force to open the door of his home, leading a neighbor to call
and report a possible break-in. The Cambridge police responded, a verbal argument ensued, and Gates was arrested. The police report reads,
"Henry Gates, Jr. was placed under arrest at Ware Street, after being
observed exhibiting loud and tumultuous behavior, in a public place,
directed toward a uniformed police officer who was present investigating
a report of a crime in progress" (Cantabridgia, 2009). History may write
this narrative in a number of ways: Henry Louis Gates Jr. is a civil rights
hero who became something of a martyr for racial profiling by police
departments in America. Gates is an arrogant Harvard elitist who tried
to use his academic status to bully law enforcement. The story that will
not get told is that despite Gates being one of the nation's most admired
and celebrated public intellectuals, Cambridge police and even his own
neighbor *have no idea who Gates is.*

So what? Why should it matter that prior to the Beer Summit on the
White House lawn, most Americans had no idea who Gates is? Why
should anyone waste time disconcerted by the lack of authentic connection Smiley has with the constituency he claims to lead? Why does any of
this matter? This book is not about bus rides and beer, though I generally
like both. It is about the role and potential of public intellectuals in the
public sphere. And, it is about rhetorical style. Merging these concepts,
this book explores the ways in which rhetorical style, in general, illuminates our history, our values, and our social mores. Distinctively, public
intellectual rhetorical style articulates the possibility of a more agentic,
activist intellectual elite, a significantly positive, proactive step on a path
to greater engagement and efficacy in political and social life. As noted
economist James K. Galbraith argues, "Some scholarship is intrinsically
apolitical but social scholarship can't be. The policies I support grow
from my ethical and political beliefs, to which my expertise (such as it
is) merely adds an element of engineering" (2004). In an era where what

is loud and soulless and fits on a bumper sticker often trumps what is introspective, meaningful, and thoughtful, public intellectual rhetorical style enables us to conceive a way to reclaim public discourse and harness it for social benefit rather than ratings bonanzas. As the University of Texas' Intellectual Entrepreneurship founder, Richard Cherwitz (2005), contends, "We have the ethical obligation to discover and put to work knowledge that makes a difference."

In thinking about intellectuals going public, we need to reexamine the project of the intellectual, in general. I come to the question of public intellectuals from a rhetorical perspective and ground this book in the rhetorical tradition as situated in the Communication discipline. However, the conversations about public intellectuals and the public sphere are multidisciplinary and transdisciplinary. For most of Western civilization's history, intellectuals of all stripes, but rhetoricians in particular, played active roles both as members and leaders of broader public constituencies (Hartelius & Cherwitz, 2010; Young, Battaglia, & Cloud, 2010; Cherwitz & Hartelius, 2007). We see in Ekaterina Haskins's work on Isocrates that he "accents his role as an *agent of knowledge*" (emphasis added) in opposition to the "theoretical detachment" Plato advocated (2004, p. 5). John Dewey, for instance, argues, "Socially engaged intellectuals must accept reality as they found it and shape it toward positive social goals, not stand aside in self-righteous isolation" (Boydston, 1990, p. 169). In her later essay "Public Rights and Private Interests," Hannah Arendt affirms that public engagement is not a means to an end but an end in itself; intellectuals, like all citizens, must engage in public life to realize intrinsic political principles like freedom, justice, equality and solidarity (in Parekh, 2008). Most notable is that she connects *agency* with public and political *action*. Antonio Gramsci advanced that "the mode of being of the new intellectual can no longer consist in eloquence but in active participation in practical life, as constructor, organizer, and 'permanent persuader,' and not just a simple orator" (1971, p. 3).

Amatai Etzioni and Alyssa Bowditch (2006) trace the decline in public engagement on the part of intellectuals in large part to the rising costs of living in New York in gracious poverty. The break between intellectuals and publics also was hastened during McCarthyism's intellectual witch hunts, which drove the vast majority of intellectuals into the academy, seeking the protective cover of tenure against the frothing-at-the-mouth invective and professional ruin of commie hunters. Now colleges and universities are, in the last few decades, some of the only places to find intellectual work, and today's "Younger intellectuals . . . direct themselves to professional colleagues but are inaccessible and unknown to others" (Jacoby, 1987, p. 7), meaning the public sphere is increasingly devoid of intellectuals who actually speak a public vernacular. Rather, intellectual life today is almost entirely confounded with academic life. Little by little, these intellectuals insulated themselves and ceased to write for, or even speak to, a broader audience (Bawer, 1998; Brouwer & Squires, 2003). Thus, as we continue to train new generations of intellectuals to write for, speak to, and work with their disciplinary peers rather than broader public constituencies, not only do we continue the cycle of intellectual isolation but we also accelerate our irrelevance to public life. In a 2004 response to a now-infamous op-ed by Stanley Fish, Michael Burawoy, former president of the American Sociological Association and professor at the University of California at Berkeley, wrote, "Academics are living in a fool's paradise if they think they can hold onto their ivory tower. . . . The chickens are coming home to roost as the public is no longer interested in our truth, no longer prepared to subsidize our academic pursuits. . . . We have to demonstrate our public worth" (2004, p. B24). An increasing corporatization of the academy, demand for intellectuals to secure external funding, and financial crises at the state and federal levels devastating institutional bottom lines, among other issues, lead all of us to consider the relevance, reach, and impact of our work. What will the academy support? What is our social contract? What is the relationship between what we do for a living and who we are as citizens?

Today we hear the echoes of Jean-Jacques Rousseau's lamentation, "We have physicians, mathematicians, chemists, astronomers, poets, musicians, painters, but we no longer have citizens" (1750). Of course, it stands to reason that intellectuals would be attracted by academic careers where they can interact with the best and the brightest, write and study, and actually get paid for this work. While it was once professional necessity for intellectuals to isolate themselves in the academy (as it was suicide to be public about politics as an intellectual during McCarthyism), it is now part of the training such that the writing and the communication coming out of academe are filtered into incredibly specialized journals read by a small band of elite peers (Galbraith, 2004). As Andrew Gamble (2004) argues,

> it will be harder in future for new generations of academics to choose to devote time to becoming public intellectuals and engage with the public domain, rather than concentrating on building their careers within the closed, self-referential networks of their professional discipline. (p. 49)

A survey of intellectuals in various disciplines on the topic of public commentary reveals the depth of this isolationist tendency. Even those making modest attempts to engage nonacademic publics most frequently cite as their primary objective to "create works which answer to the critical standards of intellectuals and colleagues whom [they valued] most," while fewer than a third of respondents cited "a desire to provide solutions to social problems" (Rhode, 2006, p. 121). In other words, many intellectuals tend to preach to their own choirs, which does little to elicit "the vitality of a public culture" (Jacoby, 1987, p. 4).

More than ever in recent memory, we are in need of legitimate thought-leaders. The 2011 Iowa Republican Straw Poll is a vivid reminder of just how much intellectuals could and should be doing. Frank Bruni reports,

> It was an intensely dispiriting spectacle because it was an entirely familiar one: the same old same old at a moment of extraordinary global uncertainty and profound national anxiety. Americans are more frightened and pessimistic—and Washington is more dysfunctional—than they've been in a very long time. (2011, August 13)

In the *London Times* review of Robert Dahl's 2007 book, *On Political Equality*, Stein Ringen argues, "What is afoot in democracy is that citizens care less for it, believe less in it, participate less in it and have less trust in governance with it" (2007, November 13). An increased engagement on the part of intellectuals is specifically relevant in addressing public disquiet. As theorist Collini explains, "the term 'Intellectuals' marks a space in which needs and anxieties are expressed about the relation between the daily round and the ends of life, and about what it might mean, with respect to such matters, for there to be some source of guidance on how to think about them" (2006, p. ix). Public intellectuals, then, are vital agents of the public sphere in negotiating and leading others through these anxious spaces. They are advocates, leaders, spokespersons, *actors*. The public intellectual "[possesses] some cultural authority who deploys an acknowledged intellectual position or achievement in addressing a broader, non-specialist public" (Collini, 2006, p. 85).

ATTENDING TO THE AESTHETIC DOMAIN OF STYLE

The argument I make here and throughout the book is that to collapse the distance between intellectuals and broader publics is to attend to rhetorical style. Style is the grounds on which we begin to reclaim the critical social project of the intellectual: engagement. If and only if intellectuals command certain rhetorical styles will they be able to use knowledge and expertise to engage the public sphere, and style is what makes them *public* intellectuals. As Collini mused in his 2006 lecture at the Royal Society of Arts, traditional intellectuals engender a public gag reflex. The public "senses pretentiousness, arrogance—on most of [the intellectual's] outings, 'so called' travels with it like a bodyguard, never far away even if not immediately in view" (qtd. in Reeves, 2006, June 1). Public intellectuals speak a public vernacular and, therefore, manage to strike a balance between being one of the gang and part of the priesthood. Certainly, intellectuals could be more rhetorically savvy in a number of ways. However, since style is a rich ground for comparing intellectuals and is the way intellectuals present themselves in public, a rhetoric of style is what is needed.

In rhetorical scholarship, style has been consciously and habitually avoided or is relegated to display or the elements of delivery pertaining to public address (Vivian, 2002). The limits of scholarly investigation into rhetoric's aesthetic domain do more than constitute a never-ending apologia for our discipline's previous sophistic and belletristic dalliances with style. As rhetoric scholar Bradford Vivian bemoans, "Modern rhetorical theory lacks a contemporary rationale and methodology for the study of style. Beyond unfortunate equations of rhetoric with grandiloquence, this scarcity in recent rhetorical scholarship corresponds to general humanistic and social scientific prejudices against the topic of style" (Vivian, 2002, p. 223). In fact, finding a substantial body of contemporary rhetorical scholarship on style for this book was a challenge. However, very recently, rhetorical scholars, including Barry Brummett, Vivian, and Carlnita Greene (and the author of this book), have made a committed theoretical return to style as both central to and synonymous with rhetoric. Largely, this reclamation of aesthetics and style in rhetorical scholarship sprang out of the extraordinary ubiquity of style, an "unprecedented investment in the aesthetic" (Vivian, 2002, p. 235). Stuart Ewen remarks that style can be found "on news magazines, sports magazines, music oriented magazines, magazines about fashion, architecture and interior design, automobiles, and sex," and that style, therefore, becomes a "key to understanding the contours of contemporary culture" (1990, p. 2). If style is everywhere, then our social and political experiences are stylized. Robert Hariman explicates that as "relations of control and autonomy are negotiated through the artful composition of speech, gesture, ornament, décor and any other means for modulating perception and shaping response," literally, our world "is *styled*" (1995, pp. 2–3). I approach this project as a rhetorician, but for all of my fellow would-be publically engaged intellectuals, we must reframe style not as a as means of generic cataloguing but as a vehicle for "understanding the dynamics of our social experience or the relationship between rhetorical appeals and political decisions" (Hariman, 1995, p. 8).

Echoing Hariman, Brummett defines style as "socially held sign systems composed of a wide range of signs beyond only language, systems that are used to accomplish rhetorical purposes across the cultural spectrum" (2008, p. 3). Today's style scholars eschew the notion that style is bounded merely as taste or as the shoes I wear or the color I paint my office. Rather, style is "the transcended ground on which the social is formed in late capitalism" (2008, p. 3). Style's ubiquitous presence in our social experience highlights consumption as the mechanism of cultural production and links, implicitly, style with identity and politics (2008, p. 54). Any demarcation between style and politics is false because "political action must always be understood in terms of what people want," and style is the way that desire manifests (2008, p. 78).

Around these sign systems, or styles, communities coalesce. Brummett's inquiry into gun culture, for instance, suggests that being part of that culture begins, not ends, with the purchase of a gun; the community convenes around "magazine ads and articles, clothing, talk, activities and attitudes" (2008, p. 149). In other words, owning a gun is the first step toward membership in gun culture, but subsequent steps follow a path to political policy support (Second Amendment), clothing choices (flannel, camouflage), cultural appreciations (John Wayne films, NRA membership), textual preferences (*Guns and Ammo*), and so on. In this way, style is the organizing function of community in our fragmented modern moment. Borrowing from Michael Maffesoli's work, Vivian calls style a "principle of unity that unites, deep down, the diversity of things . . . the postmodern form of the social link, a social link in dotted outline" (2002, p. 229).

Each of us pulls specific stylistic elements together to create an identity that is designed to be viewed favorably by a particular public. Every style "draws on universal elements of the human condition and symbolic repertoire but organizes them in a limited, customary set of communicative designs," such that "each is thoroughly conventional, yet the means for personal improvisation and intelligent, innovative responses to unique problems" (Hariman, 1995, pp. 11–12). Throughout this book, I define and operationalize style as a logos. It is the discourse of our moment, an argument intellectuals make for (or against) broader relevance. In turn, audiences resonate with certain stylistic vibrations and not others (Vivian, 2002, p. 230). Those whose styles respond to the broader and deeper vibrations of our epoch will be successful in creating unity from diversity; those who cannot or choose not even to feel the vibrations at all will fail. Increasingly, our culture assigns significance and value to the aesthetic, to style, and to an attunement to style provides for a reimagining of what Johanna Hartelius and Richard Cherwitz call "mobilized expertise" on the part of intellectuals in the public sphere (2010).

STYLE AS CULTURAL HABITUS

For this book, I add a new perspective to the growing rhetorical literature on style by reinterpreting Bourdieu's construct of habitus as the logos that is style. In this way, style is threefold: physiological, psychological, and sociological. Bourdieu's definition of style as "manifested preferences" (1979/1984, p. 56) guides this understanding. That is, style is the physiological, psychological, and sociological manifestation of preference. Or, as Vivian writes, style entails "all manifestations of symbolic enactment" (2011, p. 7). This tripartite understanding of style is also cohesive if understood rhetorically. Indeed, rhetoricians are uniquely positioned to understand and theorize style since rhetoric employs "vital tools for investigating the general proliferation of cultural, political, and personal modes of style common to late modernity (Vivian, 2011, p. 7). Like Maffesoli would argue more contemporarily, Bourdieu posits that style marks a "unity hidden under the diversity and multiplicity of practices" (1979/1984, p. 101).

Physiological

First, style is physiological and, therefore, performative. Bourdieu suggests that style *"puts into practice* a repertoire of devices or techniques, in short, the whole art of performance" (1977, p. 20, emphasis added). These "expressive forms and rituals" of style are enacted through the symbolic medium of the body (Hebdige, 1979, p. 2). Style as physiology also assumes a measure of intentionality or strategy. That style is mechanistic is naïve, suggests Bourdieu (1977). A person is sometimes said to have "style" when she recognizes a cultural vibration, and her recognition manifests aesthetically as a selection of signs that create a system of meaning. To acquire such style, imitation is a necessity. Bourdieu remarks, "[C]hildren are particularly attentive to the gestures and postures which, in their eyes, express everything that goes to make an accomplished adult—a way of walking, a tilt of the head, facial expressions . . . using implements . . . a style of speech" (1977, p. 87). All of these imitations combine to create a style that appears natural and appropriate as it manifests itself physiologically. Public intellectual style is "transmitted in practice" (Bourdieu, 1977, p. 87).

Paralleling the idea of style as performative is the notion that style creates or reflects a certain persona. Mike Featherstone (1991) articulates that "identity, presentation, appearance and lifestyle" combine to construct a persona where the body "is regarded as an extension of [one's] *persona* which must be stylized to express the individuality of the bearer" (p. 60). Goods, in turn, are an outward expression of persona. Yet, goods and physiology alone do not encapsulate style, so we follow Bourdieu and examine the psychological elements of style.

Psychological

Not only do we recognize when someone has style because his intended performance is appropriate to a certain situated persona but we also recognize when someone lacks style. By this, I am not addressing the man wearing Bermuda shorts and black socks with sandals. Although this man is certainly a fashion catastrophe, he is not without style—indeed, perhaps his style is "fashion catastrophe" or he intends his attire to be ironic or he is attending a costume party where the theme is "Old Men of the Beach." I believe we say that a person lacks style when his style is inconsistent in some way. This is a psychological reaction to form. Brummett (2004) argues that consistency (or homology) tugs on us and relates Bill Nichol's notion of "pleasure-in-recognition" (p. 10) as proof of this phenomenon. We seem drawn to styles that are familiar. Marcel Mauss (1973) describes a similar feeling. He recalls the parades in England following a victory alongside the French during World War I at the Battle of the Aisne. Because they wanted to honor the French soldiers who had fought beside them, the Worcester Regiment requested that the British infantry march to music played by French buglers and drummers. Mauss states, "The result was not very encouraging. For nearly six months, in the streets of Bailleul, long after the Battle of the Aisne, I often saw the following sight: the regiment had preserved its English march but had set it to a French rhythm" (p. 457). On the surface, Mauss may have been reacting to the strange gait and rhythm combination, but on a psychological level, he perhaps sensed that something about the marchers was "off"—that they were inconsistent with their identities or substance, that they lacked style.

Continuing in the same vein, style is as much about identity as identification. Style must be psychologically consistent for others to be comfortable; thus, it is very much concerned with identity. To be sure, physiological style is superficially malleable—fashion fads come and go as do slang words, salient conversational topics, gestures, and dance steps. However, psychological style is the identifiable core or center of a style. It is far less dynamic than physiological style and is the way it is possible for Hamlet to have said, "I knew him, Horatio" (Shakespeare, n.d., 5.1.203–4). When we say we *know* someone, it means their style is consistent, particularly, that they have psychological style that is consistent with an overall style. The person has integrity. We identify a public intellectual, in part, by her psychological style.

Sociological

Finally, style is sociological. Ewen (1990) describes style as a way of being with others. Style is "history turned into nature" (Bourdieu, 1977, p. 78) through social construction and reification and is relational. "In group life as a whole, there is a kind of education of movements in close order" that can only be obtained through social contact and practice (Mauss, 1973, p. 473). Mauss suggests, "This, above all, is what distinguishes man from the animals: the transmission of his techniques, and very probably their oral transmission" (1973, p. 461). In other words, style is socially constructed and taught. In turn, some kinds of style are rewarded (those leaning toward hegemony), and others are punished (those on the fringes). Different styles may be en vogue at different times, but all are socially constructed.

Style is also quite public. Bourdieu goes so far as to say that style is a mark of "*social position* and hence of the social distance between objective positions, that is between social persons conjuncturally brought together in physical space" (1977, p. 82). While this statement is ideologically loaded, the issue becomes clear: Style must be publicly visible and performed as well as publicly acknowledged as successful or unsuccessful. If style is a way of being in the world, that way of being must be with others and in the light of day to determine the social position or desirability of the style (and of the individual or group to whom it belongs).

In sum, the rhetorical problem of the traditional intellectual is specifically one of style. Physiologically, psychologically, and sociologically, the public perceives the private intellectual to be a failure of rhetorical style in reaching the public. He is dressed inappropriately. She carries herself strangely. He describes ideas in ways we cannot understand. She holds the floor for too long and seems to find herself to be very self-important. He does not want to talk to anyone without a PhD. She is out of touch with my life. All of these stylistic markers of traditional intellectuals fail to connect with the public sphere. Conversely, the public intellectual is one who has mastered physiological, psychological, and sociological styles that engage the public sphere. Because the public intellectual has the "right" style, he or she is able to work with and on behalf of publics in ways traditional intellectuals will never be able to do so long as they cling to their "outmoded" styles. Rather than wallowing in self-afflicted pity that scholars do not pay adequate attention to style, I want to focus my energies on what rhetorical style can be, what it can mean to the public sphere. Through rhetorical style, we can come to see the term *public intellectual* not as a noun but as a verb.

THE STATE OF THE PUBLIC INTELLECTUAL IN AMERICA

What is truly striking about the split between intellectual and public is how quickly it has become the normative standard. For most of Western history, in disciplines like rhetoric, political science, anthropology, and sociology, intellectuals have been "citizen-scholars" (Hartelius & Cherwitz, 2010). Coming from the rhetorical tradition, Hartelius and Cherwitz remind, "From its inception rhetoric's primary objective has been the integration, rather than segregation, of theory, practice, and production. For the art of situated and practical reason, whose purpose is a fitting response to social exigencies and the engineering of human action, the significance and inevitability of engagement is evident" (2010, p. 437). We can see a focus on engagement from the beginnings of Western thought to the present.

Roman philosopher Cicero's *De Oratore* is written in the form of a dialogue between Crassus, the mouthpiece of Cicero, and two other primary characters, Scaevola and Antonius. In the dialogue, Cicero, through his character Crassus, emphasizes the importance of education to the development of the whole person. For an orator to be ethical and great, "[a] knowledge of a vast number of things is necessary, without which volubility of words is empty and ridiculous" (n.d., 1.5). A real Isocratean rhetorical thread running through this dialogue in that logos is the medium through which all civil institutions and communities are cultivated and sustained. Therefore, being taught and skilled in rhetoric is critical to the creation and maintenance of community and society. There is another component, though, to Cicero's stance on a broad education. He says, as Crassus, "[N]o man can be eloquent on a subject that he does not understand; and that, if he understands a subject ever so well, but is ignorant how to form and polish his speech, he can not express himself eloquently even about what he does understand" (n.d., 1.14). In other words, without rhetoric, disciplinary

knowledge is useless to the development and maintenance of society because the scholar cannot communicate her knowledge effectively.

Generally, Crassus serves as Cicero's voice in *De Oratore*; however,
Antonius seems to be Cicero-as-practicing-orator. In book 2, Antonius
suggests that scholars are not necessarily good orators. Likely, we have
all suffered through a semester with a teacher with vast knowledge but
absolutely no rhetorical skill for teaching it. The ideal orator, for Cicero,
needs a "fund" of konoi topoi to draw on to argue what is at stake and
relate his disciplinary knowledge in an eloquent way to others to move a
community of people to honorable ends (in Conley, 1978). Cicero strikes
a balance between learning and doing. Antonius mentions that he does
not want to appear too bookish because people are persuaded in their
own language using their own conceptual frameworks, not the language
or frameworks of scholars. If one is too much the philosopher in the Socratic or Platonic sense, one will not be rhetorically effective because the
ideal rhetor has an organic emotional connection with people. The kind
of education Cicero advocates is not really about speechmaking at all but
rather about improving a person's or a community's character and utilizing
philosophy (this word stands in for *disciplinary knowledge*) for public good.

Cicero's *De Oratore* is a lengthy document that deserves greater treatment than I have the opportunity to give in this book, but his theory of
rhetoric is pertinent to the study of public intellectuals. First, it provides
a blueprint for the would-be public intellectual or engaged scholar. Cicero
carefully balances the importance of learning a discipline with the need
for knowledgeable action in the polis—in other words, just action or just
learning is not enough on its own, but the combination is what makes
one a public intellectual. Second, Cicero's treatise emphasizes the magnitude of the public—it is unimportant what a person does as a private
person; what counts is what a person accomplishes as a public citizen.
Cicero's theory of rhetoric demands a public orientation of intellectuals.
They should pursue disciplinary knowledge but only to do honorable
work in public. Cicero's rhetorical theory, therefore, orients intellectuals
as citizens of a larger community of people, not as individuals toiling
in disciplinary silos writing for peers in the priesthood. Third, while *De
Oratore* is a complex document for modern readers, a Roman audience
would have understood it perfectly well. This is because Cicero believes
rhetoric gains power only when it engages people in their own language,
and his document is a model for what that might sound like. For would-be
engaged scholars, Cicero calls for reform in intellectual writing—no
longer should intellectuals write in pedantic prose but should engage in

intellectual exchange on a level that is clear to the public. Cicero does not advocate "dumbing down"; rather, he implies that it makes no sense to write the way most academics and experts write and that to be a public intellectual requires writing like the larger public to which one belongs.

Gramsci provides an emic, political, and undeniably Marxian definition of the public intellectual: "The notion of 'the intellectuals' as a distinct social category . . . is a myth. All men are potentially intellectuals in the sense of having an intellect and using it, but not all are intellectual by social function" (1971, p. 3). In stark contrast to traditional academic intellectuals is the public intellectual or what Gramsci calls the organic intellectual. He states that the "thinking and organizing element of a particular fundamental social profession" is not determined by job title but "by [public intellectuals'] function in directing the ideas and aspirations of the class to which they organically belong" (p. 3). According to Gramsci, public intellectuals perform "an essential mediating function in the struggle of class forces" and provide "theory and ideology (and often leadership) for a mass base of non-intellectuals, i.e. workers" (p. 3). The organic intellectual is the "preferred" archetype for Gramsci because of his emphasis on every person's potential as "philosopher . . . artist" with "a conscious line of moral conduct" who "contributes to sustain a conception of the world or to modify it, that is, to bring into being new modes of thought" (p. 9). In other words, a Gramscian definition of the public intellectual does not rely on traditional markers of intellectualism like numbers of degrees earned but on expertise *and* an ability to use that experience to positively advance publics politically or socially.

Gramsci is wary of more traditional intellectuals, instead advocating the critical function of the intellectual as an emic, public philosopher. For, as Gramsci posits, public intellectuals must embrace "active participation in practical life, as constructor, organizer, 'permanent persuader.'" Gramsci is concerned here with public intellectuals dedicating themselves to constructing a better society through rhetorical action. We should move from "technique-as-work . . . to technique-as-science and to the humanistic conception of history, without which one remains 'specialized' and does not become 'directive' (specialized and political)" (1971, p. 10). The Gramscian public intellectual "shirks the contemptuous pose of the distant observer" (Dyson, 2003) in favor of the role of emic teacher and activist.

Russell Jacoby's critically important work *The Last Intellectuals: American Culture in the Age of Academe* (1987) helps make the turn to the modern public intellectual or lack thereof. Jacoby's fundamental concern is the seeming disappearance of the intellectual from public life, the disappearance of intellectuals who "employ the vernacular," "embrace a public," who are "writers on general topics," and serve as "major figures outside their specialties" (pp. 6–11). Most important, academic life values, hires, promotes, and tenures those who wear their disciplinary and departmental constraints with quiet resignation if not pride, those who *fit in*. The public intellectual, conversely, is one who *stands out*. Though standing out is not enough unto itself—the public intellectual not only stands out but stands out *in the right way*. Jacoby's sense of the public intellectual does not discount the possibility that academic intellectuals can also be public intellectuals, but it does require a different understanding of a "public" than merely an audience of peers or students. It also requires different work from the intellectual than publishing in refereed journals. Being a public intellectual demands writing "to and for the educated public"—"surrender[ing] the vernacular" of specificity or risk "[sacrificing] a public identity" (Jacoby, 1987, p. 26). In other words, the public intellectual adopts a particular rhetorical style or set of styles that the academic intellectual does not.

Recent treatments of public intellectuals warn us of the barriers to efficacy in the public sphere if intellectuals are based in the traditional academe, a place most readers of this book call (or will call) home. While most of us chose this line of work precisely because it affords us significant opportunities and space for thought and for producing high-quality work, the modern mode of the academy is increasingly an anathema to the life of the intellectual. As Richard Reeves (2006) articulates, "the potential of the long-term trend to ever-greater specialization" will "increase the distance between the skills and motivations required for professional, academic success and those driving intellectual endeavors." The logistics of tenure, promotion, and the narrowness of what "counts" as scholarship are chief among these barriers. In order to "debunk the rigid dichotomy between theory and application," we must not retain and reinforce "abacus-oriented" systems of hiring and promotion (Cherwitz, 2010, p. 65; Hartelius & Cherwitz, 2010). Beyond logistics, we must also jettison the absurd notion that intellectual work is objective and even apolitical. (This trajectory of work is accelerating and is exemplified by work like that of Kahn and Lee [2010]; Schwarz [2008]; Cheney, Wilhelmsson, and Zorn [2002]; and in special issues on engaged scholarship, Barge, Simpson, and Shockley-Zalabak [2008], and Gunn and Lucaites [2010].) These "standards" not only are dishonest, they are dangerous (Deetz, 2008). We see a culture in crisis, and rather than respond with thoughtful, meaningful solutions, we value whatever we feel is so cutting edge about our work that it "[exempts] us from the demands of 'common' discourse" (Daniels,

1996). Indeed, "we often get grants and tenure and promotion precisely by convincing those making decisions on such matters that our work on whatever topic, be it modernist poetry or television sit-coms or hypertextuality, is more complex, and with this, more intelligent or conventional than commonplace readings" (Daniels, 1996). As academics, our rewards in tenure and promotion come from decorating our isolation proudly with official trappings like a framed doctorate and a bunch of Vita-hits. In doing so, we make ourselves more and more irrelevant to the broader public. Parodying the trajectory of the academic world, Theodore Zeldin writes in his book *Happiness*,

> To remain sane, scholars had to become willing prisoners in a tiny cell, because here at least they could lay down the law about some tiny fragment of truth, like the habits of the earwig or the foreign policy of medieval Zanzibar. A few ambitious ones might become dissatisfied . . . and they might build up . . . grand theories . . . applicable to other domains

but that this system keeps intellectuals in the academy in a perpetual state of "nervous conflict" (qtd. in Reeves, 2006). And, our perpetuation of this nervous conflict comes at the cost of the public sphere. As public-intellectual economist Galbraith wonders,

> Can we really afford so little work on defining social problems, on measuring facts, on policy design? Where, if not in [the social sciences], should our University deal with poverty and racism, with prisons and schools, with immigration and inequality, with public purposes such as health care and retirement, and with the security issues of war and peace, world development and our energy budget? Public policy can't do it all. (2004)

Collini suggests, provocatively, that the question of whether or not we need public intellectuals is really "the question of whether thought, enquiry, imagination, pursued to the highest level, issue in any wisdom about how we ought to live" (Collini, 2006, p. 9). Because, Gamble (2004) worries,

> There has been a marked shrinking of the public domain . . . a space where the public interest can be determined through debate and deliberation, a public ethos generated, and a public ethic articulated. Independent, critical intellectual work is essential for it, and those who perform that work are public intellectuals. (p. 41)

Who or what, then, are public intellectuals? Collini provides a useful four-part rubric that I use in this book for understanding public intellectuals. First, a public intellectual must have achieved significant standing in a creative, analytic, or scholarly domain, what he calls a "qualifying activity." Second, public intellectuals must capitalize on a medium or a selection of media to reach a diverse audience of nonspecialists. Third, public intellectuals demonstrate concern with issues and challenges that "engage with some of the general concern of those publics." Fourth and finally, public intellectuals nurture a reputation for "being likely to have important and interesting things to say" (qtd. in Reeves, 2006).

Public intellectuals remind the rest of us of our ethical obligations to our communities and our societies. In *Nichomachean Ethics*, Aristotle uses the term *eudemonia*—today, ethicists understand the term not as ethics but as flourishing (Cheney, 2008). In other words, public intellectuals flourish and help enable society to flourish by moving away from ethics-as-obligation to ethics-as-invigoration, a move that recognizes and values a more holistic notion of our own humanity as community members (Cheney, 2008). In other words, *eudemonia* invokes honoring the idea of the public domain, a necessary condition of a functioning democratic society (Gamble, 2004). Too, public intellectuals are engaged community members that recognize the boundary between intellectual and public as a smoke screen. Pursuing public intellectual, or engaged, work means

> announcing our willingness to be *in* the world, not just *about* the world. We are not trying simply to make our claims about the world practical; we become conversation partners in the world with others.
> . . . Sophisticated methods and expertise can no longer be a substitution for saying things that matter. (Deetz, 2008, p. 290)

Distinctly, public intellectuals are active agents, even activists, whether teaching or writing or marching or prophesying. Dewey urged intellectuals to "shape reality toward positive social goals, not stand aside in self-righteous indignation" (Boydston, 1990, p. 169). Critical scholar Michael Bérubé calls for "a practice of cultural studies that articulates the theoretical and critical work of the so-called public intellectual to the movements of public policy" (1996). Indeed,

> [t]he modern state has become increasingly labyrinthine in its structures, in its networks, and in its governance. . . . The public domain becomes a sphere of political and ideological contestation in which

attempts to set agendas and define identities and the public interest, assemble coalitions and alliances, and make interventions become all-important. (Gamble, 2004, p. 43)

Public intellectuals are vital to this effort. Public intellectuals adopt a style that is tuned into the epochal vibrations of the cultural ecology. Theorist Stanley Deetz laments of the academy, "We have used incredible social and economic resources to produce a lot of stuff that is unavailable and unreadable in a time of great social need" (2008, p. 290). We would do well to remember the lessons from *De Oratore* and those that instruct us to stop sounding and looking and acting like traditional academics with all of the socially awkward baggage that term carries and start sounding and looking and acting like we have an ear to the ground, listening and feeling for the tectonic movements of our society.

BOOK OUTLINE AND CHAPTER SUMMARY

I mean this book to open a dialogue about reimagining not only the way we conceive of style but also the way we create and train scholars. This book is not a Dear John but a tough love letter for my fellow would-be public intellectuals. I offer six essays articulating successful rhetorical styles used by contemporary public intellectuals in the United States that address the connection between public intellectuals and the public sphere on the basis of style. I hope not only to describe but also to prescribe, so I offer style as an avenue for engagement and even activism, a roadmap for action by intellectuals in the public sphere.

I also offer a few notes regarding the organization and the tone in this book. This book is a strongly inductive work. Because style has been relegated to notions of delivery, has been outright ignored, or has been explicitly bemoaned, very little theoretical work exists to locate style as central to rhetorical and communication studies as well as to public life. An inductive approach is an ideal vehicle to move from case example out to theory in order to move from what we can already acknowledge as effective to spaces where we could theoretically tap style to meaningfully engage broader publics with intellectual work. The tone of this book differs from most scholarly books, and that is not an accident. I am uninterested in self-righteousness, but I am interested in self-reflexivity, and I mean to be more conversational, to employ a more publicly accessible rhetorical style in order to demonstrate that our work need not be diluted, perverted, or dumbed down in order to be readable and engaging for nonspecialists.

I begin with five styles that respond to the short-wave vibrations of our culture in that they are highly situated in the contemporary era: The Prophet, The Guru, The Sustainer, The Pundit, and The Narrator. Certainly, these styles have been efficacious in other eras and cultural and political milieus—The Prophet and The Narrator, in particular, have probably been around as long as *Homo sapiens sapiens*. In borrowing from Vivian the notion of the wavelengths (or vibrations) of an era that often compel and constrain style, our logos, a turn to metaphysics notes that the study of wavelengths encapsulates both frequency and amplitude. Frequency indicates how often a pattern recurs; amplitude measures magnitude. So, when I argue that these five styles are situated ones, I am not being ahistorical; rather, I illustrate that certain cultural, social, and political events may increase frequency and amplitude of a style that otherwise registers as a low hum. My sixth case study, The Scientist, feels the long-wave vibrations of the American mythic landscape to transcend the current moment, or any moment for that matter, marking it as an atemporal style, one whose frequency and amplitude are relatively unchanged despite tectonic shifts in culture and politics. Each of these case studies serves as a rubric for successful intellectual investment and engagement in the public sphere at a time and in a place where such an intervention is both meaningful and necessary. Although I locate one style per person, I do not mean to suggest that these are discrete styles. Indeed, a person may be capable of proficiency in multiple styles or hybrid styles. Finally, I unpack what it means in practical terms to conceive of intellectual engagement as a style, and I offer some examples of institutions where this work is already happening.

In academic circles, we have not said enough about public intellectuals, and we have said even less about style. Ignoring the not-so-hilarious irony that we are the ones in greatest need of reflection, we have relegated discussion of intellectuals and style to other writers and other audiences, mostly in the popular press. Fortunately, although still not trendy, greater scholarly attention to the political, social, and moral imperative of intellectual engagement coupled with greater investment in aesthetics marks a trend toward commitment, community, and compassion in our troubled times. By grappling with the rhetorical and material entailments of temporality, political scrutiny, public relevance, moneyed interests, and tactics of public relations, style offers a path for intellectuals to go public and to be of the public. Rigid dichotomies begin to melt away.

1

CONTEMPORARY CRISES AND
THE CENTRALITY OF STYLE

Stand in a grocery checkout line, and you see it. Browse any online news source, and it is there. Drive down the street, and it looms. Open a book. Turn on the TV. Poke around the house. Look up, look down, look all around. Style is ubiquitous, "a preoccupation of nearly all sectors of society" (Ewen, 1990, p. 3). Michael Maffesoli explains that style "becomes an all-encompassing form, a 'forming form' that gives birth to whole manners of being, to customs, representations, and the various fashions by which life in society is expressed" (1996, p. 5). Barry Brummett echoes Maffesoli in positioning style as central: "Style . . . is the transcendent ground in which the social is formed in late capitalism," the "global terrain of shared knowledge, action and judgment" (2008, pp. 3, xiii). From food to home décor, runway shows to reality television, politics to religion, and everywhere in between, style dominates as our twenty-first-century vehicle for making and perceiving and reading meaning.

This cultural preoccupation with aesthetic form opens a binary wound for those of us reared and educated in the Western tradition (Brummett, 2008; Vivian, 2011). Platonic treatments of style were consistently in opposition to substance. In the *Gorgias*, for instance, Plato locates style matters like makeup and cooking in dualistic tension with substantive topics like physical health and medicine (Brummett, 2008). Bracketing for the time being the obvious misogyny of this example (we return to this point in The Narrator), we have each been socialized to accept the style/substance dichotomy as natural and normal. In other words, it is our ideological fallback. And, until more recently, rhetorical scholarship's treatment of style has only reified the dichotomy by treating style as superficial display rather than substantive matter.

Yet, all indicators point to the imminent collapse of this ideological binary. Brummett wonders, "If our culture buys and sells signs, images, and meanings more than it does hardware—if we are a culture engrossed in *The West Wing* more than in actual politics—if more people vote for the American Idol than for nearly every political candidate who has ever run—then we live in a world where signs are becoming a reality for people" (2008, p. 11). This binary collapse probably makes even the most tolerant readers of this book uncomfortable because it reminds them of philosophy's scathing critique of rhetoric's "mere-ness," the disciplinary association with the lowest forms of sophistry. We may, however, find comfort in the psychoanalytic rhetoric of Jacques Lacan: "It is the world of words that creates the world of things" (1977, p. 65; see also Postrel, 2003). More simply, style precedes substance. Style is first in the human experience of the world. Through this lens, style *is* substantial. I have argued style is a logos that feeds Vivian's argument, "A simple difference in style can amount to a substantial difference in cultural form, political will, and embodied subjectivity. Style not only matters, as a result of its omnipresence in late modern thought and practice, but represents a kind of matter, or substance, unto itself" (2011, p. 6). If style is primary, its centrality in contemporary culture denotes a topos of great significance for scholars.

Style is also substantive because it has value, specifically, what Brummett calls *exchange value* (2008, p. 13). In *A Rhetoric of Style*, Brummett makes an important distinction between an object's use value and its exchange value. *Use value* refers to something's utility whereas *exchange value* is something's culturally perceived value. For example, if I get a free, low-end phone through my wireless carrier, that phone has use value: It makes calls, it takes calls, it stores phone numbers. All of those capabilities allow me to communicate with others via mobile phone. If, however, I spend $300 on an iPhone, not only do I get the use value of mobile communication but I also acquire exchange value as well. The iPhone brings with it all the trappings of Apple products: sleek, edgy, impeccable design, artistic sensibility, expensive to buy. I get the use value of a phone with the exchange value of the hipster I so long to be. As such, "[e]xchange value forms a kind of economy of its own" (Brummett, 2008, p. 14) because "[t]he cultural realm . . . has its own logic and currency as well as rate of conversion into economic capital" (Featherstone, 1991, p. 89). In other words, the hipster coolness of the iPhone gets transferred to me as its owner, and in the cultural marketplace, I have a sudden cache I would not have with my freebie phone that just made calls. Exchange value deals entirely in signs, in surface, but it is the way we judge value. So, style is valuable as a cultural commodity. And, in late capitalism, where what is valuable can be bought, sold, or traded in the marketplace, style is currency.

Despite style's dominance in American culture as a way of knowing, a way of being in the world, and a way that we assign value, many intellectuals have long followed Plato in dismissing style as unimportant or trivial. A generous reading on this might be that an indifference toward style—a worldly disposition—is a style in itself. I tend to lean toward a less generous reading, that intellectuals dismiss style whole cloth as unserious. For instance, academic intellectuals' clothing choices often reflect a disengagement with, or even outright hostility toward, style. In his 2001 *Chronicle of Higher Education* piece, Middlebury English professor Jay Parini writes about the inferences students make from the clothes teachers wear: "Teaching is, after all, a performance art, and, whether we want to believe it, we're putting on a costume of sorts every day. We're sending countless messages, explicit and implicit, to our students, who are reading as closely as they read the texts we assign" (2001). It seems no longer sufficient to claim professorial isolation as an excuse for opting out of the discourses of style, given that our cultural experience is largely stylized. Parini highlights the misguided dismissal of style by intellectuals in his summaries of the styles of two faculty members from whom he took classes as an undergraduate: "I am not giving into fashion. I am not a consumer," and "I am an intellectual, deeply concerned with serious matters, and fashion bores me." No doubt, academic intellectuals do not need to start subscribing to *GQ* or *InStyle*, reading them cover to cover and emulating the latest trends. That reductionist argument negates the breadth and the richness of style as a rhetoric. But pretending style does not apply to intellectuals is absurd, even irresponsible, because it suggests that intellectuals find style "beneath" them and, by extension, consider those who more adroitly navigate the world of style beneath them. It also renders intellectuals politically and socially ineffective and irrelevant—style matters (Vivian, 2011). Particularly for those intellectuals interested in connecting with a broader public, style is a central consideration to form that linkage. As Parini instructs at the end of his essay, people "find clues to our attitudes toward the world, even our politics" in our styles, and he instructs, "[I]t pays to think of [style] as a rhetorical choice, and to dress accordingly" (2001). To attend to style signifies attention to relevance. Attending to style signifies value. No one gets to claim exemption in this case.

All of this is to say that style matters. And even, style is matter. It is a cultural preoccupation that permeates our ways of knowing, of judging, and of valuing. Its history as opposite substance is collapsing, exposing the world of signs as *the world*. The rhetoric for the twenty-first century, style's vibrations can and should be felt by intellectuals who seek engagement with community, broader relevance, and greater political and social significance in their work.

A MOMENT OF CRISES

Just as important as preoccupation with style is the recognition that our moment is one dominated by crisis: a massive recession, joblessness, erosion of the middle class, addiction, political unrest, and violence. At the turn of the last century, Emile Durkheim introduced the term *anomie* to describe a society that ignores divine law, degrades norms, and is characterized by lawlessness, violence, and self-destruction (1947, p. ix). Tuning in to any mediated news or opinion source highlights the salience of Durkheim's theory of anomie. Certainly, other eras have endured crises of the same magnitude, but America's media ecology amplifies our perception of anomie, raising the dial to 11 in the *This Is Spinal Tap* sense of that figure.

Our contemporary moment of crisis iterates the significance of temporality to style. Historical, social, and political factors enable and constrain certain styles. This kind of contextual positioning also recognizes that style "has to be appealing if it is to be effective" and that there are limited "economies available to speakers in particular situations" (Hariman, 1995, p. 3). In her book *Bodily Arts*, Debra Hawhee notes the Greek rhetorical focus on *mētis*, a sort of combination of wisdom and cunning, an agility in different circumstances. In other words, based on the current social climate, only a limited selection of rhetorical styles will be read as acceptable, appropriate, or valuable in the public sphere. In the following section, I give a brief description of the US sociopolitical climate over roughly the last thirty years that has led to the dominance of The Prophet, The Guru, The Sustainer, The Pundit, and The Narrator, all rhetorical styles in response to crisis. While many, if not all, of these temporal styles have worked in other eras, their current iterations are situated in very specific, interconnected crises.

A THIRTY-YEAR SOCIOPOLITICAL
HISTORY OF THE UNITED STATES

Certainly, the last three decades have highlighted fundamental social changes both positive and negative: attention to the rights of sexual, racial, and religious minorities, a massive influx of women into the workplace, soaring divorce rates, greater access to education, the rise of the religious right, and the fracturing of the political left. Robert Dahl explains that our modern corporate capitalist system produces "inequalities in social and economic resources so great as to bring about severe violations of political equality and hence of the democratic process" (1985, p. 60; see also Dahl, 2007). In turn, these inequalities create a system of anomie or crisis spurring public intellectual rhetorical styles that must respond to anomie. And, the values that so many of us uphold in the academy, "openness, rationality, diversity, clarity and tolerance" (Gamble, 2004, p. 42), are the very values that enable the public domain to function—we should feel an especial tug toward leadership in the public sphere.

Five trends are particularly relevant to this discussion of a breakdown of democracy and a sociopolitical moment of crisis in which The Prophet, The Guru, The Sustainer, The Pundit, and The Narrator styles dominate. The first is a popular swelling of distrust in government, business, and other formal institutions where questions of ethics arise. The second is the ascendance of religious fundamentalism and extremism in Christianity, Judaism, and Islam and the call for voices of spirituality. The third is the profoundly negative turn the natural environment has taken at the hands of global warming and other human-made catastrophes that is the harbinger of disasters in the sociopolitical environment, as well. The fourth is a hypermediated culture that applauds pithy sound bites while deemphasizing deliberation and participation. The fifth is a shift in how we understand and consider evidence. Each of these trends calls forth one or more of the situated styles detailed in the following chapters, and in the last, I explicate the interwoven temporalities of these styles.

Distrust in Institutions

The last decades of the twentieth century witnessed a steep decline in social trust (Putnam, 2000). Toshio Yamigishi and Midori Yamigishi (1994) define trust as a "standing decision" to give the majority of people, both friend and stranger, the benefit of the doubt in most situations. As Wendy M. Rahn and John E. Transue (1998) report, strong social trust is associated with many positive outcomes, such as, social cohesion, economic potency, civic participation, and interest, and also works as a deterrent for engaging in unethical, immoral, or illegal behavior (p. 548). While the 1960 survey featured in The Civic Culture reports that 55 percent of American adults trusted most people and institutions—that number dropped precipitously to 35 percent by 1995 (Rahn & Transue, 1998, p. 549).

More recently, the American National Election Studies (NES) confirms a radical decline in institutional trust since the 1960s (in Griffin, 2005, p. 2). Just as high levels of social trust beget positive outcomes, low levels of social trust erode society's fabric (Putnam, 2000).

One of the most obvious derivatives of the erosion of social trust is an erosion of trust in government institutions as they are often seen as the "cause" of civic ills. Robert Putnam's landmark book, *Bowling Alone: The Collapse and Revival of American Community*, details this trend from a scholarly perspective. Putnam (2000) asserts that social trust allows for mutually beneficial social coordination, cooperation, and participation such that people can more easily gain employment, avoid criminal behavior, acquire an education, and maintain a sense of well-being in their communities. More specifically, "the proportion of Americans who reply that they 'trust the government in Washington' only 'some of the time' or 'almost never' has risen steadily from 30 percent in 1966 to 75 percent in 1992" (Putnam, 1995, p. 68). Putnam points emphatically to television as the catalyst of civic demise in this country, but the very public and shocking political scandals over the last several decades from Watergate to the Iran-Contra Affair to Monica Lewinsky to Abu Ghraib have made the political establishment the epicenter of mistrust.

However, I would be remiss if I suggested only scholars have caught onto and are concerned about a decline in institutional trust. Any major newspaper, news website, or television news channel in the United States reiterates and extends Putnam's concerns to current issues. For instance, by 1995, twenty-nine women had come forward to accuse then Senator Robert Packwood of sexual harassment and even sexual assault—he was forced to resign. The year 1998 saw Bill Clinton impeached, only the second US president in history to go through the ordeal, because of his lies to a grand jury about his affair with White House intern Lewinsky. CNN reported on June 6, 2003, that George W. Bush had likely falsified information on weapons of mass destruction (WMDs) in Iraq to make a case for military action in that country. John W. Dean, former attorney to Richard Nixon, wrote,

> Presidential statements, particularly on matters of national security, are held to an expectation of the highest standard of truthfulness. A president cannot stretch, twist or distort facts and get away with it. President Lyndon Johnson's distortions of the truth about Vietnam forced him to stand down from reelection. President Richard Nixon's false statements about Watergate forced his resignation. (2003)

In late 2005, former lobbyist Jack Abramoff was found guilty of bribing predominantly Republican members of Congress for political favors with expensive "gifts" like golf trips and overseas vacations. In April 2006, stories decried the city of New Orleans conducting its mayoral election in the absence of nearly four hundred thousand voters, primarily African American citizens. The 2008 election saw a conservative campaign against ACORN, an organization dedicated to registering and empowering traditionally marginalized citizens to vote. Eventually, ACORN was disbanded because of conservative contentions that it registered people who were dead or did not exist in order to elect a liberal, African American president. It is certainly no great revelation that people distrust government, but business institutions are also targets of mistrust.

The year 2001 was not, as predicted, a year of space odyssey but rather an odyssey through the manipulation of stock values and earning statements that brought about the collapses of some of the nation's largest corporations: Enron, WorldCom, Tyco, and Martha Stewart. Investors lost millions of dollars, and at Enron specifically, thousands of people lost their entire 401K savings in the blink of an eye. Since then, several executives have been indicted and have been or will be serving prison sentences for their roles in condoning fuzzy math and the outright falsification of data. Not surprising, these federal crimes have led to a widespread perception that corruption is at the heart of capitalist corporations. This perception, in turn, has implications for the economy as a whole. Charles Conrad (2003) states these ethical lapses "resulted from a number of trends in the U.S. political-economic system" as "adaptations to the development of a complex combination of ideologies, practices and public policies that encourage ethically questionable behavior" (p. 6).

CEO compensation is one factor contributing to the negative perception of corporate America. Because CEOs have recently been compensated based on stock valuation, CEOs are more willing to engage in behavior that puts the entire firm (and all who are stakeholders in it) at risk to increase Wall Street evaluations. Consequently, CEOs like Ken Lay of Enron, Bernie Ebbers of WorldCom, and John Thain of Merrill Lynch were paid vast sums of money and exited with proverbial golden parachutes while their employees and stockholders lost their jobs, their incomes, and their savings, and the rest of the nation lost faith. In a May 3, 2006, interview with Jim Lehrer, ConocoPhillips CEO James Mulva defended the $400 million package given to outgoing CEO of ExxonMobil, Lee Raymond, saying that if it was tied to performance, it was justified despite outcries from activist groups and even former House Speaker

Dennis Hastert, who called the move "unconscionable" given the high price at the pump. The economic collapse in September 2008 highlights more deplorable CEO conduct. Thain spent over $1 million redecorating his office as the company collapsed around him and was rescued only through a buyout by Bank of America. JPMorgan Chase's leadership, despite having received more than $25 billion in Troubled Asset Relief Program (TARP) bailout funds in 2008, publicly contemplated buying a new fleet of corporate jets to replace the ones they already had at a cost of $50 million per plane. And Jia Lynn Yang reports in the *Washington Post* that nonfinancial corporations are sitting on $1.8 trillion but are not investing any of that cash in the American people in terms of job growth (2010). The public perception that CEOs will do anything and put anyone at risk for their own self-interest results in votes of little confidence in corporate America.

Of course, other eras have suffered crises commensurate with this crisis of confidence and faith in institutions. However, this particular crisis coincides with a rise in conservative power in the United States led by staunchly religious individuals touting America's history as a Judeo-Christian nation founded on Judeo-Christian beliefs. This leads to an uncomfortable dilemma: Americans believe in God in huge numbers, yet the seemingly unchecked power that accompanies late capitalist institutions is graphically inconsistent with Judeo-Christian values like charity, responsibility, empathy, respect for all people, and humility. In times when people find their behavior, or the behavior of their leaders, inconsistent with values, the prophetic voice returns. As I explain later in this chapter, prophets are called by a higher power in a time of crisis to remind people of their covenant with God and to alert them to the fact that if they continue to violate this covenant, serious punishment will apply. Not only does a lack of trust in institutions lead to The Prophet style but it also calls for a voice of spiritual guidance in a time of crumbling faith in institutions. It calls, also, for The Guru.

A Rise in Religious Fundamentalism

Friedrich Nietzsche's proclamation that "God is dead" nearly 125 years ago seems now to be a laughable hyperbole—God is very much alive indeed. And, while mainstream churches have been losing members for decades, fundamentalist church attendance has boomed (Pew, 2003). Religion reporter Douglas Todd of the *Vancouver Sun* in Vancouver, British Columbia, estimates in 2004 that a rise in Christian fundamentalism in the United States would "affect the way we do politics, wage wars, entertain ourselves, view sexuality, interpret scriptures, deal with the gap between rich and poor, view our next-door neighbour and find inner meaning." Indeed, in the United States, the Southern Baptist church, the Churches of Christ, the Assemblies of God, the Evangelical Lutheran Church in America, and the Church of Jesus Christ of Latter Day Saints are staunchly among the top 10 Christian churches in terms of both numbers of congregations and church attendance (Glenmary Research Center, 1990). These aforementioned churches as well as other fundamentalist churches, such as, the Lutheran Church–Missouri Synod and the Church of God, comprise the most ubiquitous churches—in other words, where the church is among the ten largest in many of the fifty states (Pew, 2003). As recently as 1996, only 51 percent of people thought favorably of fundamentalists and evangelicals; ten years later, fundamentalists were viewed by 76 percent of people as favorable (Pew, 2004).

So, while we can grapple over the meaning of the words *conservative* and *religious right*, there is no doubt that fundamentalism is on the rise, not only in the United States but in Latin America, Asia, Africa, and the Middle East. Former President Jimmy Carter's *Our Endangered Values: America's Moral Crisis* (2006) attacks fundamentalism for its "rigidity, domination and exclusion" and decries fundamentalism's invasion of politics, citing, "Narrowly defined theological beliefs have been adopted as the rigid agenda" (p. 32) of certain political leaders. Maureen Dowd of the *New York Times* went so far as to characterize the current politico-religious climate in the United States as having the "feel of a vengeful mob—revved up by rectitude—running around with torches and hatchets after heathens and pagans and infidels" (2004). The GOP's vice-presidential candidate in 2008, former Alaska Governor Sarah Palin, is largely identified as the posterperson for this trend toward fundamentalist religiosity, even (and especially) in political life.

The very fact that fundamentalism is on the rise is perhaps not as interesting as the proposed reasons why it is seeing such impressive popularity. The basic idea is, we live in a world of gray areas, fuzzy borders, rapid change, increasing diversity, "alternative lifestyles," ubiquitous technology, and other uncomfortable phenomena (Bendroth, 1996). This postmodern confusion and blurring clashes with seemingly superior nostalgic values of old. Out of the discord emerge fear, distrust, and panic among some who would prefer that the world be categorizable, black and white, fundamentally planned, answerable. Candidate Palin's call that rural America (read: small town, white, Christian, conservative) is the "real America" and that people like Barack Obama (read: Ivy League, foreign, exotic, Muslim, black, liberal) are not "like the rest of us" and "pal around with terrorists" resonate in communities in crisis. Enter the healing waters of fundamentalism. Fundamentalism is loosely defined as a return to root values, a rigid adherence to those principles, and an intolerance for secularism and humanism. One has to look no further than the ascendance of the Ayatollah Khomeini in Iran in the late 1970s, the dominance of the Taliban in Afghanistan for several decades following the war with the Soviets, or our own backyard and the prominence of conservative extremists like Pat Robertson and Palin to see what fundamentalism can look and sound like. While many are apt to dismiss the rise of fundamentalism as a fleeting trend, the "chaos" that started the trend is not going away. If anything, our world becomes more uncomfortable each day, fueling fundamentalism's fire (and brimstone).

To decrease a feeling of ubiquitous "ickiness" brought on by gray area, most people seek an enlightened solution. Very few, regardless of their tolerance for ambiguity, enjoy having their beliefs, values, and sense of right and wrong challenged on a daily basis. Indeed, the meteoric rise of the Tea Party in this country is perhaps the most illustrative example of an American sentiment that if we could only return to the good old days, life would be so much better, despite any evidence to the contrary. Yet, we live in a time in which faith in government and corporate institutions has eroded substantially, so where do people turn? While increasingly fundamentalist churches in the United States provide an open door for prophetic rhetoric, this trend also opens the door to another public intellectual rhetorical style: The Guru. The Guru, as I get into later in this chapter, serves to take the confused public by the figurative hand and lead them to enlightenment, salvation, righteousness, or some other spiritual end. The Guru, although traditionally a Hindu teacher, does not subscribe solely to one religion but could be a member of any religious group or philosophical spiritual orientation.

Environmental Damage

Perhaps the least-shocking modern trend in this list is the overwhelming data implicating humankind in the destruction of the natural environment. We may not be the sole cause of this damaging cycle, but we have worked diligently to accelerate the process since the Industrial Revolution (McDonough & Braungart, 2002). Because of fossil-fuel emissions from factories and vehicles, the levels of carbon dioxide in our atmosphere will be 75 to 350 percent higher than preindustrial levels by the end of the twenty-first century (National Oceanographic, n.d.a). It now appears that stronger hurricanes, such as, Katrina, are even related to this human-advanced destruction. The United States remains against signing the Kyoto Protocol, the objective of which is to stabilize "greenhouse gas concentrations in the atmosphere at a level that would prevent dangerous anthropogenic interference with the climate system" (National Oceanographic, n.d.b).

In addition to global warming, other activities are contributing to environmental destruction. Since 1970, more than 600,000 square kilometers (or 232,000 square miles) of the Amazon rain forest have been deforested or clear-cut for commercial development (Mongabay, n.d.). Because of this deforestation in Brazil and other parts of the world, plant and animal species are in extreme danger. Much was made of the "Save the Spotted Owl" and "Save the Whale" campaigns launched by the Sierra Club, Greenpeace, and other environmental organizations, but the devastation of wildlife continues.

Finally, among the greatest dangers to the environment is nuclear proliferation. Ironically, the United States is trying to enter into negotiations with Iran and North Korea to force the countries to abolish nuclear-energy programs the United States believes are leading to weapons development even as the United States remains the world's largest nuclear superpower (Greenpeace, n.d.). The most recent Strategic Arms Reduction Treaty (START), signed by President Obama and Russian President Dmitry Medvedev in 2010 and aimed at reducing nuclear arsenals, found a chilly reception among congressional Republicans like Jon Kyl and Ron Paul. Nuclear accidents, such as, those at Three Mile Island in Pennsylvania, Hanford in Washington, and most frightening, Chernobyl in the Ukraine, led to loss of life, poisoning of water and air, and a host of birth defects and health problems that persist years and even decades later (Greenpeace, n.d.).

The United States has for decades dealt with the natural environment through well intentioned but piecemeal policy decisions—if we bury waste instead of dumping it in rivers, our problems will be solved. No? If we designate certain land as protected from human-led destruction, we will rescue the earth. No? If we recycle materials, we can use them forever. No? Clearly, piecemeal "solutions" have been proven limited or ridiculously nearsighted. Out of the ashes of environmental devastation rises the phoenix of sustainability. Sustainer-variety public intellectuals are particularly relevant in times of crisis because the solutions they advocate are long-term rather than short-lived and healthful rather than destructive. Their solutions also have a sense of permanence because the rhetoric of sustainability seeks to make overarching paradigm shifts that will ultimately eradicate the problem at hand.

However, environmental issues are likely a symptom of destruction in sociopolitical environments—cultures have gone awry because of power and money being overly concentrated among special interests to the detriment of most citizens. In addition, this trend could easily be seen as calling forth The Prophet because of this style's focus on arriving in a time of crisis to deliver judgment on the guilty.

Sound-Bite Culture

Political communication scholar Rod Hart writes in *Seducing America: How Television Charms the Modern Voter*, "The eye, the most gluttonous of all human organs, takes in all that can be taken in; it is an organ that cannot be satiated" (1994, p. 61). Hart is talking about television as the harbinger of change in political life, but his comment speaks to a larger shift in our culture—hypermediation. We have information coming at us from every possible direction: billboards offering to buy ugly houses, spam e-mail suggesting we may benefit from physical "enhancements," television news, advertisements for everything from underwear to hard liquor and back again. No wonder people feel overloaded by information. Perhaps Hart (1994) is right when he says that modern media "fill an emotional void in modern life, a void perhaps created by modern life itself" (p. 11). Perhaps because we are bowling alone, we feel alienated from one another and from our communities locally and at large (Putnam, 2000; Duke University, 2006). And perhaps hypermediation is to blame.

Not only are we inundated for as many hours as we are awake but the information itself is also often superficial and brief. We are in a moment of "off-the-rack attitudes now passing for informed . . . discussion" where "discourse is propositionless, overly truncated, sensationalistic" (Hart, 1994, p. 7). Indeed, deliberation has been replaced by the "fifteen-second spot" (Hart, 1994, p. 6) on all channels, through all mediums, all the time. Because of the truncated and sound-bite nature of many messages, people are miseducated and unengaged but *feel* as if they are informed and participating (Hart, 1994). Television news, for instance, fails to inform its audience and highly dramatized forms of the "content" "decrease viewers' recall of information, as well as the complexity with which they thought about a given problem" (Hart, 1994, p. 58).

It seems that because we are so saturated with information from ubiquitous media, our instinct is to go indoors and try to wait out the flood. Sociologist Richard Sennett declares that people have "lost a sense of [themselves] as an active force, as a 'public'" (1977, p. 261; see also Chomsky, 2010). We have gone private to avoid feeling overstimulated in public. Media have "[expanded] the private sphere" such that we are "removed . . . from the public sphere by making it seem that the public sphere has come to us" (Hart, 1994, pp. 69, 115). Our high-gloss, sound-bite existence has real consequences for deliberation—we want up-to-the-minute news that takes as long to listen to as soup does to microwave, and we would prefer it be entertaining, thank you very much. The very idea of congregating with others to deliberate social issues is not remotely in the purview of the average person, regardless of how truly informative and even inspiring that might be. If it does not fit on a bumper sticker, we look for something that does.

A lack of deliberation produces feelings of panic because there seem to be no obvious paths or solutions in sight. Also, because of their ubiquity, sound bites become a low hum—the only things that register, therefore, above the din are hyperbolic overstatements of particular positions that are never interrogated for their merit for the public sphere. Clearly, The Guru style fits well here because people seek to ease their sense of dread about a world that seems out of their control. However, the most obvious style fit here is The Pundit. The Pundit seizes upon the opportunities that mystification and ambiguity provide and becomes the color announcer of the chaotic game. Although more superficial in nature, The Pundit's commentary functions as a salve for an information-weary nation because it at least invites conversation about critical issues in the public domain, even if that conversation is around a water cooler.

Shifting Notions of Evidence

Recently, we have heard quite a lot of the adage, "Everyone is entitled to his/her own opinion, but they are not entitled to his/her own facts." Yet, this adage is only superficially heeded, if at all—"facts" in our era are very slippery. Indeed, Stephen Colbert's term *truthiness* was invented to describe this phenomenon of believing what we feel is true or right rather than relying on evidence grounded in empirical reality to make decisions, elect candidates, or create policy. A representative example occurred during the September 12, 2011, GOP/Tea Party debate on CNN in which US Representative Michele Bachmann (R–MN) chided Texas Governor Rick Perry for mandating that twelve-year-old girls receive a vaccination for human papillomavirus (HPV), by stating that not only was it big government at its worst but that the vaccine has the potential to cause "mental retardation" (Knickerbocker, 2011). Bachmann recounted a meeting she had a distraught mother who blames her daughter's developmental delays on the HPV vaccination mandated by Perry. Scholars of ethics, philosophy, rhetoric, or argument could tell Bachmann about fallacious argumentation via hasty generalization or post hoc ergo propter hoc, but that response is akin to offering a cotton ball to someone whose femoral artery is severed, hoping it stops the bleeding.

It is not that facts do not exist or that one side of the political spectrum is somehow privy to information the other side is not, but it is that this country hosts a vocal subset of people for whom facts are not particularly meaningful. Certainly, traditional standards of evidence are not politically useful. Against this kind of certitude, it seems unlikely to change the believer's mind that Barack Obama's birth certificate is not a Kenyan forgery, that climate change is real and precipitated and accelerated by human activity, that 9/11 was not an inside job, that evolution is not a hoax, or that the Founding Fathers did not intend to create a Christian theocracy in the early days of this nation. The standards of evidence an academic honors—objectivity, disciplinary authority, data, empiricism, and rigor—are not well-suited for our media ecology. As Peter Brooks (2006) describes, "The mediating organs of our culture are in disrepair—and that surely is linked to refuge [by intellectuals] in the university on the one hand, and surrender to the mass media on the other." Much of the disrepair can be traced to corporate hegemonic control of the American media system such that those with the deepest pockets control the "facts," and as Robert McChesney explains, "[j]ournalists, editors and media professionals who rise to the top of the hierarchy tend to internalize the values, both commercial and political, of media owners" (2004, p. 100). And yet, "a central issue in the health of democracy concerns the vibrancy of civil society, and a key issue for this is the problem of information" (Wright & Rogers, 2010, p. 1). In other words, information that does not jibe with corporate politics will not make it into print or onto the airwaves. Said another way, in the "free market" of information, standards of evidence and evidence itself are not politically or commercially expedient because they are not moneymakers (McChesney, 2004).

It is difficult to imagine that we will soon overthrow corporate-owned American media such that citizens demand evidentiary rigor in order to hear a variety of relevant positions and make more informed decisions (Wright & Rogers, 2010). One kind of evidence that seems to appeal to people otherwise wary of academic standards is the experiential. While we suffer from quite a lot of journalism that seems to believe that a "thus" is made from an *n* of one (e.g., "a guy I know . . ."), phenomenology feels more "real" than social scientifically derived accounts of the world. While The Guru and The Pundit could easily be called into being by this desire for stories over "hard" data, The Narrator is the most natural outcome of the trend. The Narrator gives voice, context, and relational sense to a story and is able to inform an audience or community around an event, issue, or situation without raising the kinds of red flags that seem to go up whenever traditional intellectuals try to mix it up on television.

ATEMPORAL STYLE

While style is generally constrained by history and sociopolitical forces like the situated, temporal styles explicated above, some styles are atemporal in nature because rather than drawing from recent trends, they draw from more culturally stable reservoirs like cultural mythology. Certainly, situated styles can do this work as well, but we would be remiss not to attend to all the stylistic possibilities. Styles like The Scientist, then, are culturally rather than temporally bound for two key reasons. First, they resonate with more people than do other public intellectual styles because The Scientist's styles begin at the ground floor of our collective experience, and, second, they have resonated and will continue to resonate in other eras because they are not "trendy" but "classic." They are the Jackie O's of public intellectual styles. I want to assuage fears that I am blinded by science, that I am somehow essentializing atemporality in the realm of science. I am not. What I mean to articulate is that because scientists have a much-longer history of "selling" their projects to attract benefactors, we might learn from some of their tricks not situated in an era: Asking questions about "universals," such as, the existence of God, and writing for a lay public to garner funding enable these rhetors to hone a style that can facilitate stronger and richer engagement between intellectuals and publics simply by virtue of getting an important project off the ground.

As mythology expert Joseph Campbell describes, "Myths are public dreams. . . . Dreams are private myths. Myths are vehicles of communication between the conscious and the unconscious, just as dreams are." For Campbell, myth and mythology tell "as much about humanity—its deepest fears, sorrows, joys and hopes—as dreams tell about an individual" (1972). As Campbell explains, a myth is a "symbol that evokes and directs psychological energy" (1972). These symbols carry with them substantive meaning about the philosophical and ideological underpinnings of a culture. Mythology teaches observers what a culture believes, what it values, what it wants, and how it wishes to be perceived. For Campbell, mythology serves four cultural purposes:

> 1. Through its rites and imagery it wakens and maintains in the individual a sense of awe, gratitude and even rapture, rather than fear, in relation to the mystery both of the universe and of man's own existence within it.
> 2. It offers each of us a comprehensive, understandable image of the world around us, roughly in accord with the best scientific knowledge of the time. In symbolic form, it tells us what our universe looks like and where we belong in it.
> 3. It supports the social order through rites and rituals that will impress and mold the young.
> 4. It guides the individual, stage by stage, through the inevitable psychological crises of a useful life: from the childhood condition of dependency through the traumas of adolescence and the trials of adulthood to, finally, the deathbed. (1972)

In other words, cultural mythology has direct bearing on the individuals within that culture. In this way, myth and dreams are interconnected: Dreams are individual-scale versions of cultural myths; myths are culture-scale versions of individual dreams. Every person is the product of cultural influence from birth to death, and we become increasingly familiar and invested in the collective dreams of our culture. That is, "everyone is a creature of myth, that the ancient legends and tales of the race are still the master keys to the human psyche" (1972, p. 1).

In making the case for war against Iraq, much was made of the United States' responsibility to shine the light of democracy into the dark, despotic corners of the Earth. We are the New Israel, says our cultural mythology, not a country that consumes 25 percent of the world's oil and, therefore, must make sure we can get our petroleum fix. After both the *Challenger* and *Columbia* accidents, NASA and its partisans invoked the myth of manifest destiny and argued that we are a nation of explorers and it was our duty to keep sending humans into space. In the 2008 election season, the myth of equality, of a classless society, of the melting pot were all part of the narrative of both presidential tickets. As products of a culture, we take personal ownership of these myths as "ours."

The rhetoric of science demonstrates a keen awareness of cultural mythology. Reading the *New York Times* "Science Page" and *Science* magazine illuminates the ways people talk about science. On the homepage of each source alone, words jump out at readers, including "wonder," "beauty," "life," "space," "cutting edge," "innovation," "beginning," and "revolution," each a cultural god term in its own right (Weaver, 1953/1985). Each fits into a cultural mythos that speaks to individuals—Americans are explorers and discoverers, we are the first to create and to innovate and to develop. For example, in his speech to Rice University in 1962 known as the "We Choose to Go to the Moon" speech, President John F. Kennedy states,

> For the eyes of the world now look into space, to the moon and to the planets beyond, and we have vowed that we shall not see it governed by a hostile flag of conquest, but by a banner of freedom and peace. We have vowed that we shall not see space filled with weapons of mass destruction, but with instruments of knowledge and understanding.
>
> Yet the vows of this Nation can only be fulfilled if we in this Nation are first, and, therefore, we intend to be first. In short, our leadership in science and industry, our hopes for peace and security, our obligations to ourselves as well as others, all require us to make this effort, to solve these mysteries, to solve them for the good of all men, and to become the world's leading space-faring nation.

Kennedy makes a truly American case to go to the moon, calling on collective mythology to speak to individual dreams. Translating Campbell's understanding of mythology for style, science, like mythology, inspires awe about the mysteries of the universe, works with the best knowledge of the time to explain our place within it, and guides us through life from cradle to grave (1972, p. 4). As such, The Scientist marks an intriguing case for those of us who want to connect our intellectual pursuits to the public sphere because it gives us a model for extraordinarily broad appeal and national, or even international, relevance.

DIMENSIONS OF STYLISTIC COMPARISON

Each of us is a bricoleur, or one who cobbles together stylistic cues from a variety of available sources and puts them together to be read as a style, a sort of publicly performed logos to be read and judged by others. Robert Hariman (1995) explains, "Each . . . style draws on universal elements of the human condition and symbolic repertoire but organizes them into a limited, customary set of communicative design" (p. 11). Yet, despite our individual distinctiveness, there are sites on which we can compare and contrast styles to get at their efficacy and their potential for use by other would-be public intellectuals. Five dimensions are specifically germane: fluidity, degree, location, media, and resources.

On a university campus in his or her native environment, the academic intellectual looks completely natural. Intellectuals look like they belong in a classroom wearing tweed, surrounded by students, covered in chalk dust, papers hanging out of a worn briefcase. However, if the intellectual walked into an interview in an office in the private sector, he or she would be shockingly out of place. Fluidity, then, is a dimension that allows us to understand how easily a public intellectual moves between "worlds." Is the public intellectual like water, maintaining its core integrity but being able to flow in different directions and in different contexts? If so, we might call a public intellectual's style fluid. Traditional intellectuals, on the other hand, are nonfluid—their rhetorical style that works so beautifully in the campus environment makes them conspicuous in other environments. Their style does not travel well. Public intellectuals, on the other hand, are fluid but perhaps to varying degrees in diverse situations. Knowing how fluid and in what situations helps us to understand the importance of fluidity to public intellectual style.

Closely related to the dimension of fluidity is degree. What I mean by degree is the level of "publicness" and the level of "intellectualness" that a public intellectual possesses and demonstrates. Of course, public intellectuals are both public and intellectual simultaneously, but the two worlds push and pull on public intellectuals such that balance is precarious. In turn, there are probably public intellectuals who are more heavily public than intellectual (Rachel Maddow), and there are those more intellectual than public (Dr. Maya Angelou). Degree provides a way of gauging in what circumstances and with what habitus a public intellectual is more public or more intellectual. Degree can also measure change over time. If crises escalate, public intellectuals may be more dedicated to the public than to more traditional intellectual work; if crises deescalate, another path may emerge. Knowing this, we can better comprehend the contexts that produce a habitus with a higher degree of publicness and one with a higher degree of intellectualness, and we can better comprehend the implications of such a habitus in society.

In popular and academic literature on public intellectual figures, location is a common dimension of study. It is a useful one here, as well. Location addresses the questions: Where are public intellectuals? In academe? In the private or public sector? All of these? Different locations demand different styles. An iceberg remains an iceberg at the North

Pole but an enormous puddle in San Diego. While it is still authentically water, location dictates its ultimate form. We may note that because of tenure requirements and other structural impediments, academics find it increasingly difficult to be public intellectuals. I point to the case of Cornel West, rebuked by his own alma mater and then-employer, Harvard University, for doing too much in the way of public works. Another example is Professor Robert Jensen of the University of Texas, who, after his letter to the editor in the *Houston Chronicle* condemning the United States for its role in spurring on the events of September 11, 2001, was lambasted by UT President Larry Falkner: "Jensen is not only misguided, but has become a fountain of undiluted foolishness on issues of public policy" (Nichols, 2001). Location can also help scholars acknowledge the existence of public intellectuals outside academe—a line of thought that has been slow in developing.

Not only is it compelling to note where we find public intellectuals but also how public intellectuals communicate. The use of media is a way to examine this distinction between public intellectual styles. How do different public intellectuals express themselves? Is it always face-to-face or in another physically present way, such as, public address? Do they appear on television or write for a newspaper? Do they blog? All of these tools may be used, but channel selection has always been of interest to communication scholars and remains of relevance in this case, as well. For example, it is my anecdotal opinion that there is an inverse relationship between the amount of time a public intellectual spends on television and the amount of perceived intellectualism that person maintains. In other words, the more Sanjay Gupta, MD, appears on CNN as a medical correspondent, the less impressive an intellect he is perceived to be by other doctors. This begs the question: Do different media have different reputations? Part of unpacking media use will be understanding whether popular media channels like television are less "intellectual" in some way than more time-honored media channels like print news. By studying the public intellectual's use of media, issues like this may be addressed.

Resources are central to style. By resources, I include all things financial, but I also include training, credentials, education, media access, and opportunity. Not all public intellectuals are wealthy, or, at least, they may not have begun their lives that way. All do, however, obtain training and education in some area of expertise. What are those different areas? What counts as "appropriate" training (i.e., does one need a PhD to be a public intellectual? Does one even need a BA?)? For example, in the last decade, many would identify Bill Gates as a public intellectual because of his extensive work in complex humanitarian crises related to education and medical science through the Gates Foundation. Yet, famously, Gates dropped out of Harvard before earning his BA (he has since gone back to finish). Just as notable, many who hold advanced degrees are not public intellectuals. Further, as was just discussed, public intellectuals may access different media resources to do work. And, different opportunities present themselves depending on context, location, fluidity, and the other dimensions I have explained. Above all, public intellectual style is "a particular expertise disposed, like any other *techne*, to displace any other kind of intelligence" (Hariman, 1995, p. 3).

Historical moments are characterized by particular rhetorical styles that "work" in that time. We are currently in a time characterized by crisis: a crisis of faith in institutions brought on by political scandal and corporate corruption. A crisis of intolerance brought on by a rise in fundamentalism and, therefore, a narrowing of what it means to be ethical or even "OK." A crisis of the environment brought on by human production since the Industrial Revolution. A crisis of a lack of space and climate for deliberation brought on by hypermediation and the "me" generation. And, a crisis of information and evidence. Out of these crises come five situated rhetorical stylistic responses: The Prophet, The Guru, The Sustainer, The Pundit, and The Narrator. Out of our cultural tradition emerges an atemporal stylistic response: The Scientist. The next chapter develops Cornel West as an example of Prophet style.

2

PROPHET STYLE: CORNEL WEST

Cornel West can be found in many places. First, he is the 1943 Professor of Religion at Princeton University, though he has held faculty positions at Union Theological Seminary, Yale University, Harvard University, and the University of Paris, Sorbonne. Second, he is a contributor to CNN, C-SPAN, and NPR. Third, he performed on a CD of rap music and spoken-word art called *Sketches of My Culture*. Fourth, he appears in *The Matrix* films as "Counselor West." Fifth, his other nonfiction works, notably *Race Matters* and *The Cornel West Reader*, were bestsellers along with the work I examine here, *Democracy Matters: Winning the Fight against Imperialism*. Notable, The Prophet positions him/herself stylistically as the heir apparent of the Hebrew tradition, a mystical denouncer of sin, claiming authority from a higher power, using "intellectual" media (NPR, print) to castigate sinners, all the while maintaining a more marginalized, and, therefore, more authentic, persona.

THE PROPHETIC STYLE

Prophet style emerges out of a long tradition of Judaic prophecy from biblical times. The prophets of the Old Testament, such as, Ezekiel, Daniel, and Jeremiah, were called by God to live the ultimately difficult life of prophecy: lives of pious isolation and the task of damning their fellow Jews for breaking basic covenants with God. Six major characteristics of prophetic rhetoric that hold for public intellectual prophets are: having authenticity, being called by a higher power, speaking a "higher" form of truth, speaking in a kairotic moment of crisis, standing apart to offer judgment, and describing a community's betrayal of God and the road to redemption. I am examining Cornel West's description of his prophetic philosophy in *Democracy Matters*, his media appearances, and his own life to elucidate his prophetic public intellectual skill on two levels. First, West's rhetoric demonstrates mastery of the prophetic archetype by clarifying his status as an authentic, called prophet of God and American politics who rises in a time of crisis to deliver judgment and outline a hopeful path to redemption for the sinners in his midst. Second, West's own rhetorical habitus reinforces the prophetic rhetorical form through his work to limit and ultimately eradicate American imperialism and its ramifications both at home and abroad, and his "lived" philosophy of "deep democracy" serves to regenerate activism and community. West's work and life shows him not as a strictly religious prophet, though he is a theologian and professor of religion; but because his focus is entirely sociopolitical, his brand of prophecy belongs to the category of public intellectuals known as Prophets. He speaks to several communities: African Americans, activists, and the empowered elite. Considering style as habitus means focusing on the physiological, psychological, and sociological performances of Cornel West to understand how he embodies Prophet style.

Physiological Style

Cornel West does not look like a typical theologian: He is never seen wearing the robes of ministry, he does not maintain a conservative hair style, and he does not pose for photo opportunities, smiling, Bible in hand. This is because West is predominantly a thinker-activist who uses the teaching of theology to inform his political and social philosophies. Therefore, his physiological style is somewhat unconventional relative to what most consider appropriate for a man of God. Yet, because there are constraints on the kinds of styles that resonate in certain eras (Hariman, 1995; Brummett, 2008), West's ability to recognize the limits of the stylistic embodiments of the traditional "man of God" enables him to be more effective in communities that might otherwise reject the do-gooder in the clerical collar. West still wears an afro, and his taste in clothing seems to channel Malcolm X—plain black suits, white shirts, black bowties. In fact, West looks more like a holdover from the late 1960s black-power generation, but his appearance is thoroughly in line with his overall rhetorical style: the thinking person's activist.

However, listening to West, it becomes clear that this prophetic public intellectual embodies and performs theologian, intellectual, and activist and rarely as discrete categories. In terms of the performance of theology,

West's written work and public speaking engagements are rife with references to scripture and religious philosophy. Quoting biblical prophets adds to the strength of this rhetorical move. West offers examples from scripture, "to do justice, to love kindness and to walk humbly with your God" (Micah 6:8) and "to keep the way of the Lord by doing righteousness and justice" (Genesis 18:19)" (West, 2004, p. 114). West invokes the history of the prophetic:

> Let us begin with the long and rich prophetic tradition among Jews, past and present. . . . We recall that the Jewish invention of the prophetic, to be found in the scriptural teachings of Amos, Hosea, Isaiah, Micah, Jeremiah and Habakkuk, not only put justice at the center of what it means to be chosen as a Jewish people but also made compassion to human suffering and kindness to the stranger the fundamental features of the most noble human calling. (2004, pp. 112–14)

In using actual quotations from biblical prophets in scripture interspersed with a categorical understanding of the history of prophecy, West exhibits a rich knowledge of both the historical tradition and the language of the prophetic. In doing so, he begins to make the implicit case for himself as modern-day prophet.

Certainly, with West's academic pedigree and distinguished teaching career at some of the world's finest institutions of higher learning, we would expect West to perform or embody intellect, and he does not disappoint. In an interview with CNN, West argues, "Classroom reasoning should be applied to gritty urban realities: Sensitive race issues like whether reparations should be paid to black America for slavery have to be confronted by whites and blacks before any true healing can occur" (Associated Press, 2002). West marries philosophy from Søren Kierkegaard to the teachings of Gandhi and King. And, he teaches some of Princeton University's most popular courses. As Ronald Walters, professor of political science from the University of Maryland, offers, "Cornel is foremost a philosopher. . . . He has one of the quickest minds among scholars I know and puts together unique perspectives on issues" (Associated Press, 2002).

Finally, West performs and embodies activism. Aside from the Malcolm X vibe he gives off from his appearance, West uses his physical body to take action on critical political and social issues. For example, West was the intellectual leader of the Nation of Islam leader Louis Farrakhan's Million Man March and worked with rival gang members to end street violence in the black community. In a February 22, 2000, interview with C-SPAN about his nonfiction work, *The Cornel West Reader*, West asks, "Why are black men 7 percent of the population and 50 percent of the jail population . . . ? It is a national crisis for me." As the Associated Press reports, "West is primarily a thinker who uses his life experiences and interpretation of other works for a more impassioned, seat-of-the-pants style of professorship" for which he is famous, or even infamous, given one's perspective (2002).

Not only is physiological style embodied and performative but it is also a reflection of an inner persona. In other words, physiological style involves embodying a worldview. For West, his life, religious ideology, and political philosophy are grounded in the ideals of democracy: equality, justice, respect, and humanity. Toward this end, West's physiological style can be described as democratic. He does not employ the vocabulary of the traditional academic, despite his tenure among the intellectual elite. He is very clearly a student of Cicero and of Gramsci. For example, in detailing the legacy and goals of prophetic Judeo-Christian life, West explains simply, "The prophetic goal is to stir up in us the courage to care and empower us to change our lives and our historical circumstances" (2004, p. 115). West's rhetorical style marks a belief in speaking accessibly for as many as possible. Not only does his speaking style embody this democratic worldview but his use of media does as well. West has never felt confined to the classroom even if his primary occupation is university professor. Rather, since achieving mass popularity on the wings of his book *Race Matters*, West has been on the lecture circuit, a regular contributor to C-SPAN and NPR, in *The Matrix* series of films, on CD with his spoken word/rap, and most recently, online with his web presence. In other words, West embodies democracy by trying to speak and reach as large an audience as possible without it costing huge dollars to catch a glimpse.

Psychological Style

Having psychological style is having consistency between what one says and how one lives. For West, this consistency emerges through his indictment of current sociopolitical and even religious practices alongside his personal democratic practice, itself an implied indictment of the current moment. It has always been a hallmark of prophetic rhetoric that The Prophet arrives at a kairotic moment of crisis to articulate God's judgment and provide a pathway to righteousness. West follows in this tradition in his indictment of this sociopolitical moment generally and the George W. Bush administration and its policies specifically.

West begins *Democracy Matters*, published during Bush's presidency, in fact, with a chapter titled, "Democracy Matters Are Frightening in Our Time," where he establishes that the entire book will be dedicated to looking "unflinchingly at the waning of democratic energies and practices in our present age of the American empire" because "[t]here is a deeply troubling deterioration of democratic powers in America today" (2004, p. 2). Instead of the kind of deliberative democracy the American Constitution outlines, "elite salesmanship to the demos has taken the place of genuine democratic leadership" (2004, p. 3) and where the three antidemocratic dogmas of free-market fundamentalism, aggressive militarism, and escalating authoritarianism rule (2004, pp. 3–6). West sums up the sad situation succinctly:

> In short, we are experiencing the sad American imperial devouring of American democracy. This historic devouring in our time constitutes an unprecedented gangsterization of America—an unbridled grasp at power, wealth, and status. And when the most powerful forces in a society—and an empire—promote a suffocation of democratic energies, the very future of genuine democracy is jeopardized. (2004, p. 8)

Certainly, we can point to other times in this country in which we faced crises: slavery and the subsequent secession of the American south from the Union leading to the Civil War; presidential assassinations; denial of basic rights to people of color, women, religions other than Christianity, and sexual practices outside of mainstream heteronormativity; and Vietnam. So what is more troubling about this contemporary moment that would bring the prophets to the fore? West states, "[T]he course and unabashed imperial devouring of democracy of the Bush administration was a low point in America's rocky history of sustaining its still evolving experiment in democracy" (2004, p. 10). He argues that the Bush era was a disaster and that his reelection to a second term was further evidence of a broken covenant with, in this case, the god of democracy.

Continuing in his democratic psychological style, West also condemns American Christianity as it is practiced in fundamentalist circles: "[T]he dominant forms of Christian fundamentalism are a threat to the tolerance and openness necessary for sustaining any democracy" (2004, p. 146). West asks a series of provocative questions: "Does not the vast concentration of so much power and might breed arrogance and hubris? Do not the Old Testament prophets and teachings of Jesus suggest, at the least, a suspicion of such unrivaled and unaccountable wealth and status? Are not the empires the occasion of idolatry run amok?" (2004, p. 151). The questions he asks are quite obviously rhetorical, a device used to soften the blow of The Prophet's message by asking the audience to engage in deliberation and reflection. Since West is a public intellectual prophet, he does not limit his focus to religious or theological concerns but rather turns his keen attention outward to the broader scope of sociopolitical troubles and tanglings in which the American people find themselves.

The foremost job of The Prophet, though, is to cast judgment on a guilty people for their decision to break their covenant with whatever higher authority The Prophet serves. This is a lonely and unhappy mission. Biblical prophets were intensely discontented men—they had been called as the mouthpieces of God to deliver very damning tidings to the Jewish people and so lived as outcasts and loners because few others want to befriend someone who spends his life judging them unfavorably. Although this is an unfortunate mission, The Prophet accepts it because he or she feels that not to do so would be to turn a back to God, a decision far worse than serving as judge and jury of a guilty nation. The public intellectual prophet, like the biblical prophets of old, must also cast judgment and must use considerable evidence as an intellectual to justify his or her chastisement.

Cornel West gives a judgment of the ills associated with the stripping of democratic practices in the United States and around the world. However, the public intellectual prophet cannot simply condemn everyone in his or her path but rather must select those people who are the most egregious offenders, those against whom The Prophet has the most damning evidence. Why? Because, unlike biblical prophets who were accepted on the basis that God called them, public intellectual prophets have to answer to evidentiary standards of the intellectual elite. Intellectuals are fundamentally curious, well-researched people, and without that basis, West would summarily be dismissed as taking a superficial swing at an issue he is clearly unprepared to hit out of the park.

West selects four major groups for judgment: the Bush administration, the religious "right"/fundamentalists, academics unwilling to engage the culture at large, and US political policy at home and abroad. He says the Bush administration marked a sharp decline in America's shaky experiment in democracy, and, "We must not allow our elected officials—many beholden to unaccountable corporate elites—to bastardize and pulverize the precious word *democracy* as they fail to respect and act on genuine democratic ideals" (2004, p. 3). In addition, he holds that the Bush administration was particularly guilty of corporate and religious cronyism leading to an unholy and undemocratic alliance among corporate, religious, and political elites. This marriage, he explains, "undermines the truth of informed citizens in those who rule over them. It also promotes the pervasive sleepwalking of the populace, who see that the false prophets are handsomely rewarded with money, status, and access to more power. This profit-driven vision is sucking the democratic life out of American society" (2004, p. 4).

His prophetic judgment continues. If the Bush administration dug democracy's grave, religious fundamentalism in America is putting the nails in the coffin. West makes the argument that Constantinian Christians (his term for Christian fundamentalists) today demonstrate many parallels with the Romans who put their savior to death on the cross. In addition, he chastises Constantinian Jews for their complicit alliance with the United States in condoning racist and violent policies against Palestinians and others of Arab descent. He also reminds those who practice Islam that their treatment of women in their own countries is not part of the democratic tradition he claims was envisioned by the Prophet Muhammad. He warns about all of these groups, "Even the most seemingly pious can inflict great harm" (2004, p. 169).

Because, as West claims, "[t]his love of democracy has been most powerfully expressed and pushed forward by our great public intellectuals and artists" (2004, p. 15), he is critical of academic elites who do not engage the larger culture. He suggests that in colleges and universities, where democratic traditions should be cemented and taught, market forces have started to invade: "A market-driven technocratic culture has infiltrated university life, with the narrow pursuit of academic trophies and the business of generating income from grants and business partnerships taking precedence over the fundamental responsibility of nurturing young minds" (2004, p. 186). In essence, West castigates his fellow academics for worshipping at the altar of high-profile grants and selling their democratically engaged souls for a business partnership rather than using their authority, and the platform that authority provides, to make real change and bring legitimate solutions to bear on social problems.

Finally, West condemns US policy at home and abroad. America's domestic policy of "free-market fundamentalism" is a growing danger. West blames this brand of fundamentalism, saying it "puts a premium on the activities of buying and selling, consuming and taking, promoting and advertising, and devalues community, compassionate charity, and improvement of the general quality of life" (2004, p. 5). Not only is our domestic policy making a shambles of democracy but our foreign policy also makes others in the world question whether we have any democratic fiber at all. He places blame on aggressive militarism: "This new doctrine of U.S. foreign policy goes far beyond our former doctrine of preventative war. It green-lights political elites to sacrifice U.S. soldiers—who are disproportionately working class and youth of color—in adventurous crusades" (2004, p. 5). It also implies that the nation with the most military might is somehow the most "morally" capable of policing the world (2004, p. 5).

West's own philosophy and life work as a kind of salve for all of the wounds caused by a lack of democracy. Specifically, he accomplishes this authentication as public intellectual prophet by listing his credentials as an engaged scholar, a public intellectual. He castigates the troubling corporatization of the academy for trumping the nobler goal of educating and nurturing youth:

> It is imperative for the adults who have made the life of the mind their life's calling to be engaged with the wider community and play a vital role in furthering the national discourse on the important issues of the day by exercising the ways of truth telling that engage youth. (2004, p. 186)

In other words, it is critical for intellectuals to *go public.*

The problems West illuminates in academe make his own practice as a teacher/thinker/activist even more important. His work as a citizen-prophet is consistent with his indictment or judgment of our current moment of undemocratic crisis. He explains, "I have made not only a serious commitment to teaching and writing in the academy but also a substantive conviction to communicate to the larger culture" (2004, p. 186). In support of this claim, he recounts his teaching prison inmates, appearing on C-SPAN and NPR as a guest of Tavis Smiley, cochairing the National Parenting Association, appearing in *The Matrix* film series, assisting with the Pass-the-Mic Tour with Smiley and Michael Eric Dyson, and supporting the efforts of Russell Simmons and KRS-ONE in using hip-hop to reach a new generation of potential political activists (2004, pp. 187–88). In addition to his public outreach, West contributes to his own academic discipline with books like *The American Evasion of Philosophy: A Genealogy of Pragmatism* and *Keeping Faith.* He concludes his list of accomplishments by recounting his version of his decision to leave his own alma mater, Harvard University, because of the "technocratic" regime of then-President Lawrence Summers. West seemingly counts this among his successes rather than professional failures because he remained resolute that he was enough of an academic that he did not need to prove himself further and could devote time to both teaching at the university level as well as engaging the culture. In the end, the life of the public intellectual prophet is potentially no easier than the life of the biblical prophets of old—there will always be those who not only broke the covenant but do not care to hear you cast judgment or to hear your call to redemption.

Inasmuch as psychological style is about consistency between word and deed, it is also about identity—an outward mark of a consistent identity. Three characteristics describe the prophetic public intellectual's identity in terms of psychological style: authenticity, responsibility, and judgment/hope. Let us look at each in more depth.

The first essential characteristic of prophetic public intellectual rhetoric is to prove that one is a truly authentic public intellectual prophet and not merely an insane person, coming off the street to rant about the evils of the world, retreating to his or her private world, perhaps never to be heard from again. While West certainly has an impressive command of prophetic history, language, and goals, he also sets himself up as a prophet in another way. He turns from a more general comprehension and adroitness of the Judaic prophetic tradition from scripture to a more specific tradition of prophetic rhetoric: the black church. West explains, "Prophetic witness was a driving force in Martin Luther King Jr.'s vision for the civil rights movement, and lay behind the solidarity of Jews and blacks in the enactment of that movement" (2004, p. 19). Truly, "much of prophetic Christianity in America stems from the prophetic black church tradition" (2004, p. 158). West begins to align the suffering of the Jewish people despite their status as the chosen people of God with the more contemporary suffering of black people in America despite their religious devotion: "The Socratic questioning of the dogma of white supremacy, the prophetic witness of love and justice, and the hard-earned hope that sustains long-term commitment to the freedom struggle are the rich legacy of the prophetic black church" (2004, p. 158). In turn, he aligns himself with this black prophetic tradition because "to have been designated and treated as a nigger in America for over 350 years has been to feel unsafe, unprotected, subject to random violence and hated" (2004, p. 20). West names black prophetic Christians "from Frederick Douglass to Martin Luther King Jr." as among the formidable Americans who "fueled the democratizing movement that at last confronted the insidious intransigence of the color line" (2004, p. 158).

Not only have black Americans fought to eradicate the color line, West explains, "the black American interpretation of tragicomic hope in the face of dehumanizing hate and oppression will be seen as the only kind of hope that has any kind of maturity in a world of overwhelming barbarity and bestiality" (2004, p. 20). By arguing that black Americans have long been victims of violent oppression and subjugation yet have, in many political and social instances, turned the other cheek and, instead, provided the nation and the world with a blueprint for justice, West elevates the struggle of the American civil rights movement to the status of the Jews leading a movement of a people out of Egypt to the promised land of Israel. This elevation of the black struggle in America and his overt alignment as a black American within that struggle, in turn, authenticates his status as a prophet. And, his calling upon iconic black figures like Douglass and King only adds to this distinction because it highlights West's lineage within the black prophetic tradition.

To match his rhetoric, West has worked diligently as a spokesperson and activist in the black community and for black causes. I mentioned earlier that West worked with Farrakhan to organize the Million Man March and with other black activists to begin a dialogue among rival gangs to end street violence. Not only does he teach classes on religion and theology but he also is one of the nation's leading voices in the classroom on African American studies. He publicly engages ideas of special concern to this community. For example, in a May 26, 2004, interview on NPR's *Tavis Smiley Show*, West addressed the controversial comments made by Bill Cosby at the fiftieth anniversary celebration of *Brown v. Board of Education*, in which Cosby, according to Dyson, degraded black Americans by chastising their "lack of parenting, poor academic performance, sexual promiscuity and criminal behavior amongst what he called the 'knuckleheads' of the African-American community" (2005). West disagreed, arguing instead that Cosby was a sort of social parrhesiast, speaking the truth to the black community in a loving way. West stated, "I think that is both Biblical and true. If you love and serve, you're bearing witness. That is all you can do in this space and time before you meet your maker, brother" (West, 2004, May 26).

In addition to being authentic, part of The Prophet's identity is being responsible for taking on the burden of the call to prophecy. In terms of everyday living, West claims,

> Prophetic witness consists of human deeds of justice and kindness
> that attend to the unjust sources of human hurt and misery. It calls
> attention to the causes of unjustified suffering and unnecessary
> social misery and highlights personal and institutional evil, includ-
> ing the evil of being indifferent to personal and institutional evil.
> (2004, p. 114)

His description points to the fact that the goal of The Prophet has
changed relatively little over the centuries, despite what The Prophet
might look like or the subject matter on which The Prophet casts judgment. Indeed,

> [t]he especial aim of prophetic utterance is to shatter deliberate
> ignorance and willful blindness to the suffering of others and to
> expose the clever forms of evasion and escape we devise in order
> to hide and conceal injustice. The prophetic goal is to stir up in us
> the courage to care and empower us to change our lives and our
> historical circumstances. (2004, p. 115)

West's commitment to this responsibility is obvious in his actions:
teaching, traveling on the lecture circuit, and appearing on "democratic"
media like radio and television on a regular basis. It is his books that I
think best exemplify his commitment, however. While his other actions
certainly paint a picture of a man engaged in prophecy, his books go much
further in their indictment of the status quo as well as their treatment
of unjust and undemocratic practices with regard to race, class, sexual
orientation, and gender. *Race Matters, The Cornel West Reader,* and *Democracy Matters* all spent time on the *New York Times* Bestseller List,
and although not cost-free, books are a largely democratic medium, as
each of these books can be checked out through local libraries. West's
philosophy can also be accessed online through a number of sources,
such as, those of Democracy Now! and Pragmatism Cybrary. His 1993
lecture "The Responsibility of Intellectuals in the Age of Crack" is one
such example of West's assumption of responsibility for the call in his
own actions.

Judgment is the third part of the prophetic public intellectual's
identity. Since biblical times, judgment has been the central job of The
Prophet. Ultimately, West's identity as judge serves to highlight the issue
that undergirds all others: a democratic collapse in this country. Democratic ideals, says West, are the foundation upon which all else rests, and

without them, we not only cede our legal rights but our humanity. Thus, the action of The Prophet must be to illuminate a path to redemption for all sinners.

The prophetic public intellectual rhetorical style offers a sense of hope, a light at the end of the tunnel that signals that redemption is possible should the public change its sinful ways. This is an important element of prophetic rhetoric because it makes clear that this is a covenant with a two-way street—if one party can repent, the other can forgive. Giving his ultimate vision for American democracy, West states that to right ourselves, we must

> shore up international law and multilateral institutions that preclude imperial arrangements and colonial invasions; that should also promote wealth-sharing and wealth-producing activities among rich and poor nations abroad; and that should facilitate the principled transfer of wealth from well-to-do to working and poor people by massive investments in health care, education, and employment, and the preservation of our environment. (2004, p. 62)

In addition, West's vision includes "accountability and responsibility in democratic public life, including vibrant debate and dialogue," a "recasting of Islamic identity," and learning from "modern science, modern politics and modern culture" (2004, pp. 122, 132, 135).

In order to redeem our national covenant with democracy, Americans must also embrace youth culture and not dismiss it as silly or naïve. Youth culture is something of a euphemism for popular culture or even style. Although many intellectuals, particularly in rhetoric, have taken courses on popular culture, the larger academic trend is to conflate popular with unworthy of study. West emphasizes the dangers of this dismissal, saying that American youth "long for energizing visions worthy of pursuits and sacrifice that will situate their emaciated souls in a story bigger than themselves and locate their inflated egos . . . in a narrative grander than themselves" (2004, p. 177). We can begin to acknowledge the contribution of youth culture by engaging young people in their own language, a theme familiar to public intellectuals. West's action mirrors this concern. I have discussed previously that West has been involved in providing rhetorical space and opportunity for gang members to cooperate to end street violence. In addition, West uses hip-hop as his medium in completing two CDs, *Sketches of My Culture* and *Street Knowledge*, that bridge generations in an inherently democratic way in an everyday language.

West offers his most complete vision for redemption when he tells us, "The historic emergence of Athenian democracy and the Greek invention of Socratic dialogue must instruct and inspire our practice of democratic citizenship in present-day America" (2004, p. 204). He goes on to reconstruct the history of Western democracies to encourage the practice of Socratic questioning and dialogue, particularly on matters of public concern. Socratic questioning

> shatters one's petty idols, false illusions, and seductive fetishes; it undermines blind conformity, glib complacency, and pathetic cowardice. Socratic questioning yields intellectual integrity, philosophic humility, and personal sincerity—all essential elements of our democratic armor for the fight against corrupt elite power. (2004, pp. 208–9)

Ultimately, we must avoid "the paralyzing paranoia of Manichaean thinking, the debilitating hubris of dogmatic arrogance, and the myopic self-righteousness of nihilistic imperialism" (2004, p. 212) to find redemption. We must also embrace the prophetic tradition because "it generates the courage to care and act in light of a universal moral vision that indicts the pervasive corruption, greed, and bigotry in our souls" (2004, p. 215). The prophetic, in its best use, opens up hearts and minds to suffering and social misery and requires us to fight our own indifference to this suffering. With these panels of our democratic "armor," we can "absorb any imperial and xenophobic blows," "face any anti-democratic foe and still persevere," and "fight any form of dogma or nihilism and still endure" (2004, pp. 217–18). As God declares in Exodus 22:23, "I will surely hear their cry . . . [f]or I am compassionate."

West is the founding member of an organization called the Tikkun Community, which serves to "heal, repair and transform the world." It is an interfaith movement cochaired by Dr. West, Rabbi Michael Lerner, and Sister Joan Chittister. Part of the Tikkun Community (which also publishes a print magazine) is the Network of Spiritual Progressives. The focus of this group is to accomplish four major tasks: (1) to advocate a new "bottom line" in America that looks beyond profit and power to understand how institutions maximize love, caring, peace, and respect; (2) to challenge a misleading use of religion by the religious "right"; (3) to challenge leftist antireligion and antispiritual sentiments; and (4) to challenge philosophical liberalism and its antecedent, staunch individualism (n.d.). This entire project reveals West's active commitment to redemption. In addition, West is actively involved in a number of political and social organizations, the Democratic Socialists of America and the National Parenting Organization's Task Force on Parent Empowerment, and was a member of the Reverend Al Sharpton's presidential exploratory committee. West acts as the prophetic public intellectual style demands: as authentic and responsible, as judge and advocate of hope.

Sociological Style

The public has called for Prophet style. Faith in government, business, and other institutions has been replaced by a sense of outrage—those in power who espouse Judeo-Christian beliefs of respect and charity are the very same people who throw ethics out the window when it comes to their own behavior. The Prophet enters in this time of crisis to judge those who have sinned and to offer a road to a renewed covenant. Perhaps it seems ironic that the Prophet could also be part of the answer to the rise in religious fundamentalism. However, today's public intellectual Prophet is not necessarily a servant of God but the mouthpiece of some divinity, be it some philosophical ideal like justice or the logical ideals of science. Therefore, to counteract a herd mentality that accompanies a rise in religious fundamentalism, the Prophet enters with another version of truth.

For West as the prophetic public intellectual, the social construction of style means that not only is he authentic but also that he speaks a higher form of truth to the public. And, perhaps more significant, that the public judges this truth-telling as a higher form and faithful to the prophetic style. A higher form of truth rhetorically elevates the public intellectual prophet as being somehow more closely linked to the divine. In biblical tradition, prophets would work to convince their Jewish audiences that the prophets were the incarnate mouthpieces of God, speaking God's literal truth. In modern times, prophets have a difficult time making this claim—audiences are far too wary of anyone claiming to be God's trumpet. However, prophets must prove that their message is a higher form of truth because they have to be beyond reproach, trustworthy, and credible to a much greater degree than the average person. If they fail to establish their higher truth speaking, their rhetoric may still be impactful but not as powerful as if they are successful in their persuasion.

Cornel West accomplishes this prophetic task in a two-part rhetorical strategy: He denigrates the rhetoric of the Bush administration and its allies as false truth, then he elevates prophecy and the prophetic tradition as the "real truth." Much of West's rhetoric is dedicated almost solely to the task of proving that prophetic public intellectuals like him speak a higher form of truth. West moves that fundamentalist Christianity has

> gained far too much power in our political system, and in the hearts and minds of citizens. This Christian fundamentalism is exercising an undue influence over our government policies, both in the Middle East crisis and in the domestic sphere, and is violating fundamental principles enshrined in the Constitution; it also providing support and "cover" for the imperialist aims of the empire. (2004, p. 146)

West blames neoconservatives for this frightening trend, most obviously, the former Bush administration. Tracing the history of fundamentalism in America, West offers the legacy of Roman Emperor Constantine as the genesis—West articulates, "Immediately after his conversion, Constantine targeted numerous Christian sects for annihilation . . . as he consolidated power by creating one imperial version of Christianity" (2004, p. 148). What resulted was what West describes as Christian schizophrenia—on the one hand, the teachings of Christ promote justice, fairness, respect, and tolerance; on the other hand, the way Christianity emerged in Western practice after Constantine is based entirely on imperialist authoritarianism. West reminds us, "This terrible merger of church and state has been behind so many of the church's worst violations of Christian love and justice—from the barbaric crusades against Jews and Muslims, to the horrors of the Inquisitions and the ugly bigotry against women, people of color, and gays and lesbians" (2004, p. 149). Out of the schizophrenic turmoil rises fundamentalism Constantinian Christians led by those referring to themselves as the religious "right." We see Constantinian Christian rhetoric, according to West, when the far right discusses a ban on same-sex unions or justifies war against an Islamic enemy through a "religious" lens.

Yet, West, a Christian theologian himself, is quick to laud another brand of Christian—the Prophetic Christian: "In criticizing Constantinianism in American Christianity, however, we must not lose sight of the crucial role of prophetic Christianity as a force for democratic good in our history." He goes on to list critically influential social movements like the abolitionist, women's suffrage, trade unions, and civil rights movements as having been founded and led by prophetic Christians. Even more important for West's democratic project, Prophetic Christians have "done battle with imperialism and social injustice all along" (2004, p. 152). In other words, Prophetic Christianity is the antidote to Constantinian Christianity—it is the higher form of truth.

Prophetic Christianity is the higher form of truth for three key reasons, according to West: (1) it is more historically based, (2) it is more moral, and (3) it is more like the life of Jesus Christ. Let us look at each of these in turn. West makes the claim that for himself and for other prophetic public intellectuals, Prophetic Christianity is more historically based primarily because it is rooted in biblical tradition, whereas Constantinian Christianity is rooted long after the life of Jesus Christ. Proverbs 14:31 reads, "He who oppresses a poor man insults his maker / He who is kind to the needy honors Him." West explicates the history of the prophetic connection to democracy: "Prophetic Judaic figures appeal to us as individuals to join in transforming the world as communities. They shun individual conversion that precludes collective insurgency. They speak to all people and nations to be just and righteous" (2004, pp. 17–18). He then goes on to connect the alleviation of social ills with the prophetic in a democratic system: "Prophetic Judaic figures also target the sole reliance on the force of power . . . 'heal your wound" (Hosea 5:13). Escalating authoritarianism is a species of injustice that tightens the rope around one's neck ("'for not by force shall man prevail,' 1 Samuel 2:9)" (2004, p. 18).

He further makes his case that the prophetic is more historical because of its appearance in the Bible by quoting a number of biblical prophets as proof. For instance, Amos spoke in the name of a "God who decides the destiny of all nations" (Amos 9:7); Isaiah spoke to "all you inhabitants of the world, you who dwell on earth" (Isaiah 18:3). By making the observation that the audience matters, West again underscores the importance of rhetorical style to the prophetic public intellectual. To be a prophetic public intellectual is not to speak to colleagues or peers in arcane or disciplinary vernaculars but to speak to a public in a public language. Notice also the scope of the audience. West selects verses that show prophets addressing a large public if not the entire world. While I would contend that all public intellectual rhetorical styles, including the prophetic, are more effective when targeted toward specific publics, it is still important to recognize that The Prophet is motivated by his or her calling to address issues for humanity as a whole. And, of course, despite its negatives, today's mass mediated world offers connections to much of humanity simultaneously, making media selection an increasingly valid criterion for public intellectuals, in general.

Not only is Prophetic Christianity the higher truth because of its historical background but it also is the higher form of truth because it is more moral or ethical. West recounts, "The Jewish invention of the prophetic commitment to justice—also central to Christianity and Islam—is one of the great moral moments in human history" (2004, p. 17). He continues, "Prophetic witness consists of human acts of justice and kindness that attend to the unjust sources of human hurt and misery. Prophetic witness calls attention to the causes of unjustified suffering and unnecessary social misery" (2004, p. 17). According to West, then, Prophetic Christianity is more ethical because it is centered in religious tradition. Although the prophetic was a Jewish invention, West relays that the "prophetic commitment to justice is foundational in both Christianity and Islam. The gospel of love taught by Jesus and the message of mercy of Muhammad both build on the Jewish invention of the prophetic love of justice" (2004, p. 19).

West makes public his higher form of truth through his immense visibility. In turn, this visibility allows audiences to judge the fidelity of his performance of prophetic public intellectual style, a key characteristic of the sociological dimension of style. By using a variety of particularly democratic media, such as, radio, television, film, and books as well as the Internet and face-to-face communication, West can be seen almost anywhere, virtually anytime. His message of judgment and redemption through his higher form of truth is available to many if not most, and, therefore, his dual goal of engaging and then helping to transform the culture can be better realized. Amen.

DIMENSIONS OF COMPARISON

As I described previously, there are five main dimensions I explicate to compare the five public intellectual styles I am exploring. These are fluidity, degree, location, media, and resources. Cornel West is a highly fluid prophetic public intellectual. He has an impressive academic intellectual pedigree, having graduated magna cum laude from Harvard University, earning a PhD from Princeton University, and having taught at both his alma maters as well as Union Theological Seminary and the Sorbonne. In addition, he has written more than twenty books and is a dedicated teacher. For his stature as an academic, however, West is astoundingly politically and socially active. He has appeared on CNN, C-SPAN, and NPR; he has put out two rap CDs; he starred in *The Matrix* film series as "Counselor West"; he was a participant in the Million Man March and Russell Simmons's Hip-Hop Summit; he is the honorary chair of the Democratic Socialists of America; he works for PETA's Kentucky Fried Cruelty Campaign. He is something of a celebrity intellectual and said in an interview with PBS, "I've always wanted to use whatever celebrity status I have for the struggle for freedom, the struggle for goodness" (PBS, 2003). However, the prophetic style is extreme—The Prophet, because of his or her calling by a higher power, has to negotiate a balance between authenticity and popularity to pronounce guilt on a nation and offer hope for redemption.

Cornel West is very highly intellectual as well as very highly public, but the way he balances these things in different moments is valuable to understand. West has clearly read his Cicero. Although he has written over twenty books, his most notable works, *The Cornel West Reader*, *Race Matters*, and *Democracy Matters*, are clearly researched and written by an intellectual but are spoken in the voice of the public. In other words, West is able to balance both the maintenance of rigorous standards of intellectual work with the standards of sounding like an engaged, smart but *one of us* guy. He refers constantly to "elite power" as if he is totally outside of it. In addition, as crises loom, West becomes more public rather than less. He seems to believe that crises points are the moments in which intellectual interventions are most necessary. What this balance tells us about prophetic public intellectuals is that, like their biblical counterparts, they take rhetoric and timing very seriously. Prophets must speak in the voice of the audience on whom they pronounce judgment or risk the audience misunderstanding or dismissing The Prophet as some deranged person out of touch with lay reality. Furthermore, The Prophet becomes more public in times of crisis just as the biblical prophets of old—crisis, in fact, is a major marker of prophetic rhetoric.

Location is our next object of interest. In *Democracy Matters*, West devotes a sizeable chunk of chapter 6 to clearing the air on his reasoning for leaving Harvard after a very public dispute with President Summers. West claims he left because Summers was unsupportive of West's public works like his rap CDs and his role in *The Matrix* and its sequels because Summers felt they conflicted with the goals of Harvard University and West's teaching load. Public intellectuals, in general, have a challenging time remaining in academe for this very reason—the more public they are, the less seemingly intellectual they are to other traditional academics and the more often they are accused of selling out. So, we would generally expect to find The Prophet in other places besides academe. Since the prophetic public intellectual is an accuser of nations, it makes sense to find him or her in roles where he or she can accuse: politics, the pulpit, protests. West is able to be colocated because of Princeton University's flexibility in his role, though many other public intellectuals have failed at this location.

The Prophet accuses nations, and so we should expect that his or her media resources are more mass than interpersonal. Cornel West demonstrates this clearly. He has appeared on a number of television shows, is a regular on-air contributor to *The Tavis Smiley Show*, has been in films, has two rap CDs, writes a blog, and is a regular lecturer. Even his university courses have seven-hundred-plus students in attendance. While biblical prophets relied solely on a public but in-person forum for delivering their message of guilt and redemption, West and his prophetic public intellectual colleagues today have more media resources of which to take advantage. As chapter 2 discusses, it is likely that the more these public intellectuals appear on television or in film or on the radio, the less seriously they are taken by their intellectual peers, particularly if they are academics. In other words, the more "mass" the media, the greater the reduction in intellectual praise. On the other hand, there is a medium that can bolster the prophetic public intellectual or stave off the criticism that accompanies mass media participation. Books. Although books have the capacity to reach great numbers of people, they are taken as more "establishment" for intellectuals than is television or film. West has remained, by most accounts, a respected academic likely because he has balanced his mass-media appearances with writing twenty-plus books on philosophy, African American studies, and politics.

Finally, the last point of comparison between public intellectual styles is the use of resources. Certainly, most academic intellectuals would not seriously entertain the idea that academics is where the big money is, but West, because of his public appeal and his ability to capitalize on wide-reaching media experiences, is likely better paid than the average professor. More important, he seems to have access to people with money. Why might this be important? He has access to media resources that others do not have. Very few people are ever asked to be part of a major motion picture, and fewer still with a series of films as popular as *The Matrix*. I argue that prophetic public intellectuals, particularly religious ones, are going to have better access to financial and media resources because their messages are very much en vogue in a time of crisis of faith. In terms of training and credentials, West has obvious academic pedigree other prophetic public intellectuals lack. However, as long as the prophetic public intellectual can prove to his or her audience that he or she was authentically called, that serves as the only credential The Prophet needs to deliver the message.

In all, the prophetic public intellectual rhetorical style requires The Prophet to prove authenticity and that he or she has been legitimately called by a higher power. In turn, The Prophet must deliver harsh judgment in a time of particular crisis, followed by a plan for redemption should the audience repent and recover its covenant with the higher power. This style is extreme—it requires a lonely road for The Prophet, a life in many ways on the rhetorical fringes. However, in a time of rising religiosity (or at least rising fervor), escalating crisis, and hypermediation, the prophetic voice is significantly more prominent. West demonstrates both the limitations and the possibilities of the prophetic public intellectual style—he is criticized by some academics for being a "less serious" scholar since his newfound celebrity status but is celebrated by many because of his public work and activism. With West as an example, the prophetic public intellectual can expect great things.

Chapter 3 moves from The Prophet to The Guru, a public intellectual who bridges worlds to guide confused people to the light.

3

GURU STYLE: DEEPAK CHOPRA

Among the foremost tenets of Hinduism is the importance of finding a guru, one who can impart what disciples believe is transcendental knowledge. In the Hindu text the *Bhagavad Gita*, the student is told by God in the form of Krishna: "Acquire the transcendental knowledge from a Self-realized master by humble reverence, by sincere inquiry, and by service. The wise ones who have realized the Truth will impart the Knowledge to you" (4:34). *Guru* is loosely translated from Sanskrit as "teacher" but can also mean "heavy with spiritual knowledge" and the light who leads those in darkness to God (Cornille, 1991, p. 207). Because the Western tradition lacks an equal term or understanding of the Hindu guru, the guru has come to signify virtually anyone who develops a following or anyone who can teach others the way to some path of enlightenment. A Google search of the word reveals some of these less spiritual definitions, such as, guru.com, a site that specializes in freelance technology talent; Guru Bicycles, an Urban Dictionary entry, and a 2007 film.

The public intellectual guru does not need to be a Hindu teacher or practitioner by any means; instead, The Guru style underscores the both/and nature of the public intellectual, a master of two worlds. For instance, Christiane Northrup's work aligning spiritual support with science enables women to navigate menopause with greater understanding of the process, and she has written passionately about mothers and daughters improving their health by strengthening their relationships. Another example would be Michael Pollan, John S. and James L. Knight Professor of Journalism at Berkeley and acclaimed food activist and author, who takes his journalistic perspective on food production in the United States to bear on activist issues like equal access to nutrient-dense food. Whatever their both/and,

public intellectual gurus are, however, spiritual leaders of a flock of followers, formally or informally, helping to shepherd followers to knowledge,
enlightenment, and, ultimately, to God. Thus, public intellectual gurus are
teachers of a practice and a lifestyle that leads their followers closer to the
spirit. Like Hindu gurus, public intellectual gurus must have real disciples
and must strive to pass along an undiluted brand of spiritual wisdom or
knowledge to the disciples such that once the guru is no longer alive or
taking new disciples, his or her teachings will live on in the disciple that
rises to become the next guru. In other words, guru imparts knowledge,
guru is replaced by the next generation guru. The circle remains unbroken
in this way. The guru is not a teacher but the teacher, always shrouded
in intellectual mystery, using media to cultivate an intimate relationship
with followers, marshaling the resources of two worlds.

DR. DEEPAK CHOPRA: THE GURU OF AYURVEDA

Dr. Deepak Chopra was born in New Delhi, India, in 1947 and attended
the prestigious All India Institute of Medical Sciences in 1968. Upon grad-
uation, Chopra moved to the United States to complete his residency in
endocrinology at the Lahey Clinic in Burlington, Massachusetts, and at the
University of Virginia Hospital. Subsequently, he taught at Tufts University,
Boston University, and Harvard University medical schools and became
chief of staff at the Boston Regional Medical Center. He began an excep-
tionally successful private practice as a board-certified endocrinologist
in the early 1980s. And yet, something seemed "off" to Dr. Chopra about
his medical practice. Western medical practice traditionally accepts a
definition of health as simply the absence of disease. Eastern philosophies
on medicine, however, consider the balance of mind, body, environment,
and spirit when determining the overall health of a patient. As a student
of Indian and American medical practices, Chopra was uniquely qualified
to meld the two schools, and he founded the Chopra Center for Wellbeing
in Carlsbad, California, in 1996 (Chopra Center, n.d.b).

The Chopra Center teaches a practice known as Ayurveda, an ancient
holistic health care practice that asserts "nothing exists in isolation, so
that everything you interact with, your diet, family, work or relationships, has an effect on your health and wellbeing" (Chopra Center, n.d.b).
Ayurveda posits that we all inherit an individual mix of mind/body principles known as doshas: vata, pitta, and kapha (Chopra Center, n.d.b). If
these doshas are in harmony, we experience optimal mind/body/spiritual
health. If any one dosha dominates, our overall health is out of alignment,

and we will suffer physically, psychologically, and spiritually from the imbalance. To aid in achieving the healthful balance that Ayurveda prescribes, experts in traditional Western and holistic medicine lead classes in yoga, meditation, and Jyotish astrology, a mathematic form of Vedic Indian astrology that translates to "science of light" and can "help us realistically evaluate our strengths and weaknesses in order to optimize our full potential" (Chopra Center, n.d.b). In addition, Chopra offers seminars, goes on speaking tours, has created a blog, writes for the *Huffington Post*, has written over sixty-five books translated into thirty-five languages that have sold more than twenty million copies, and regularly appears on PBS on his shows *Super Brain* and *The Happiness Prescription*.

Physiological Style

Regardless of The Guru's mastery around which he or she garners a following, he or she is a physiological embodiment of East meeting West in the sense of the spiritual meeting the logical. After looking at dozens of still photos and video clips of Deepak Chopra, one thing is clear: He does not look like a doctor in the Western traditional sense. No lab coat, no stethoscope around his neck, no orthopedic shoes. I do not mean that he does not look like he is medically competent or scientifically gifted but rather that he is anything but sterile or institutional in appearance. Chopra has transformed from practicing endocrinologist to spiritual health guru over the past two decades, and his physiological style followed suit. Chopra generally dresses in very simple colors, often black and white. He is fond of Nehru-collared shirts and jackets, perhaps his injection of his Indian heritage into his Western practice. His hair is always impeccable, his hair is almost all gray, his clothes are neat, his face is clean shaven, and his overall posture and demeanor is relaxed. Interestingly, his appearance over the last twenty years has changed relatively little—he does not look dated or out of touch, but he looks as if he has not aged much and certainly does not look like a man nearing seventy. Physiologically, therefore, he is the perfect advertisement for the kind of clean living he endorses both as a physician and as a spiritual healer and guru through his center and other public endeavors.

Because physiological style involves the performance of a persona, Chopra must appear the embodiment of the guru. Certainly, it would seem contrary to his station as prominent physician to appear in sandals and long, flowing, white robes as traditional gurus might be dressed. However, it would be equally contrary to his status as the poster prophet for alternative medicine to appear in public wearing a lab coat, glasses, and stethoscope and carrying a clipboard. Chopra must walk the same kind of line all guru public intellectuals walk—not too much the scientist/intellectual, not too much the messiah.

The Guru is, first and foremost, a teacher. I mentioned briefly that Chopra always performs a sense of innate calm spirituality as if he is his own best patient for his brand of Ayurveda healthcare for the contemporary American. However, the relationship between guru and student is critical to understanding guru style. Obviously, Chopra is not the student but the master, but like any benevolent guide to enlightenment, he considers his relationship with the student to be one of spiritual intimacy. So, regardless of how many devotees or disciples any public intellectual guru has, each relationship must appear to be managed as if it is the most important one. Each student's journey to knowledge and truth is equally valued by The Guru. To perform this physiologically and stylistically, Chopra works on two levels: through physical performance and through manner of speaking. In terms of his physical performance, videos of Chopra reveal a very camera-savvy guru. Chopra works the camera as if he is having a cherished, private moment with a single disciple. He sits close to the camera and makes direct eye contact throughout. He has a relaxed posture and natural, conversational gesture. He speaks in the ideal "twelve inch" voice as if the disciple is sitting right in front of him, regardless of the fact that his audience is on the other end on a webpage. He also insists that others call him by his first name rather than Dr. Chopra. As a guru, Chopra realizes the significance of intimacy when talking spirituality. The Guru relationship historically has been face-to-face. It is an intimate relationship. The modern Guru, though, uses mass media to forge and maintain relationships with followers. Yet, he or she does so in what is perceived as an intimate way.

Disciples will then watch Chopra online or on television as if he is sitting right in front of them, and they are sitting at the feet of their "master." Americans saw this technique work profoundly when former President Ronald Reagan addressed the nation from the Oval Office to deliver a televised eulogy to the *Challenger* astronauts. It felt as if our own grandfather was telling us it was going to be OK, and we perceived a certain amount of intimacy despite the message being delivered on television. Chopra channels that same skill as a Guru. Indeed, few would select a Guru, arguably the most important relationship these disciples will ever forge, whose attention is or seems to be divided or whose attitude is dismissive or unengaged. Chopra physiologically performs Guru style through his embodiment of spiritual intimacy.

Not only must The Guru teach student disciples but he or she must also teach in an intimate way. Chopra selects his words carefully to convey this critical need for intimacy. He constantly uses the word *you*—as in, "your body and your mind" and "you are contributing to your own environment." Rather than addressing his audience as some nebulous group somewhere in cyberspace or on the receiving end of a television or radio broadcast, Chopra chooses words that make his audience feel as though he is speaking to each one of them individually and not on any sort of mass scale. Using the second person accomplishes this sentiment. In his best-selling book *How to Know God: The Soul's Journey into the Mystery of Mysteries*, he is equally intimate in the way he says things, for instance: "Also, you might argue that just because God is seen in a certain way by us, that doesn't mean he *is* that way. I don't believe this is black or white" (2000, p. 8). He goes on to say, "I believe that God has to be known by looking in the mirror. *If you see yourself in fear, barely holding on with survival at stake, yours is a God of fight or flight*" (2000, p. 9). These transitions between "I" and "you" mark rhetorically intimacy—his book, like his media appearances, reads like a personal letter to a close friend instead of a mass-produced, mega best seller that sits in the homes of hundreds of thousands of readers. Again, The Guru's style demands spiritual intimacy, and, again, Chopra performs it physiologically in word choice.

Public intellectual gurus must also embody spirituality and "religious" conviction. The language of the spirit is poetic in many instances—the book of Psalms, the use of parables in Sunday-morning preaching, Walt Whitman. Chopra keenly understands how to embody spirituality through his poetic rhetoric. Indeed, his advice is often in the form of poetry. For example,

> God is a protector to those who see themselves in danger.
> God is almighty to those who want power (or lack any way of
>   getting power).
> God brings peace to those who have discovered their own inner
>   world.
> God redeems those who are conscious of committing a sin.
> God is the creator when we wonder where the world came from.
> God is behind miracles when the laws of nature are suddenly
>   revoked with warning.
> God is existence itself—"I Am"—to those who feel ecstasy and a
>   sense of pure being.
> (*How to Know God*, p. 44)

If in the place of poetry, Chopra were just to state things like, "Look, it's obvious you see yourself as being in danger for some reason, so it makes sense that you would see God as a protector," he would not adequately perform The Guru style's calm spirituality. Rather, he would sound like any garden-variety counselor. By using poetry, though, his disciples get the sense that he is somehow more divinely inspired than most, marking him the kind of guru with whom one would feel comfortable studying.

Not only is physiological style performative but it also is a specific kind of performance, one that reflects an inner persona. For the public intellectual guru, that inner persona is as teacher. As previously described, the word *guru* is generally translated from Sanskrit as "teacher," and the bond The Guru cultivates with his or her disciples is a teacher-student relationship. But, The Guru is no ordinary teacher since his or her tutelage is not in a traditional discipline, in a standard classroom, from September to May. The guru is not *a* teacher, the guru is *the* teacher. For this reason, I argue that The Guru serves as more of a model for audiences than other kinds of public intellectuals. Students commit to one guru for life as their sole bridge to enlightenment. Therefore, for this kind of public intellectual to achieve appropriate style as a guru, it is imperative that he or she reflect through physiological style an inner persona of *the teacher*.

Chopra demonstrates the physiological style of teacher in a number of ways. First, he does it through his clothing. As mentioned earlier, Chopra does not dress like a physician in that he avoids looking remotely "institutional"—no lab coat, no pocket protector, no suit or tie, no glasses. Instead, he chooses neutral-colored clothing like black or white and often wears Nehru collars. As Chopra is incredibly media savvy, his choice of dress is no accident. Donning neutral colors does not call attention to Chopra's attire, allowing attention to be focused on his message of the health of Ayurveda. The selection of Nehru collars pays homage to the Indian tradition of the guru and harkens to the East, a rhetorical move that serves to remind students they are dealing with an authentic guru. Second, he does it through his overall demeanor, specifically, his posture, gait, and facial expression. Image after image reflects a man who is relaxed and calm—he is never overly animated and is thoughtful and reserved. He is also someone who makes media appearances intimate events—he leans into the camera, he uses familiar and comfortable gestures, he wears a fairly neutral expression on his face. Third, he does it through his physical environment. Chopra has created the Chopra Center for Wellbeing, and he uses this environment to conduct classes and lectures on everything from yoga and meditation to the ways in which quantum physics and the soul intersect. In other words, he created a *teaching* center as his place of business. Just to really drive the point home, one of the programs at the Chopra Center is the "Teacher's Path." So, he has constructed a physiological reflection of guru style in his center.

Psychological Style

The Guru's rhetoric focuses on seeking God or other higher power by walking a path of enlightenment through his or her teachings. Chopra wonders "whether we can open the door and allow helpful angels into our reality, along with miracles, visions, prophecy, and ultimately that great outside, God himself" (2000, p. 3). He answers his own inquiry: "God is a process. Your brain is hardwired to find God. *Until you do, you will not know who you are*" (2000, p. 14). His behavior echoes this search for God. The Chopra Center for Wellbeing is dedicated to this search, and Deepak Chopra is at the heart of the organization: His smiling countenance greets you warmly when you visit the website of the Chopra Center. In addition, Chopra, in his blog at Intent Blog, explores topics, such as, the connection between spirituality and health and issues of spiritual concern like Taoism, Kabala, the Dalai Lama and his mission of peace, and questions like, "Do we have a self?" and "Do soul mates exist?" Chopra explores these issues of God and spirituality with both readers and other contributors. In addition, Chopra talks about how he has been on his own spiritual path to God.

> The experience of God feels like flying. It feels as if I'm walking above the ground with such equilibrium that nothing can sway me from my path. It's like being the eye of the storm. I see without judgment or opinion. I just watch as everything passes in and out of awareness like clouds. (2000, pp. 5–6)

So, not only is Chopra teaching others to take their path of enlightenment to spiritual fulfillment but he also writes and speaks about his own journey and his own discovery. This is critical, of course, for guru style because The Guru must be enlightened already; otherwise, potential followers would select another guru to work with who already knows God. Like The Prophet, The Guru must be a bit mystical because although he or she does not have to be authentically called or to live a life of isolation to some degree, The Guru does need to seem to possess an otherworldly spiritual logic or risk being called a poseur.

Gurus are teachers, and as teachers, they must pass on their knowledge such that others may become teachers as well. This is part of their visibility as public intellectuals. As such, they must teach and model their philosophy to their disciples. Chopra believes the way to knowing God is to discover within oneself a soul, and he encourages his students to do just that. He writes that the soul "doesn't feel or move; it doesn't travel with you as you go about your life," but, instead, "the soul is really a junction point between time and the timeless. It faces in both directions. . . . But it would be a mistake to think that the soul and the person are the same" (2000, p. 275). So where does that leave Chopra's philosophy? Ultimately, for Chopra, the soul is the "carrier that takes us beyond; it is the essence connecting us to God" (2000, p. 274). As psychological style is about consistency between word and action, Chopra has to demonstrate his own search for and finding of a soul:

> When I experience myself in the world, I am not experiencing
> my soul, yet it is somewhere on the periphery. . . . If everything I
> know about myself since birth is separate from my soul, it must
> not be a material thing. (2000, p. 275)

Chopra seems to have found his soul through practices like yoga and meditation. Proving that it is true that there is no place like om, the Chopra Center offered the opportunity to "Meditate with Deepak" for a weekend in Marco Island, Florida. During this weekend, Chopra took disciples on a journey of discovery about how

> meditation is one of the most effective tools we have for gen-
> tly washing away the stress, tension, fear, and conditioned
> thought-patterns that cloud the mind. As we meditate, we regain
> our connection to an inner core of peace that allows us to stay vi-
> brant, healthy, and creative—even when chaos is swirling around
> us. (Chopra Center, n.d.e)

All Gurus balance the spirit with logic in some form or fashion, and Chopra is no exception. He is concerned with the balance between mind and body in terms of his psychological style. Chopra sells his "Seduction of Spirit" seminar as one that is offered a few times as year at the Chopra Center to transform the lives of students as "an immersion into present-moment awareness that transforms you at the cellular level" (Chopra Center, n.d.e). This connection between mind and body means "[t]he person has to be reduced to the merest point, a speck of identity closing the last miniscule gap between himself and God. At the same time, just when separation is healed, the tiny point has to expand to infinity" (2000, p. 164). If part of The Guru's rhetoric involves a connection among mind, body, and spirit, in order for The Guru to have psychological style, he or she must then behave in a way consistent with this kind of balance. For instance, in the "Soul of Healing" seminar program Chopra used to offer, it was recommended that all participants undergo a medical examination by Chopra or one of his MD colleagues on staff for the event. This was no ordinary exam, however. It involves the participant undergoing not just a physical exam but also an examination of psychological and spiritual health to get a better understanding of the person's level of balance or imbalance. Chopra believes in creating "a personalized body/mind/spirit health-enhancing prescription is formulated, including recommendations on diet, stress management, exercise, emotional healing, nutritional and herbal supplements, and sensory modulation" (Chopra Center, n.d.a). He himself describes following such a regimen and believes that the results have led him to a new plateau of consciousness and health. This self-proclaimed level of conscious, spiritual achievement has garnered some angry responses. When Chopra was on *Larry King Live* on CNN with a strict, biblical preacher, the preacher turned to him and said, "I've read your books. I know you think you're God" (2006). However, Chopra's understanding of the balance among mind, body, and spirit is based in Indian Vedanta tradition, which dictates that the guru may say, "I am the universe," without it being a sacrilegious, scandalous, or blasphemous utterance. Instead, it is a corrective to the pathological rigidity and myopia of fundamentalism. It is a state of being that Chopra has achieved through meditation, yoga, diet, and a lifetime of learning, and now it is a state that he as guru tries to help others realize.

Psychological style also involves an outward presentation of an inward identity. We know The Guru is a teacher, but what does that involve in terms of his or her identity? Three identity components are central for The Guru: one who has experienced an awakening, one who sees the light, and one who bridges two worlds. First, in terms of his awakening, Chopra testifies, "It is no wonder that finding God is called *awakening*. A fully awakened brain is the secret to knowing God" (2000, p. 26). After one is awake, "literally all the paradoxes of religion start to unravel, and God's ways make sense for the first time" (2000, p. 34). For Chopra, his own personal spiritual awakening led him to feel that,

With the loss of time comes a complete absence of ordinary
identity. The personality that I feel myself to be dissolves beyond
the material level, and with that, I lose the need for the landmarks
that I have gathered since birth. (2000, p. 209)

To publicly confirm this spiritual awakening in terms of his psychological style, Chopra describes on his Intent Blog what he calls his "Chinese
Menu" approach to awakening. Some of the things that he does to project
outwardly his inner identity of awakening are: stopping for a moment
to say to himself, "I am conscious," and see what it feels like, asking for
viewpoints outside of his own and taking them seriously, giving gener-
ously of his time and money, and reading the inspirational words of the
great sages (2006, September 23).

Chopra also counts as part of his identity what I am labeling as "seeing
the light":

I am proposing that no one is alive who hasn't taken just such a
journey [into higher awareness]. The "way," whether it is used in
the Christian sense of a path or the Taoist sense of the hidden
stream of life, means following the light. None of us could be
here without having roots where light is born, in the quantum
domain. (2000, p. 211).

For Chopra, this idea of light being the quantum domain is central to his
philosophy as a guru, blending quantum physics with religious philosophy. In its simplest form, it means humanity's "shared home" (2000, p.
243), or the place we can all achieve if we follow a path of awareness into
the quantum domain. Chopra demonstrates his achievement of seeing
the light through his creation of the Chopra Center for Wellbeing—ultimately, the entire center is dedicated to helping people come to our
"shared home" by teaching them paths and activities that bring awareness
and teach teachers to help other students do the same. In addition, the
Chopra Center sells literal lights. At the store of the center's website, if
you type *light* into the search field, the first several items that appear are
candles, the Joyta Soothing Aroma Candle to be exact. This candle is
designed to balance the Pitta Dosha, and users are instructed to "[e]njoy
during meditation or simply throughout your day as a reminder to be
present and celebrate the gift of life." In other words, you can achieve light
through awareness and discover a shared home, and you can purchase

light to help you achieve awareness through meditation. Either way, seeing the light seems integral to The Guru psychological style.

The final element of The Guru's psychological style is the outward appearance of bridging worlds, something Chopra does with great ease. In his case, Chopra bridges East (spirituality) and West (logic), but there could be many instantiations of this "bridging." Chopra quotes quite a lot of Eastern philosophy and philosophers. For instance, he cites an ancient Vedic hymn:

> In the beginning,
> There was neither existence nor nonexistence,
> All this world was unmanifest energy . . .
> The One breathed, without breath, by Its own power
> Nothing else was there . . .   (p. 31)

However, as mentioned in describing Chopra's "Soul of Healing" seminar, his teachings and seminars often involve a full medical examination that establishes baseline physiological health as well as identify imbalances in emotional and spiritual health. Much of his rhetoric is dedicated to balancing East and West. For instance, on the popular blog *Huffington Post*, he laments in one of his posts, "Mind-Body Bridge," the fact that "the average senior in America is taking 7 prescription drugs" when "American medicine should be helping people build a mind-body bridge. The human body contains enormous wisdom, and we could be tapping into it" (2006, September 25). He goes on to detail the benefits of practices such as meditation, prayer, and yoga on blood pressure, stress, heart disease, and stroke. In other words, the guru's rhetoric literally and figuratively bridges East and West. In terms of his behavior, I have discussed a number of ways Chopra acts as a bridge between East and West—he has created the Chopra Center for Wellbeing, he is an active practitioner of his own "medicine" in the form of meditation and prayer, he has developed a philosophy that combines quantum physics, Western medical training, and Eastern religion that is embodied in his Ayurveda practices. Chopra himself is a kind of embodied bridge between East and West. He is a person of Indian descent living in the United States; he is a student and fervent enthusiast of Taoism, Hinduism, and other Eastern religious ideologies but is extraordinarily well versed in Christian philosophy. So, Chopra as guru bridges East and West through his very life and action.

Sociological Style

Sociological style involves understanding style as something that is socially constructed and publicly visible. In the first place, it involves audience co-construction. Let us return to the sociopolitical trends from
chapter 2 that imply the need for The Guru style. While it is conceivable
for The Guru to respond to a number of trends because a Guru can be a
master of just about anything that is perceived to have a higher "spiritual"
authority, The Guru responds predominantly to a felt need for answers.
This is an uncomfortable time. We are bombarded by mediated information from all sources and feel overwhelmed by the sheer magnitude of
noise coming from all sides. For most, this feeling engenders a desire for
something concrete and tangible, something black and white. As Fantine
sings in *Les Misérables*, we want someone to take our hand and lead us
to salvation. The Guru public intellectual emerges to do just that.

For The Guru, sociological style involves leading others to God or other
higher authority in publicly visible ways. In his book *How to Know God:
The Soul's Journey into the Mystery of Mysteries*, Chopra creates a socially
centered and publicly visible roadmap or outline into the ways the body,
mind, and spirit know God, which, for Chopra means becoming aware,
seeing the light, and realizing balance in life. It is socially centered and
publicly visible because anyone can read and follow this roadmap—it does
not require that one sign up for expensive seminars through the Chopra
Center or "hire on" Chopra as one's personal guru. Rather, the guidelines in
this book, and the advice found in many of his other over sixty-five books,
are a monetarily inexpensive way to know God. In addition, it legitimizes
Chopra as a guru because his books have sold twenty million copies and
are translated into thirty-five languages around the globe—there are clearly
disciples in search of the teacher. To begin, Chopra outlines in "Seven Levels
of Miracles" that individuals may have experienced and what happens to
the body in each level. For example, in level 3, called the "Restful Awareness
Response," Chopra claims, "Miracles involve synchronicity; yogic powers,
premonitions, feeling the presence of God or angels," and gives the example of "Yogis who can change body temperature or heart rate at will,
being visited by someone from far away who has just died, visitation by a
guardian angel" (2000, p. 20). Toward the end of the book, he proclaims,

> According to our three ways of finding God, no one is ever
> trapped without hope:
> 1. We can always cross the horizon to a new reality.

2. Clues are left to tell us how to grow.

3. Second attention enables us to read these clues.   (2000, p. 297)

Most important, Chopra shares the rules that have been effective for him and for others:

> Know your intentions. . . .
> Set your intentions high. . . .
> See yourself in the light. . . .
> See everyone else in the light. . . .
> Reinforce your intentions every day. . . .
> Learn to forgive yourself. . . .
> Learn to let go. . . .
> Revere what is holy. . . .
> Allow God to take over. . .
> Embrace the unknown.   (2000, pp. 301–4)

Essentially, Chopra gives a spiritual path for his followers or for those who would like to follow, and this path is publicly visible.

In addition, The Guru must make this philosophical balance publicly visible. Chopra has created several organizations that are publicly visible to spread his message of mind, body, and spiritual health and balance. Through the Chopra Center, he invites people to join communities of teachers, medical providers, and volunteers, and each of these groups can utilize the center and its services or can be a part of the message board and share ideas, comments, and thoughts. He is also on Sirius Satellite Radio (Sirius Stars 102) with a call-in show where he discusses everything from healthful vegetarian recipes to politics. More recently, Chopra has become a contributor to the *Huffington Post*, where he has dozens of posts on topics like "Obama and the Rise of Secular Spirituality" and "Terror Attacks in Mumbai." Finally, he has two groups and one foundation: Alliance for a New Humanity, devoted to "accelerating a global movement for a better world"; and the Peace Is the Way Global Community, committed to creating a "critical mass of peaceful global citizens" and inviting people to join the "neuronal network of the planetary mind" (Chopra Center, n.d.e); and the Chopra Foundation, dedicated to "advance the cause of mind/body spiritual healing, education, and research through fundraising for selected projects" (Chopra Foundation, n.d.). Each of these activities is a publicly visible way of leading others to God and, for that reason, comprises the public intellectual guru's sociological style.

Finally, real gurus are recognized as such. While some gurus may be recognized by a small flock, others, like the Dalai Lama, are recognized around the world. However, the central issue is whether the guru's actual or would-be followers believe him or her to be *the* teacher, regardless of how many followers that person has. In other words, The Guru must be identifiable by others as a "real guru" if this type of public intellectual is stylistically accurate. Like many authors, Chopra has a list of endorsements in the first several pages of his books. However, endorsements for Chopra's book *How to Know God* continue for seven pages and include such Eastern luminaries as the Dalai Lama and His Holiness Vasudevanand Saraswati, and Jagad Guru Shankracharya of Jyotirmath World Headquarters and such Western figures as Andrew Weil, MD, director of the program in Integrative Medicine at the University of Arizona, and Candace B. Pert, PhD, professor, Department of Physiology and Biophysics, Georgetown University School of Medicine. For example, His Holiness Vasudevanand Saraswati explains,

> Deepak Chopra has blessed the world by spreading the light of vedic knowledge and the timeless teachings on nonduality. Vedanta has inspired and transformed the lives of seekers for thousands of years. However, every age needs a voice that can articulate ancient Wisdom in a contemporary framework. Dr. Chopra has given the seekers of self-knowledge a clear and scientific road map to understand and realize the ultimate reality. I congratulate him for his brilliant work. (in Chopra, 2000, endorsements)

And Pert exclaims,

> Deepak Chopra has really done it this time—a brilliant, scholarly yet lyrical synthesis of neuroscience, quantum physics, personal reminiscence, Eastern, Western, and spiritual thinking. Dr. Chopra's new theory of seven stages of understanding God is extremely relevant to the ongoing transformation in medicine today from the old soul-less paradigm to the new one with spirituality and emotions occupying center stage. (in Chopra, 2000, endorsements)

The acclamations are not limited to his immensely popular books, however. Not only is he a popular speaker at such impressive institutions as Harvard University Medical School and Divinity School but he is also on the faculty of the Kellogg Graduate School of Management and was named one of the "Top 100 Icons and Heroes of the Century" by *Time* magazine in 1999. More than a dozen of his books have appeared on the *New York Times* best-seller lists. Aside from these "official" designations, Chopra receives accolades as a public intellectual guru in the form of testimonials about the Chopra Center for Wellbeing and through his blog at Intent Blog. For instance, James, age fifty-four, from Duarte, California, comments about the primordial-sound meditation seminar the Chopra Center offers, "Before I started meditating my blood pressure was 150 and above. Since taking the PSM course, my average blood pressure is now about 133, and I only take half of my medication now!" (Chopra Center, n.d.d). Nancy, age fifty-seven, from Boulder, Colorado, says about her experiences with Dr. Chopra, "I felt blessed, a true sacred moment in life conducted with a perfect blend of love, light, and laughter" (Chopra Center, n.d.d). The replies to his posts on *Huffington Post* are equally enthusiastic, as "john l close" posts,

> Thinking out of the box of the Skull.
> Brain matter scattered throughout the body like stars in the solar
>   system.
> Complementarity scattered and interacting in perfect harmony.
> Emergence osculating with the precision of integrated
>   knowingness. (Chopra, 2013, August 12)

And "AuroraCarlson" posts, "This is a very elegant invitation, a door opened to respectful dialogue and evolution together, for the good of all. This is the way forward for humanity! Thank you Deepak Chopra and Jim Walsh for this beautiful initiative!" (Chopra, 2013, June 25). Virtually every person who replies to Dr. Chopra's blog posts calls him Deepak, as do many of the people providing testimonials on his Chopra Center website. It is as if these people feel such a strong sense of intimacy with him that they consider him their personal guru; whether they have actually ever encountered Chopra in person or not seems irrelevant. His style as a true public intellectual guru is so strongly recognized that it transcends the physical limitations of being co-present for his teachings.

DIMENSIONS OF COMPARISON

Chopra, like all Gurus, has a highly fluid public intellectual style. He is a board-certified endocrinologist and a former faculty member of both

Tufts University and Boston University Medical Schools. He is currently an adjunct faculty member of Northwestern University's Kellogg Graduate School of Management. He was also the chief of staff at the Boston Regional Medical Center. He has been a keynote speaker at Harvard Medical School, Harvard Business School, Harvard Divinity School, Kellogg Business School, Stanford Business School, and the University of Pennsylvania's Wharton Business School. He has written more than sixty-five books and sits on the board for the National Institute of Health. Deepak Chopra is clearly recognized as a leading intellectual in the fields of medicine and alternative, holistic health. Simultaneously, Chopra is very public. His books have been translated into thirty-five languages and have sold more than twenty million copies worldwide. As mentioned earlier, more than a dozen of them have appeared on the *New York Times* best-seller list. He is a regular contributor to PBS, Sirius Satellite Radio, Intent Blog, and the *Huffington Post* and directs education at the Chopra Center for Wellbeing. In addition, he travels regularly as a speaker to locations all over the world and is involved in a number of political and social efforts to improve health and promote peace around the world. He explains truly difficult concepts, such as, quantum physics and medical jargon, in a relatively easy-to-understand manner, and his teachings are available in so many formats, it would be hard to miss his public intellectual endeavors. Chopra's highly fluid style is characteristic of guru public intellectual style, in general, because The Guru must be recognized as such by both other experts and teachers as well as some corpus of disciples; otherwise, he or she cannot be considered a guru.

Turning to degree, The Guru navigates the line between being *a* teacher and being *the* teacher. Certainly, Chopra is highly intellectual and highly public and leans more toward the "intellectual" side of the coin. Yes, The Guru must be public in order to be noticed and recognized as authentic and thus to acquire a following of students, a key element to being a Guru. However, it is more important for The Guru to be revered as having uncommon wisdom that is unavailable to most people, even to those who study or follow religion, generally. There must be something profoundly mystical and special about The Guru's spiritual understanding and knowledge that can only be transmitted to disciples willing to commit their lives to The Guru's teachings. In other words, not every theologian or spiritual intellectual is a Guru—that is an elevated distinction. As such, The Guru maintains a higher degree of intellectual-ness than public-ness.

The question then becomes, If The Guru is more intellectual than public, where do we locate him or her? The Guru must be found teaching and practicing wisdom in a spiritual setting. Chopra can be found most often as director of education for the Chopra Center for Wellbeing. So, most often, Chopra is located as teacher. However, Chopra can also be found teaching around the world and serving in leadership positions in his groups and his foundation. His Kellogg MBA course, The Soul of Leadership, is extremely popular (Kellogg School, 2013). Followers may also find him posting to his blog or listen to him on the radio or watch him on television. It is perhaps unsurprising that The Guru, because he or she must maintain a higher degree of intellectualness, is generally located in more-institutional, formal settings like centers, foundations, and the like. However, because The Guru must also acquire and maintain a following and a sense of intimacy, he or she must find "spaces" for this work to occur. It is quite likely that once The Guru acquires a following, word of mouth will bring others to whatever location The Guru chooses.

There is an irony in the mediated intimacy the contemporary Guru maintains with his or her followers. Chopra is clearly a media-savvy guru—his Chopra Center website is elaborate and includes a number of multimedia functions, including several video clips of Chopra discussing topics of interest to those seeking spiritual, physical, and emotional well-being. He regularly contributes to his blog. He has an extensive list of publications, and some of his books are available on CD and ebook formats. He appears on television and on satellite radio. He interacts face-to-face with Chopra Center clients. He does large lectures at academic institutions. Despite the level of intimacy that Chopra and other public intellectual gurus must cultivate with followers in order to be recognized as true gurus, it seems unimportant or superfluous to most that the contact they may have with Chopra is through a television screen or on a monitor. In a shift from traditional guru relationships, which were based, in part, on an intensive face-to-face commitment to spirituality, colocation and face-to-face interaction are not prerequisites for the modern Guru in terms of media usage.

The Guru must be the master of two worlds because like all public intellectuals, he or she is obligated to straddle worlds, one foot in each. In this way, The Guru is the master of channeling resources. Chopra, like all public intellectuals, made excellent use of his training resources in terms of selection of schools and his position within the medical community in his practice. Because of his extremely successful endocrinology practice, he was able to make the leap into his real passion: combining Eastern philosophy with Western medical practice and, ultimately, to create the Chopra Center for Wellbeing. All of this takes tremendous financial resources, which Chopra has. No program at the Chopra Center is inexpensive. However, Chopra does use his financial resources in responsible ways, such as, creating centers for peace and balanced health as well as leading others to find spirit and "the light." Chopra, as already described, is well versed in media resources and takes the fullest advantage of his ability to connect with audiences whether in person or in a mediated channel, such as, television, radio, or the Internet. Chopra may be wealthy, but the guru is not supposed to be vocal or overtly concerned about resources, unless it means building up spiritual reserves. Resources in this book are material needs rather than spiritual ones, so Chopra has to keep his rhetorical focus away from his own financial resources and onto his abilities to teach others to find spiritual well-being.

The Guru is the ultimate teacher. He or she possesses a unique brand of spiritual knowledge that is obscured for most, even those who practice organized religion or a variety of spiritual philosophy. The guru must be recognized as authentic by other enlightened spiritual sages and must garner a following of disciples. The guru's physiological style involves projecting outwardly the inner persona of the teacher—calm, spiritual, and intimate. Psychologically, The Guru shows consistency between rhetoric and behavior by demonstrating the achievement of having found God or spirit, being in touch with a soul, and having a balance among mind, body, and spirit. The Guru is also a product of a spiritual awakening, having seen the light and, in the United States, mixing East and West. In terms of sociological style, The Guru constructs a publicly visible path or roadmap for followers in order to lead them to the light and is socially recognized for this ability both by other gurus and by students or disciples of the teaching. Through the public intellectual guru's rhetorical style, we have a greater understanding of the powerful motivation that is provided by spirituality, and, ultimately, we may be better prepared to tap into that motivation for political and social change in the public sphere.

Chapter 4 introduces a public intellectual style that includes natural as well as sociopolitical environments in its purview: The Sustainer.

4
SUSTAINER STYLE: WILLIAM MCDONOUGH

Sustainability has a "religious" following. Though likely coined by *The Ecologist* in the early 1970s, the United Nations World Commission on Environment and Development (WCED) in 1987 takes credit for introducing the term *sustainability*. The WCED defines sustainability as "the viability of natural resources and ecosystems over time, and the maintenance of human living standards and development" (1987, p. 43). Sustainability is associated largely with the environmental movement and, more specific, to green building and design. However, as the WCED definition overtly states, sustainability also involves creating and maintaining responsible and altruistic social and political systems. We can understand sustainability as a long-term commitment to the health of environmental, political, and social systems such that these systems can sustain themselves over time in a prosocial manner. In turn, the people who practice sustainability are what I call Sustainers. Regardless of its origin and scope, sustainability has gone "sexy," according to the August 2006, edition of *Dwell* magazine, which, I suppose, makes one of the world's foremost green designers, William McDonough, the sexiest man on our green and blue planet. Sustainers are so public they become "local" to the community and to the case, trying never to take what they cannot add back, innovating resources for communities and for the earth.

WILLIAM MCDONOUGH: IT'S NOT EASY BEING GREEN

William McDonough is a world-renowned architect and designer who since he began practicing as an architect in the late 1970s has been at the forefront of eco-efficient, green, or sustainable design and living. In fact,

McDonough built the first solar-heated house in Ireland in 1977 while still a student at Yale University and the first so-called green office for the Environmental Defense Fund in the United States in 1985. He has founded two design firms, William McDonough + Partners, Architecture and Community Design, and McDonough Braungart Design Chemistry. His sustainable philosophy is at work in a number of places around the world from the United States to China and back again, including Maui Land and Pineapple, Fuller Theological Seminary, Bernheim Arboretum and Research Forest, IBM, and Nike.

Several characteristics are central to Sustainer style, in general. Like prophetic rhetoric, the public intellectual Sustainer style relies first on a scathing indictment of current practices and the effects of those practices. Sustainers are also creative visionaries—rather than viewing sociopolitical or environmental problems as things to be tweaked until they are less bad, Sustainers work to invent new products and processes such that they eradicate the problems entirely. Ultimately, all in this and subsequent chapters, Sustainers are designers whether by profession or by style. I focus on the Sustainer here because he or she is one type of visionary working to sustain particular environments physiologically, psychologically, and sociologically.

William McDonough and his partner, Michael Braungart, a chemist, write in their acclaimed book *Cradle to Cradle: Remaking the Way We Make Things*, "Loss of resources, cultural depletion, negative social and environmental effects, reduction of quality of life—these ills can all be taking place, an entire region can be in decline, yet they are negated by a simplistic economic figure that says economic life is good" (2002, p. 37). McDonough and Braungart even recast something as seemingly positive and socially responsible as recycling as simply the lesser of evils—instead of creating and using products or systems that are infinitely sustainable, recycling results in "downcycling" (2002, p. 4), or the reduction of the product or service to an unusable and even dangerous form. Industry takes the brunt of The Sustainer's environmental and social wrath. The authors note that although the reduction of waste emissions is an important goal for industry, "even tiny amounts of dangerous emissions can have disastrous effects on biological systems" (2002, p. 54).

Of course, this destruction of natural and human environments is hardly a new phenomenon. Rather, McDonough and Braungart point to the West's Industrial Revolution as the harbinger of much of our misguided thinking and practices as they relate to eco- and sociosystems. The Industrial Revolution has spawned a system of production that puts billions of pounds of toxic material into the air, water and soil each year; puts valuable materials in holes all over the planet, where they can never be retrieved; measures productivity by how few people are working; and erodes the diversity of species and cultural practices. (2002, p. 18)

McDonough has dedicated his professional life not to making designs and buildings that are "better" for environments and people than the ones currently being built but, instead, redesigning design itself. For McDonough and other Sustainer public intellectuals like him, this kind of paradigm shift and transcendence is fundamental to their style.

Physiological Style

For The Sustainer, physiological style means he or she must perform creativity and reflect a worldview that incorporates a long-term vision for the sustainable health of sociopolitical and natural systems. McDonough is an ideal embodiment of these elements. He looks like an architect. In every still photo, interview, and other media clip available, he is dressed both artistically and functionally—in all black with funky accessories—a polka-dot bow tie, a checkered vest. He is confident and poised, standing or sitting with a relaxed but composed posture. He speaks with unbridled enthusiasm, even optimism that seems catching—there is a strikingly youthful energy about McDonough despite his tenure in the field of architecture and design. Like all Sustainers, he is obviously intelligent and engaged but has an approachable demeanor distinguished by his choice of simple ways of explaining his philosophy and his practice. He avoids jargon; rather, he has created his own language of clear but colorful jargon: upcycling, industrial re-evolution, cradle-to-cradle, disassembly plant, ecological intelligence, nutrivehicle. He commands attention, partly because he demonstrates mastery of his craft but also partly because he is physically activated by his passion for that craft.

His physiological style is, in addition to quintessential aesthetic qualities, a performance of his personal creativity and his choice of career. In other words, he just *looks like an artist* through his physiological performance of creativity. This is true for Sustainers, in general. For instance, McDonough prefers using and wearing environmentally intelligent fabrics. He and his design team were challenged by Röhner, a Swiss textile client, to create such a fabric. They turned first to a blend of cotton and PET or polyethylene terephthalate, a fabric made of recycled, plastic soda bottles. However, the by-products of PET are potentially dangerous, inhalable chemicals and dyes and a fabric that would not go back into the soil effectively. So, his team decided instead to "design a fabric that would be safe enough to eat: it would not harm people who breathed it in, and it would not harm natural systems after its disposal. In fact, as a biological nutrient, it would nourish nature" (2002, pp. 106–7). Not only are his clothes appropriately artistic, some of them are edible, a literal embodiment of the inventiveness that is critical to Sustainer style.

The items McDonough carries with him are also a performative embodiment of creativity and design. He is often interviewed about his philosophy and practice by magazines like *Time, Newsweek,* and *Atlantic Monthly,* and he frequently carries *Cradle to Cradle.* Perhaps this seems unremarkable, the author carrying a copy of his own book. This is a scene from virtually any book signing. However, what is unique about the situation is that his book is not made from a tree. It is, as he calls it, a "prototype for the book as a technical nutrient, that is as a product that can be broken down and circulated infinitely in industrial cycles—made and remade as 'paper' and other products" (2002, p. 5). The "book" is practically indestructible yet is upcyclable (his preference to recyclable, which he calls "downcycling"), waterproof, fireproof. It is made of plastic resins and put together by Melcher Media so that it looks like a traditional book. McDonough's "prop" for discussing his sustainable philosophy and practice is itself a product of that philosophy and practice and is another performed embodiment of his creativity as a Sustainer public intellectual.

For McDonough, creativity also involves a thorough respect for diversity. He believes,

> When given the opportunity, people choose something other than that which they are typically offered in most one-size-fits-all designs. . . . People want diversity because it brings them more pleasure and delight. They want a world of four hundred cheeses. (2002, p. 139)

He performs this diversity through his choice of clients and the cultures in which he is asked to design and to speak. In other words, he embodies the diversity that creativity requires through his choice of place. His client list is as impressive as it is diverse: universities and colleges like Oberlin College's Adam Joseph Lewis Center for Environmental Studies, the China Housing Industry Association "Cradle-to-Cradle Village," Barcelona's Grupo Habitat Emrasario "Habitat," and Brazil's Complexo Industrial Ford Nordeste Master Plan and Workplace Concepts. Clearly, his physiological style carries cross-culturally because he has worked around the world for decades, and this fit is due, at least in part, to his embodiment of diversity. For McDonough, "diversity enriches the quality of life in another way: the furious clash of cultural diversity can broaden perspective and inspire creative change" (2002, p. 144).

In addition to his choice of clients, his own office environment is an extension of his personal performance of creativity into his physical surroundings. Like any highly skilled and very highly compensated executive, McDonough works in offices that are luxurious; unlike most of these uber executives' offices, McDonough's are "green." Perhaps unsurprising, The Sustainer believes in embodying his own philosophy on his body and in his environment as part of his physiological style. The offices are decorated with fabrics that are upcyclable, sustainable woods like bamboo; upcyclable insulation is so effective the offices require little to no air conditioning and heating; and natural light sources are made the most of so thousands of light bulbs are not disposed of each year. The "Design Approach" section of William McDonough + Partners' website states,

> We are a collaborative, principles-driven design firm that sees the unique characteristics of each place and project as a source of inspiration and innovation. The foundational principles we bring to each project derive from our vision of the future: a delightfully diverse, safe, healthy and just world—with clean air, soil, water and power—economically, equitably, ecologically, and elegantly enjoyed. (William McDonough + Partners, 2013)

McDonough surrounds himself with sustainable practices and products as an extension of his personal physiological style. And, he is always ready to create and invent and then literally "wear" sustainability. He encourages, *"Be ready to innovate further.* No matter how good your product is, remember that perfection of an existing product is not necessarily the best investment one can make" (McDonough & Braungart, 2002, p. 184).

Not only is Bill McDonough's physiological style a performance of the creativity that is central to Sustainer public intellectual style but it is also a performance of his chosen career as a designer. McDonough calls design a "signal of intention" (2002, p. 9), and, therefore, his physiological style demonstrates intent on his part to look and carry himself a specific way. And for McDonough, his intention is respect, an intention he "wears." This question is answered again in the clothes he wears, the clients he accepts, the cultures he visits, and his general philosophy as a Sustainer public intellectual. Like all Sustainer public intellectuals, McDonough embodies his sustainable philosophy by wearing not only clothing that is artistic and functional but also safe for the environment and made by people who are not exploited as slave labor. He asks clients to adopt not only environmentally green practices but also culturally green practices. His own firm, in turn, is an example of respectful practice. McDonough's physiological style is a reflection of an inner persona, a particular worldview. McDonough shares this worldview: "We wish to grow education and not ignorance, health and not sickness, prosperity and not destitution, clean water and not poisoned water. We wish to improve the quality of life" (2002, p. 78). McDonough's physiological style (including the environments he creates) *intends* creativity, diversity, and respect: "Don't just rethink the recipe, reinvent the menu" (2002, p. 179).

Psychological Style

Specifically, McDonough's psychological style calls attention to the consistency between his talk and his action. For Sustainer public intellectuals, there is a heavy reliance on the rhetoric and practice of sustainability. The rhetoric of sustainability can be broken into two major themes: (1) the indictment of current practices and outcomes of such practices and (2) solutions to our current crises. As mentioned in the introduction to this chapter, industry, generally, and the Industrial Revolution, specifically, suffer the great majority of the wrath of the Sustainer, but even the current environmental movement's practices are called into question in The Sustainer's indictment. McDonough explains,

> Instead of presenting an exciting and inspiring vision of change, conventional environmental approaches focus on what *not* to do. Such proscriptions can be seen as a kind of guilt management for our collective sins, a familiar placebo in Western culture. (2002, p. 66)

The general attitude of today's environmentalist (not today's Sustainer) is to sacrifice and shrink waste and our ecological "footprint" to zero, but The Sustainer believes that this "be less bad" approach is ultimately a failure of imagination (McDonough & Braungart, 2002, p. 67). The Sustainer's vision is not to be less bad, it is to be all good. The Sustainer public intellectual indicts the systems that take without putting back and tries to remedy these systems by offering radically alternative ways of thinking about problems and solutions, in general.

Critical to the psychological style of The Sustainer, then, is to live the practice of sustainability such that he or she maintains consistency between rhetoric and practice. McDonough spends an enormous amount of time explaining his practice and spends the rest of his time living it. Particularly in his younger days, McDonough was an environmental activist who regularly protested destructive practices of industry and government. While he is not seen at protest rallies anymore, he created two firms, William McDonough + Partners and McDonough Braungart Design Chemistry, dedicated not to being "less bad" but to "be involved in making buildings, even products, with completely positive intentions" (2002, p. 11). These firms allow McDonough an avenue for sustainable practice in action, to manifest the Sustainer public intellectual worldview in "chemical research, architecture, urban design, and industrial product and process design to the project of transforming industry itself" (2002, p. 15).

Ironically enough, one tenet of Sustainer psychological style that is consistent is change. That is, these are public intellectuals who are fundamentally open to paradigm shifts, to dynamic ideas, and to creativity and invention. Perhaps it seems odd that those who want to sustain rely on an openness to change, but part of the Sustainer practice is to question that things must be made and processes must be maintained in a certain way. Hence, part of McDonough's practice is questioning progressive taken-for-granteds, such as, eco-efficiency and recycling, and call into question the design of these systems. He says, "We leave aside efficiency the old model of product-and-waste, and its dour offspring, 'efficiency,' and embrace the challenge of being not efficient but *effective* with respect to a rich mix of considerations and desires" (McDonough & Braungart, 2002, p. 72). In other words, change and openness to it are central to Sustainer psychological style. McDonough's designs reflect this strategy of change. For instance, McDonough designed office-furniture manufacturer Herman Miller's office spaces

> in a way that celebrates a range of cultural and natural pleasures – sun, light, air, nature, even food—in order to enhance the lives of the people who work there. . . . In its every element, the building expresses the client's and architect's vision of a life-centered community and environment (McDonough & Braungart, 2002, pp. 74–75)

Returning to McDonough's challenge to create a fabric that is so safe it is edible, his challenge was turned down by more than sixty European chemical companies because of its complexity, but, finally, one company did step up to the plate to take a swing with McDonough. With the help of this company, McDonough and his team created an edible fabric—in fact, they created a process for creating the fabric such that when inspectors came to examine the amount of waste produced by the new process, they felt their instruments were broken: "They could not identify any pollutants, not even elements they knew were in the water when it came into the factory" (McDonough & Braungart, 2002, p. 108). These projects reflect The Sustainer's rhetoric and practice of "reestablishing our fundamental connection to the source of all good growth on the planet" (McDonough & Braungart, 2002, p. 131). In all design challenges, McDonough and his team consider a variety of factors that will enable them to continue to walk the talk, so to speak. Among them are chronic toxicity, biodegradability, and potential for ozone depletion and whether all by-products meet the same criteria (McDonough & Braungart, 2002, p. 175). So, the psychological style of The Sustainer is about consistency between word and deed—consistent engagement, consistent questioning, consistent change, and consistent invention are all hallmarks of Sustainer psychological style.

The three characteristics of the Sustainer public intellectual's identity are responsibility, a focus on the local, and a long-term vision. It should not be a shock that Sustainer public intellectuals both advocate and live responsibly. Even acts as simple as purchasing athletic footwear do, for McDonough and other Sustainers, elicit feelings of "social inequity and . . . guilt" (McDonough & Braungart, 2002, p. 4) because of the labor conditions of the workers who produce the shoes and the processes of production that are generally detrimental to the natural environment. McDonough wonders, "Maybe we want our things to live forever, but what do future generations want? What about their right to the pursuit of life, liberty, and happiness, to a celebration of their own abundance of nutrients, of materials, of delight?" (McDonough & Braungart, 2002, p. 114). He states that his professional goal is to help create "a delightfully diverse, safe, healthy, and just world, with clean air, soil, water, and power—economically, equitably, ecologically, and elegantly enjoyed, period. What's not to like?" (qtd. in McGregor, June 12, 2006).

In the scope of his practice, McDonough has taken on the role as chair of the China-US Center for Sustainable Development. In this role, he is leading the design of urban spaces—more than four hundred million people are expected to move from rural to urban areas in China by 2020—and planning transportation and the mix of green space for the world's most populous nation, China. In fact, in Liuzhou, McDonough is moving sugarcane farmland that would otherwise be displaced onto the area's rooftops as insulation. Waste water will be converted through a treatment plant into fertilizer, and buildings will feature windows set at an angle to make the most of natural light and heat. Another example is the William McDonough + Partners' new line of cradle-to-cradle–inspired greeting cards. As the ReProduct website details,

> Each card comes with a unique two-way return postage-paid envelope that allows its constituent materials to be safely reused rather than discarded. Both the cards and the envelopes are made from a Certified Technical Nutrient plastic material. Cards returned using the self-mailing envelope will be used by Shaw Carpet as raw material for new carpet tiles. (ReProduct, 2007, October 18)

In other words, behaving responsibly toward people and environments enables the expression of the Sustainer identity in public space.

In addition to being responsible, the Sustainer public intellectual considers the local to be vital to his or her identity—the Sustainer sustains local places first before turning attention to global issues. McDonough spent part of his childhood living in Tokyo. He vividly remembers the paper walls, futons, and steam baths of Japanese homes; even those with very few material resources were simple but impeccably clean, and, as he notes, "I was again struck by how simple and elegant good design could be, and how suited to locale" (McDonough & Braungart, 2002, p. 7). This sense of and connection to the local have been hallmarks of McDonough's career and are elementary to Sustainer public intellectual style perhaps because of The Sustainer's elevation of respect for diversity—such an inclination propels The Sustainer to find local idiosyncrasies beautiful and interesting rather than provincial or trivial. McDonough explains, "In healthy, thriving natural systems it is actually the *fitting-est* who survive. Fitting-est implies an energetic and material engagement with place, and an interdependent relationship to it" (McDonough & Braungart, 2002, p. 120). The Sustainer public intellectual understands that people are more likely to work to protect a known and particular people and a personally meaningful, specific landscape than they are general human beings somewhere unfamiliar on the other side of the globe. Indeed, sustainability is local. Elaborating on this, McDonough opines,

> We begin to make human systems and industries fitting when we recognize that all sustainability (like all politics) is local. We connect them to local and material energy flows, and to local customs, needs, and tastes, from the level of the molecule to the level of the region itself. (McDonough & Braungart, 2002, p. 123)

Making manifest this local identity is McDonough's Cradle-to-Cradle Village in Huangbaiyu, China. Rather than using imported materials or labor, McDonough and his team have made use of compressed-earth blocks and straw bales from local land and farmers to construct the homes in the village. In addition, because the population of this largely rural area in the Liaoning Province of northeast China makes a living farming corn and raising sheep and are quite poor, McDonough and his team are working with their Chinese counterparts to develop local rural enterprises to boost villagers' incomes and allow them an easier method for financing the new homes (Project targets, 2006). Because heating and cooking are great obstacles for the Huangbaiyu locals because of their remote and northern location, the homes have been built to consume only one-third of the typical amount of energy needed to heat a home and to prepare meals. In addition, fuel for heating will be available from the newly built and locally run biomass gasification plant (Project targets, 2006). Although McDonough is clearly not a local citizen of the village, his admiration of diversity and his identity as a person invested in local communities allow him to transcend the boundaries of nation-states and bring a sustainable philosophy to other parts of the world. In this way, Sustainer public intellectuals are locally global.

The last major component of the Sustainer public intellectual's identity is a sense of longevity or a focus on the long-term outcomes of a product's or process's design. This also speaks to the visionary nature of The Sustainer's style. McDonough's longevity philosophy is best captured in his own language when he hypothesizes, "Imagine a building like a tree, a city like a forest" (McDonough & Braungart, 2002, p. 139). This philosophy means conceiving of the design of a single building as a living thing that will be a contributing component of an entire ecosystem, feeding and sheltering all of its inhabitants. For a designer like McDonough, this means "considering not only how a product is made but how it is to be used, and by whom. In a cradle-to-cradle conception, it may have many uses, and many users, over time and space" (McDonough & Braungart, 2002, p. 139), and having an eye toward this long-term plan is what separates The Sustainer from the garden-variety ecologist. The Sustainer asks, "What would it mean to become, once again, native to this place, the Earth—the home of *all* our relations?" and answers, "This is going to take us all, and it is going to take forever. But then, that's the point" (McDonough & Braungart, 2002, p. 186).

In his work to create Oberlin College's Adam Joseph Lewis Center for Environmental Studies, he worked with local residents and professor

David Orr to create a building site in the same way a tree works. But the design goes further than that. It seeks to actually reverse the damage the US Industrial Revolution perpetuated (William McDonough + Partners, 2013). This approach works on three assumptions: "waste equals food, use current solar income, and respect diversity" (William McDonough + Partners, 2013). Ultimately, the Adam Joseph Lewis building exports energy rather than sucks it up as a resource. And, with a continual eye not on the bottom line but on the future of the Oberlin environment, McDonough + Partners trumpet, "Just as the building's materials promote long-term human and ecological health, the vibrant atrium at the building's core enriches the social character of the place, functioning as the 'town hall' for Oberlin's southern campus" (William McDonough + Partners, 2013). By striving to reverse damage caused by the Industrial Revolution, Oberlin's center has moved cleanly into the future. By designing a building that repays both the natural and human environments of Oberlin College over the long term, McDonough lives his own standard and turns his identity outward to benefit the local public sphere of a college campus.

Sociological Style

The Sustainer is the public intellectual stylistic response to the destruction of both our natural and social environments. Americans have heard for decades about our beloved industry's contribution to holes in the ozone layer, to global warming, and to clear-cutting. In turn, these environmental disasters spawn social and political disasters: a rise in cancer, concerns over our use of fossil fuels, wars in the Middle East, loss of jobs in this country as the need increases for imports.

For Sustainer public intellectuals, the way that we interact needs a radical paradigm shift—instead of interacting superficially with a barely passing notice of others, we need a return to a commitment to legitimate community in order for our human "systems" to become sustainable over time. We must, according to Sustainers, ask ourselves "not only what has worked in the past and present, but what will work in the future. What kind of world do we intend and how might we design things in keeping with that vision?" (McDonough & Braungart, 2002, p. 145). If we intend to sustain human community, we cannot continue to design spaces and technologies that isolate people from one another. McDonough notes, "To concentrate any single criterion creates instability in the larger context and represents what we call an 'ism,' an extreme position disconnected from the overall structure" (McDonough & Braungart, 2002, p. 147). This kind of sociological style is reminiscent of Thomas Jefferson's words to

James Madison: "The earth belongs . . . to the living. . . . No man can by natural right oblige the lands he occupied, or the persons who succeeded him in that occupation, to the payment of debts contracted by him. For, if he could, he might, during his own life, eat up the usufruct of the lands for several generations to come, and then the lands would belong to the dead, and not the living" (McDonough & Braungart, 2002, pp. 185–86).

This philosophy must be performed sociologically if it is to be a style and not merely a political commitment. This paradigm shift to community is exemplified in McDonough's Kanawha Museum of Life and the Environment outside of Charlotte, South Carolina, in the small town of Fort Mill. The museum is the central showpiece of an entire master-planned community that McDonough hopes will feature "a very rich mix of housing types. We want to have granny flats, places to rent and small studios—we want to make sure housing is available to the ordinary income earner" (Smith, 2006). The county's Culture and Heritage Foundation president, Frank Barnes III, states that the

> "Fort Mill residents will get a cultural facility that tells the story of sustainable development" in the museum and "a *community that lives the story*" (Smith, emphasis added). McDonough & Partners describe the planned community as "a new model for the interaction between people and place" to ultimately "encourage the search for a deeper understanding of how human communities connect."(William McDonough + Partners, 2013)

Indeed, McDonough + Partners has an entire area of practice devoted solely to the transformation of human communities. Other projects in this area include the Coffee Creek Center in Chesterton, Indiana, which "fosters vibrant mixed-use neighborhoods, walkable streets, and convenient transportation," and the Fuller Theological Seminary's North Campus Comprehensive Residential Master Plan, in which

> buildings are organized around two housing types that emphasize community—courtyard housing and stacked flats. By reinforcing the traditional American campus idea as a well-defined urban precinct, the design solution seeks to foster a spiritually centered living and learning community that preserves public open space in a cohesive, adaptable, and culturally diverse setting. (William McDonough + Partners, 2013)

The emphasis, for McDonough and other Sustainer public intellectuals, is a sociological style of community.

Not only does The Sustainer's sociological style mark a paradigm shift in terms of social construction of knowledge about human community but it is also publicly visible in the form of public texts. McDonough certainly wants people to know he is an authentic Sustainer in terms of his style, and hundreds of clients undeniably have embraced his Sustainer style as faithful. McDonough has been interviewed by and featured in newspapers from small-town America, like the *Charlotte Observer*, through to major news magazines, like *Time* and *Business Week*. In addition, there is a documentary film titled *The Next Industrial Revolution* that is narrated by actress Susan Sarandon. The hour-long video is dedicated to exploring how McDonough is combining ecology and commerce to, as the film states, "change the world." A six-hour interview with McDonough on his cradle-to-cradle philosophy was captured on a six-CD set *The Monticello Dialogues*. And, as previously mentioned, the firm has now started a line of greeting cards based on the cradle-to-cradle philosophy and book. Finally, he has a number of websites including those of McDonough himself, McDonough + Partners, and McDonough Braungart Design Chemistry. Despite his stature in the field and his own contribution to a number of university and college campuses as a designer and as a faculty member, his work and philosophy are not the subjects of academic research, debate, and writing—the texts about him and the texts he contributes in a lay context are always those of the lay public. Sustainer public intellectuals must be publicly visible in terms of their sociological style because, of course, they are *public* and not private intellectuals but also because they address an audience around the world. They believe their ideas too important for too many to circulate only in the confines of specialists and academics.

DIMENSIONS OF COMPARISON

Returning to the five dimensions of comparison, we begin with fluidity. In the case of William McDonough, he is a highly fluid Sustainer public intellectual. He holds a bachelor's degree from Dartmouth College and a master's in architecture from Yale University. In addition to his two firms, William McDonough + Partners and McDonough Braungart Design Chemistry, he is also a consulting professor of civil and environmental engineering at Stanford University, the chair of the board of overseers for the Center for Eco-Intelligent Management, a venture partner with VantagePoint Venture Capitalists, and from1994 to 1999, served as the Edward E. Elson Professor of Architecture and dean of the School of Architecture at the University of Virginia (McDonough, 2013). Despite his significant stature within the design, architecture, and ecology communities, McDonough lives his life serving communities around the world. Through his projects to bring his cradle-to-cradle philosophy to life, he embeds himself in the public, learning how specific communities operate, what materials are native to a place, and how to make architecture and design feel native and make them contribute more than they take away. All of this requires his fully embodied presence as both a designer and as a member of a greater human community. He states,

> I believe we can accomplish great and profitable things within a new conceptual framework—one that values our legacy, honors diversity, and feeds ecosystems and societies. . . . It is time for designs that are creative, abundant, prosperous, and intelligent from the start. (William McDonough + Partners, 2013)

While Cornel West and the prophets are more evenly distributed between "public" and "intellectual," McDonough and the Sustainer public intellectuals demonstrate a greater degree of "publicness" in their style. Certainly, this is not to discount Sustainers as subpar intellectuals or to suggest that McDonough is somehow less capable a thinker than West. It is, though, to say that Sustainers, because they are trying to bring ecological activism mainstream, must be more public than intellectual for that movement to be possible. To demonstrate this, see McDonough and Braungart's *Cradle-to-Cradle*, any number of interview texts, or any film footage of McDonough as a speaker or interviewee. The chiefly noticeable element of each of these mediated texts is that all are in the language of the lay person, not "architectese" or design-speak. I mentioned earlier in the chapter that McDonough has created his own sort of vernacular to describe things, such as, *upcycling* instead of *recycling* or *nutrivehicle* instead of *automobile*. Even though McDonough is a capable specialist and an acclaimed designer, his manner of speaking is very publicly accessible. Also contrary to prophetic public intellectuals, as crises escalate, McDonough maintains the same degree of "publicness" rather than assuming a greater public role. Sustainers are used to weathering crises—in fact, the entire sustainability movement arose out of a perceived ongoing crisis situation: environmental destruction. For that reason, they are not as bound to a particular kairotic moment; rather, they "sustain" their level of public participation through all types of social and political situations.

Turning to location, the Sustainer public intellectual can largely be found in the community, that is, in whatever public he or she is currently working. McDonough is incapable of doing his job solely in an office setting, surrounded by other design professional peers and sending his ideas off to someone else to complete. His philosophy of respecting the diversity of native cultures and the natural habitats in which they exist prohibits him from isolating himself, even if his "day job" is as architect, designer, ecologist, or professor. For instance, McDonough Braungart Design Chemistry is dedicated to their "Cradle to Cradle Design paradigm," which is "powering the Next Industrial Revolution, in which products and services are designed based on patterns found in nature, eliminating the concept of waste entirely and creating an abundance that is healthy and sustaining" (2013). This strategy of "Eco-Effectiveness" is not done in a vacuum. Indeed, Sustainers have to take their show on the road. Yet, for a Sustainer like McDonough, there is a balance to be struck between local and global in terms of location. So, while McDonough and his teams greatly value and participate in the local, the Sustainer's goal is to change the global by changing many locals. So, The Sustainer, though located "locally," always has his or her eye focused globally.

The Sustainer public intellectual also avails him- or herself of media for communicating an important ecological message to the world's neighborhoods. McDonough seems almost masterful at this stylistic task. He has several websites cited through this chapter, a book, a line of greeting cards, a documentary film, a six-CD box set of his interviews, a speaking tour, academic positions, face-to-face work with clients and countless interviews in popular press, many of which have also been cited in this chapter. Media diversity is important for The Sustainer because of his or her focus on respecting local customs—if, for instance, McDonough is working in a community that has a lower socioeconomic level and where people are not always online, it does not make sense to use electronic media for his message, but, instead, it may make perfect sense for him to speak to villagers face-to-face and do an interview with the local newspaper. However, the work will later be described on his websites or in interviews with larger press outlets such that it has a higher degree of visibility. Technological innovation is also critical to The Sustainer because electronic media, for example, use less natural resources to produce and disseminate messages than does print press. So, media use is based, for The Sustainer, on the project, but all technologies are available.

And lastly, the use of resources. Obviously, media are among the resources used by The Sustainer, but resources are a touchy subject for the Sustainer public intellectual. The idea, ultimately, is to give back a greater amount of resource than one has taken in any given circumstance.

Resources for other public intellectuals may make a huge mark, but Sustainers try to leave very little trace of themselves on ecological systems in particular. McDonough is clearly highly paid, no one disputes that. However, he works diligently to help clients pay for his services through sustainable community businesses that help to subsidize his work. He certainly made use of valuable training resources through his education and apprenticeships but gives back much in this way by training other designers and community members to be more eco-effective themselves. He has been given many opportunities to share his philosophy and his life's work, but much of his press is dedicated to telling the stories of locals in a particular community who made something extraordinary out of the most ordinary of resources. So, The Sustainer works to put back at least as much, if not more, than he or she takes away in terms of resources. Without that kind of orientation, The Sustainer is not a Sustainer but a regular environmentalist or concerned human being. Sustainers' street cred is based on giving back vast amounts of resources and trying to take as little as possible, to leave a smaller ecological footprint.

McDonough is one example of a Sustainer, but he exemplifies the characteristics critical to Sustainers, in general. The Sustainer public intellectual style requires an indictment of current practices and their outcomes, but more important, it requires a transcendent paradigm shift of a vision for natural and human products and processes. There is a strong dedication to respect, diversity, and local communities while maintaining an overarching goal of changing the world. Sustainability is finally in fashion, allowing Sustainers a more amplified voice not only in ecology but in industry as well. Sustainers pride themselves on being part of humanity, never isolated or removed from it. They are doing more than just trying to make the world a better place. They are reinventing what counts as better in the first place.

Thus far, I have highlighted prosocial public intellectual rhetorical styles. Chapter 5 marks a move to the "dark side" of situated public intellectual style as I take on The Pundit.

5
PUNDIT STYLE: PAUL BEGALA

As the pithy usurps the substantive in contemporary mediated discourse, punditry abounds in America—turn on any network or cable news broadcast, and you will undoubtedly run across them (and probably want to run over them). Very few pundits would qualify as public intellectuals, but Paul Begala is an exception worth noting given punditry's ubiquity in the public sphere. Begala was born in New Jersey and raised in Texas and is a two-time graduate of the University of Texas at Austin, holding both a BA and a JD from the institution. He taught briefly at the University of Texas before going to work with partner James "Ragin' Cajun" Carville (together they make up the political consulting firm Begala and Carville) for then-governor Bill Clinton of Arkansas. After an unlikely but resounding victory in the Clinton campaign, Begala found himself thrust into the national spotlight as a political strategy consultant. Begala and Carville scored more victories for Democrats Diane Feinstein and Zell Miller, among others. He also served as strategist for Hillary Rodham Clinton's 2008 bid for the Democratic nomination.

Begala served as one of the key spokespeople for the Clinton administration's policy efforts while consulting with President Clinton during his tenure in the White House. During this time, Begala helped John F. Kennedy Jr. launch his political magazine, *George*, and worked as contributing editor and author of the "Capital Hillbilly" column. The author of five books including *Is Our Children Learning? The Case against George W. Bush*, and *Take It Back: Our Party, Our Country, Our Future* (coauthored with Carville), Begala is a regular op-ed contributor to a number of news publications and the former cohost of the CNN debate program *Crossfire*. Currently, Begala serves as Research Professor of Public Policy at Georgetown University and a Sanders Political Leadership Scholar at the University of Georgia School of Law and appears regularly on programs like Wolf Blitzer's CNN news show, *The Situation Room*, and Candy Crowley's *State of the Union*. The Pundit downplays the intellectual for the public and the political, making effective use of media resources to be seen by as many people through as many different channels and for as much of the time as possible.

PUNDIT STYLE BASICS

In contrast to the public intellectual styles that I have detailed so far, The Pundit is less effective in fostering deliberation. This is not to say that Paul Begala is a bad person or that Begala as an individual is always working against the best interests of our culture—it is to say, though, that punditry itself often runs counter to democratic desires. In 2006, sociologists at Duke University published a study examining nineteen years' worth of data on the link between social ties and the social health of the United States. The Duke study confirms the thesis of Robert D. Putnam's *Bowling Alone*, that spending larger amounts of time at work and smaller amounts of time doing social activities degrades civic concern and participation (Duke University, 2006). In other words, the more people bowl alone, the worse the social health of our nation. If those surveyed by the Duke sociologists are extrapolated to the larger population, Americans feel like they do not have time for lengthy dialogue. Hence, we have The Pundit public intellectual.

That said, there are pundits that encourage dialog about pressing issues (e.g., Anderson Cooper), but we should be concerned that this type of pundit is few and far between. Most pundits are of another sort—a political commentator on a very superficial level, providing a mediated gloss on concerns of the day and moving on to the next hot topic seconds or minutes later. We should also be concerned about the amount of attention punditry receives. Yet, there are lessons we can learn from The Pundit: Wit is not anathema to wisdom, demeaning the popular makes you unpopular, concision increases the likelihood that the entirety of the message is received, and acting as if you are an expert attending a dinner party is a winning comportment. In these ways, we should regard The Pundit not as a fully formed democratic agent akin to the other public intellectual styles in this book but as an omnipresent figure in our public and mediated spheres with enormous potential to do great things. It is through this lens that we look at the work of Paul Begala.

Physiological Style

Conservative talk-show host Rush Limbaugh refers to him as "the Fore-head," but whether or not Paul Begala has a canyon between his eyebrows and hairline, his physiological style clearly works for him. The Pundit has to walk a particularly fine line between the perception of the audience that he or she is an expert in something but also that he or she is not stodgy or patronizing like those other experts (read: traditional intellectuals). Of course, all public intellectuals walk this line to a degree, but The Pundit is specifically aware of this requirement, likely because punditry is seen most often on television—if the average American is going to invite you into her living room, you had better know something that she does not but dish it quickly. She has other things to do. In other words, Begala has to portray the physiological style of "every person's expert." To accomplish this, Begala is always seen in a conservative, "politician" suit, neat haircut, and clean shaven. This is the garb of the political expert, and Begala wears it like he was born in it. Looking like the politicians he supports and critiques allows Begala the ability to craft himself as *the* strategy analyst and expert on all things political.

However, Begala would be unsuccessful as a Pundit public intellectual if he was only seen as a political expert, however pithy he may be, if he did not also seem like a fun guy to invite to a dinner party at your house. While his clothing and physical comportment scream "expert" (or at least "Brooks Brothers"), his folksy and straightforward manner of speaking shout, "I'm one of you, despite how I'm dressed!" Of course, Begala is not really "one of the guys"—he is a professor of public policy at Georgetown, hosted his own very popular CNN show, and is called upon to represent the Democratic party line on television several times a week. However, he seems like one of the gang, and that is because of his physiological style. Begala is funny without being cruel ("Prayers with George W Bush and family after reported heart stent surgery. Politics stops at the pericardium") (Begala, 2013, August 6) and smart without being pedantic ("This is important: NYTs reports NYers health insur premiums in individual mkt to fall 50% or more under Obamacare") (Begala, 2013, July 17). Because of this folksiness, Begala is able to walk the line between expert and dinner-party guest.

Quite simply, Begala conveys a worldview through his physiological style. For Begala as a political strategist pundit, he views the world through an undeniably political lens. This framing is most evident in the way he describes the world. For instance, Begala is a regular contributor to several political blogs, one of them TPM Café. In a post dated February 14, 2006, Begala describes Vice President Dick Cheney's hunting accident in South Texas involving attorney Charles Whittington.

> To quote Mary Matalin to vouch for Cheney's safety, as the *Post* does, is absurd. I love Mary—she's married to my best friend. But she was 1500 miles away, drinking a fine Rhone, no doubt. And I daresay she's never been hunting in her life. And yet the *Post* quotes her reassuring us that Cheney "was not careless or incautious." Baloney. That's like quoting me on Mrs. Bush's inaugural ball gown. I didn't attend the event, and I don't know squat about the subject. (2006)

Self-deprecating humor aside, Begala takes a subject that is *not* political prima facie and politicizes it by chastising Vice President Cheney and questioning the credibility of Matalin, conservative strategist. If we extend the argument, Begala takes on the Republican Party. Begala exists in the world as if all things are politically polarized, and that is represented in his style of speaking.

Since The Pundit must constantly be available for pithy commentary, he or she must have a physiological style that reflects this occupational requirement. As mentioned previously, Begala dons the suit of the politicians for whom he strategizes, lending him street cred as a political insider. However, it serves a second purpose in terms of reflecting an inner persona. By always being seen publicly dressed in a suit, Begala gives the impression that he is a man who is ready, at any moment, to discuss the news of the day. And, of course, this is his job. Begala is successful, though, because he understands the level of stylistic preparedness necessary for the life of the professional pundit.

Psychological Style

Psychological style is, first and foremost, about consistency between talk and action. As described in the preceding paragraph, The Pundit is always available as punditry, as public background noise—that is its nature. So, physiologically, this requires The Pundit to be available both in terms of physical proximity to a medium to disseminate a message and also clothing and manner of speaking that convey expertise in a given area. Part of being always already available as The Pundit public intellectual is having something to say about virtually anything under his or her umbrella field of expertise. Begala is no exception. Certainly, a quick, informal poll would reveal that most people feel Begala is entitled to consideration as an expert in politics, but what kind of politics? A more informed opinion would reveal a more limited swath of expertise: traditional electoral political activities, such as, campaigning, public relations, communicating party platform, and the like for the Democratic Party. Begala himself would probably admit, off the record, no doubt, that he is not an expert on social movements, globalization, or education. Even in his most honest moments, Begala would have to admit he is no policy wonk. Yet, The Pundit must cast the widest net possible in terms of expertise in order to get as much face time as possible on whatever medium is most readily available. A quick Google search on quotes by Paul Begala lends credence to this argument: "Again, President Reagan was sort of an amiable presence out at the ranch by the last 6 months of his presidency. He had no effect on national policy at all"; "Defining the terms of the debate generally dictates who's gonna win it"; "I'm a Catholic, but I used to love going to Vacation Bible School with my fundamentalist friends"; "It seems to me the American people never really forgave the Democrats for being right about Vietnam"; "See, I think if it just became who's sleeping with whom, then there's no reason to prefer one party over the other, 'cause the truth is we're all sinners" (Paul Begala Quotes, n.d.). Once a Pundit like Begala has media phronesis, he can opine on just about anything from Catholicism to sex, Vietnam to Reagan, without having his credibility called into question. We should certainly attend to the implications of unquestioned musings by most pundits—it is alarming how much opinion passes for fact in our era of truthiness. Still, the problem lies less with individual pundits and more with a broken system. Peter Brooks argues, "The mediating organs of our culture are in disrepair" (2006). And as Richard Reeves (2006) explains regarding mediated intellectuals, "The risk in these conditions is that barriers to entry are lowered, so that even if the prevalence and status of intellectuals remains unchanged, the quality of their product diminishes."

Begala's actions outside of his quipping on all things political further support a high level of consistency between talk and action, a stylistic trend that sets him apart from pundits that spout often uninformed opinion under the guise of fact. Begala used to appear several times a week on CNN when *Crossfire* was still on the air. When it was cancelled, Begala was tapped to be the "voice of the left" on Blitzer's program, *The Situation Room*. Despite the fact that Begala is not the primary host, nor even the only commentator on the left, he is on television at least once a week. Notable, when Begala is introduced, he is introduced as a Georgetown professor, not a political strategist, reinforcing his more intellectual approach to punditry. He occupies time and space on other media, as well. He writes for Bloomberg online and serves as one of its radio personalities on politics. Begala contributes regularly on a number of blogs, including Talking Points Memo, BuzzFlash, Bernaise Source Media, Camus Progress, and the *Huffington Post*. He has a very active blog on CNN, where he comments on such things as presidential debates. For instance, on October 8, 2004, Begala wrote about the third debate between George W. Bush and John F. Kerry, "Bush was asked to name three mistakes he's made. He can't name one. Breathtaking arrogance. He's had the hardest job in the world for almost four years and he cannot name a single mistake. Either he's the Second Coming of the Messiah, or he's so damned arrogant he's dangerous" (2004, October 8). He is always available for the last word.

Not only must The Pundit be readily available but he or she must also be available in the right places. All public intellectuals have an area of expertise, and The Pundit is no different. So, we would expect to find The Pundit occupying spaces particular to his or her area of perceived expertise. For Begala, this means he must be available to be seen in political contexts, in general, and heard on the "left," in particular. For starters, Begala lives and works predominantly in Washington, D.C. For a political-strategist pundit, this nation's capital is an obvious choice. Begala highlights this choice, saying that he and Carville "want to be where the politicians are and where the voters are. I love being in Washington [D.C.]; it's often the nerve center" (CNN, 2003). In addition, in the 2008 and 2012 presidential elections, citizens of Washington, D.C., cast more than 90 percent of their votes for the Obama-Biden ticket. In other words, for a single city, it would be challenging for Begala to pick one that has a higher concentration of citizens on the political left. There, in addition to his television work that I have already described in some detail, Begala is Research Professor of Public Policy at Georgetown University. The course he teaches for the spring semester is "Politics and the Media," where he instructs students about the intersection of the press and politics. He says in his course description,

> If you don't read a daily paper and aren't prepared to discuss current issues affecting politics and the press, you don't belong in this class. Finally and most importantly: robust debate will be required, as will a decent respect for the opinions of others. So bring both a thick skin and a civil tongue; both will be necessary. (Georgetown University, n.d.b)

Begala may be most famous for his political consulting and strategy firm, Begala and Carville, that he runs with Carville and that most notably helped a then-little-known Arkansas governor named Bill Clinton with the 1992 presidential election. As his biography for Georgetown notes, "As a former top-ranking White House official, a University professor, a political consultant and a corporate communications strategist, Paul Begala has spent his career at the intersection of politics, policy, and press" (Georgetown University, n.d.b).

In addition to his actual physical home and work locations, Begala can be found on the "left" by anyone, anywhere with access to a television, a radio, an Internet connection, a bookstore, or a library. So, even if Begala-philes live outside the D.C. area and cannot see him in person, this Pundit lives his life visibly on almost all communicative media. Begala is on CNN on *The Situation Room*. He is on the radio on NPR, *Imus in the Morning*, and other shows. He appears on *PBS NewsHour*. He writes for *Newsweek* and pens a political blog for CNN. He contributes to a number of liberal blogs. He has written five books, including his latest (2008) *Third Term: Why George W. Bush (Hearts) John McCain*, and two coauthored with consulting partner Carville. He is often asked to write op-ed pieces for newspapers like the *Washington Post*. Quite surely, Begala is consistent in talk and action in terms of his psychological style.

The other component of psychological style is identity. Begala has cultivated his identity as a pundit public intellectual—I refer to his identity as "every person's liberal geek." It should be obvious by now that Begala is on the political left and is available through most mediated sources as a strategist in this capacity. However, because Begala is a public intellectual in The Pundit category, he must also represent accessibility in terms of his identity. Hence, people feel comfortable inviting him into their homes on a regular, if not daily, basis. He achieves this accessibility, I believe, through his simplistic descriptions of complex political policy and process and his use of folksy humor. For instance, he stated about the need for reform in the Catholic Church,

> Since every cardinal is a product of the status quo, it is difficult to imagine 115 men chosen by the present system electing a new pope committed to fundamental change. Monarchs don't start revolutions. But we people of faith are praying for a miracle. Angelo Roncalli was supposed to be an elderly caretaker. Instead, as Pope John XXIII he dragged the church into the 20th century—well, at least into the 19th. The hierarchy needs reform, to say the least. A

fumigation is more like it. Here is a thought exercise to illustrate how blind the princes of the church have been to their true duty. (Begala, 2013, March 11)

While the issue of whether to usher in an era of progress in the Church is undoubtedly important, Begala's treatment of it suggests its resolution is just a matter of getting some folks in a room and chatting. While The Pundit is not where other public intellectuals are in terms of fostering deliberation, he or she is effective in getting issues like comprehensive sex education into the national conversation. Other examples exist in abundance. In the February 28, 2005, taping of *Crossfire*, Begala "debates" conservative cohost Bay Buchanan about our progress in Iraq. He muses,

> Of course, we were told Mr. Bush's invasion would be a cakewalk. We were told our troops would be greeted as liberators. We were told that killing Uday and Qusay would change everything, that capturing Saddam would be the turning point. We were told that the handover of sovereignty was the key, and we were told that elections last month were the light at the end of the tunnel. Through it all, we were told everything but the truth. I just don't know how much more Mr. Bush's kind of progress our troops can stand. (CNN, 2005, February 28)

And, famously, Begala hails from Texas, which gives him some "authority" in using down-home humor. His folksy brand of humor is clear when he quips,

> Texas is the nearest thing to heaven there is. We love our state but we are embarrassed by our weak government. We ignore 400,000 souls in Third World conditions with no electricity and running water. We pay our teachers less than our football coaches, and we get the results you'd expect. (CNN, 2000)

Another example of his witticism can be found in his CNN blog entry on October 13, 2004, "As we say in Texas, don't piss on my boots and tell me it's raining." As every person's liberal geek, Begala successfully boils involved political issues down to the most simplistic terms in a humorous way.

Sociological Style
The first element of sociological style is that all styles are socially constructed. The public audience must co-create The Pundit style, in other

words. This is where our sociopolitical trends come into play. The clear effect of the hypermediation and sound-bite nature of our contemporary moment, people perceive that they have very little time. The 2006 study conducted by sociologists from Duke University demonstrates, primarily, a trend among the approximately fifteen hundred people surveyed about their social networks that most felt they spent more time at work and had less time to do anything else. As boundaries between work and "normal" life collapse because of the ability to take the office home on a laptop, this feeling becomes even more pronounced. For people who want it all right now, punditry emerges as a legitimate form of public discourse. If we have to wait longer than a few minutes or even seconds to learn what is going on in our political landscape, we flip channels or boot up an online resource because it "saves" time, and time is scarce, and time is money. So, the public, in many ways, calls forth The Pundit public intellectual as a response to this need for brain-cell saving news. Certainly, we should not rejoice in this reality, but it should provoke the rest of us to consider how we, individually and collectively, can change our media ecology for the better.

In addition to co-creating Pundit style, the public must also judge The Pundit's performance as authentic or faithful for this public intellectual to be successful. Clearly, the public has pronounced his performance as authentic to Pundit sociological style. Although it has been cancelled, Begala's CNN program *Crossfire*, despite its 4:30 P.M. timeslot, was CNN's seventh-highest-rated program in 2004 and had been on the air since 1982 featuring a number of prominent voices from the left and right (Media Bistro, 2005). Students line up for his Georgetown courses on political topics. After the 2010 midterms, Begala and fellow Georgetown professor and journalist E. J. Dionne debated Kevin Madden, press secretary for Mitt Romney, as to the lessons for 2012 and beyond to a sold-out crowd. As of December 1, 2009, Begala's newest tome, *Third Term*, garnered a 4.5-star rating on Amazon.com, and Begala and Carville's 2006 book, *Take It Back*, sold 17,734 copies in two months, according to Nielson Bookscan, and received an average reader-rating of 4 stars on Amazon. com. So, in terms of authenticity, Begala has been embraced by the public.

The second part of sociological style is being publicly visible. Style cannot occur in a vacuum. As a Pundit, Begala is undeniably visible. Begala, I have no doubt, believes that he utilizes the media to help audiences understand issues. And, I have already gone into many pages of detail about Begala's media visibility. Few Pundits, in fact, are more publicly visible than Paul Begala.

DIMENSIONS OF COMPARISON

Begala seems to be fairly fluid, although likely less so than other public intellectuals. It is a fact that Begala is an intellectual. He holds a doctoral-level degree in law, runs a thriving political strategy consultancy with partner Carville, worked closely with President Clinton, and teaches public-policy courses at Georgetown University. Begala is certainly capable of teaching classes on public policy—after all, he was at the center of public policy for Bill Clinton and worked as the spokesperson for that administration. Yet, it is likely that Begala lives too far outside the traditional academic realm to be taken seriously by his traditional academic colleagues. Most public intellectuals with day jobs in academe face a similar set of perceptual obstacles from their peers. By virtue of his career trajectory, Begala must be publicly visible, a choice that delegitimizes him among traditional academics and intellectuals. So, he is not terribly fluid, though movement is evidently possible.

Degree is the second point of comparison for this project and is closely related to fluidity. The Pundit lives most of his or her life in the public, rather than intellectual, world. Although Paul Begala is a highly educated person holding both a BA and a JD from the University of Texas at Austin and although he counts Georgetown University professor as his day job, The Pundit cannot live predominantly in that world. Intellectual life is about critical and analytical thinking, about asking tough questions, and, ultimately, about *depth*. The Pundit engages in summary, superficial questioning and is concerned with *breadth*. This is not to say that the public is unintelligent—that would be patently false. It is to say, though, that the public's attention span tends to be quite short. Without much spare time, activities, such as, critical thinking and in-depth questioning and analysis, take an almost permanent backseat to having high-level information at a moment's notice in a moment's time. While the intellectual world digs into issues, questions, and problems, the public world soars above them at about thirty thousand feet. Therefore, Begala as Pundit must concentrate the bulk of his time in the friendly skies because popularity is paramount to The Pundit. He is a sort of flight attendant on the airline of political discourse. Welcome aboard.

The third issue here is location, or where to find Pundit public intellectuals. While some public intellectuals maintain a reasonable degree of privacy even with public visibility, The Pundit is plainly visible. Again, Begala teaches in a classroom with limited seats and goes home every night to a house without a television crew. He has some private space.

His job literally *is* public—The Pundit has to be intellectual in public all the time. There is no "private" intellectual time for this style. When he is not on television, he is online. When he is not online, he is on the radio. When he is not on the radio, he is writing op-ed pieces. We locate The Pundit solely in the public eye—as Rosa Eberly (2000) notes, a classroom can be considered a kind of public. His extreme visibility to a mass audience is what makes Begala a captivating intellectual. He is just nerdy enough to seem brilliant but is overwhelmingly savvy in his ability to win an audience through media.

The next point of comparison is somewhat of a "duh" moment: media usage. Indeed, I have spent the bulk of this chapter detailing Begala's mastery of media. Pundits, in general, require media for exposure to an audience. Pithiness does not get very far toward publishing a disciplinary article in a peer-reviewed journal. But it gets The Pundit amazingly far toward a career in front of the camera, over radio waves, or through the Internet. American culture, as I said earlier, dictates brevity and prefers to avoid deliberation and debate regardless of the fact that informed dialogue could mend much of what is broken in this country. Instead, we embrace the short, the pithy, the diluted, the simple. In truth, we embrace The Pundit.

The last point of comparison is the use of resources. Pundits, generally, and Begala, specifically, capitalize on resources. Begala has made the most of his education—he has parlayed his knowledge of the law into an indisputably impressive strategy consulting firm. He then capitalized on his "win" for Bill Clinton and has gone on to be one of the most prominent voices in popular culture related to the Democratic Party. For this, he is both admired and despised. The Pundit has the requisite style to be the kind of person people invite into their homes. This is not true of the other styles I have outlined in this book. The Pundit seems like the kind of person we would like to drink a beer with, and for that reason, The Pundit is able to make incredibly effective use of resources available to him or her in ways that other public intellectuals cannot or would not even be asked to do. Pundits are, by their very nature, popular, and they become that way through their use of media and other resources. They stay that way because we like them. And, because we let them.

In the traditional academic circles in which we run, there is a very real undercurrent of hostility toward popular media and toward the popular, in general, a view spurred on by the Frankfurt School in the 1940s and 1950s that has yet to be eradicated. To be sure, there are elements of popular culture that are superfluous, ridiculous, and unworthy of scholarly consideration (e.g., actress Lindsay Lohan). The Pundit is one case of throwing the baby out with the bathwater. Of course, Paul Begala, like other Pundit public intellectuals, has his limitations, and we should not lower our standards for democratic deliberation and practice. However, rather than writing off The Pundit, we can learn the stylistic qualities that make The Pundit popular and, in many ways, efficacious. These qualities may seem at odds with traditional intellectual work, but that is precisely the point.

Chapter 6 details a highly gendered style, The Narrator, in order to begin to unpack challenges unique to nonmale public intellectuals.

6
NARRATOR STYLE:
CHRISTIANE AMANPOUR

In Alice Walker's *The Color Purple,* the protagonist, Celie, serves also as narrator. As a rhetorical device, Celie-the-narrator tells Celie-the-character's story in a way that gives readers a sense of history, of place, of politics, of society, of relational dynamics, of the struggles of power. Celie-the-narrator represents faceless and voiceless other Celies in the world. She is the book's conscience, its rudder, and its soul. When director Steven Spielberg made his version of *The Color Purple* into a film, he maintained Celie-the-character but removed Celie-the-narrator. In turn, Spielberg's film stifles "Celie's dialogue with God and herself, [obscuring] her story of self-empowerment through relationship and community" and diminishes Celie to the role of distant onlooker (Lister, 2010, p. 24). Ultimately rendering a feminist narrative a foil for normative patriarchal structures, "Spielberg's film recasts Celie's story to fit cultural myths, rather than highlighting her alternate path to power in its racial and sexual specificity" (in Lister, 2010, p. 24). Celie is robbed, literally, of her voice.

The role of the Narrator, in general, is to convey a story and, along with the author and audience, is one of the three principal voices in storytelling. Unlike the author and audience, though, The narrator is known as the viewpoint character, the voice that gives the audience the lens through which they will view the narrative, the frame for understanding the characters, the plot, the moral, and the context of the story. Good narrators do not merely report but translate, instruct, and constitute a community. The Narrator style melds experience, experts, and audience, taking us on a story with an ever-changing backdrop and cast, connecting stories with real people and real communities via a savvy media approach. As James Jasinski (2001) explains, narrative can have an instrumental or constitutive function. Narrative functions instrumentally when it is "used to respond to *exigencies* in a rhetorical situation and manifest direct or indirect arguments or persuasive appeals" (p. 393). Narrative functions constitutively when it helps "to shape and transform how a community understands its world, and when they offer inducements to create, recreate or transform the social world" (Jasinski, 2001, p. 393). The Narrator, then, frames identity and subjectivity, time and temporality, community and political culture, and language (Jasinski, 2001, p. 399).

In communication theorist Walter Fisher's work on narrative, he quotes Alasdair MacIntyre, who argues, "Man [*sic*] is in his actions and practices, as well as in his fictions, essentially a story-telling animal" (1984, p. 1). In other words, narration is not a "fictive composition" but a "theory of symbolic action—words and/or deeds—that have sequence or meaning for those who live, create, or interpret them" (Fisher, 1984, p. 2). In laying out his narrative paradigm, Fisher joins the argumentative with the aesthetic, revealing the public sphere as a place where stories, rather than formal or informal logic, move citizens to action. Narrative is particularly persuasive because it is connective and relational—it binds people, histories, regions, and themes. Rabbi Michael Goldberg explains,

> Neither "the facts" nor our "experiences" come to use in discrete packets disconnected which simply await the appropriate moral principle to be applied. Rather, they stand in need of some narrative which can bind the facts of our experience together into a coherent pattern and is thus in virtue of that narrative that our abstracted rules, principles, and notions gain their full intelligibility. (qtd. in Fisher, 1984, p. 3)

In Fisher's terms, narratives serve to recount and account for an event or situation. Recounting can be history or biography; accounting involves theory and argument (Fisher, 1984). The Narrator, then, is the person that "relates a truth about the human condition" through narration (Fisher, 1984, p. 6).

Two other entailments of Fisher's narrative paradigm seem particularly germane. First, stories resonate with human beings on a visceral level because the stories are value laden. In Narrator public intellectuals, we are prudent to discern patterns among competing values that permeate their rhetoric and actions. In the tradition of wise women (see Steiner-Adair, 1988) and in more recent work on women's political rhetoric (see Campbell, 1989; Dow & Tonn, 1993), values like nurturance and care consistently mark women's rhetorical and behavioral choices. In turn, we would expect different value lenses to be applied by women Narrator public intellectuals than by their male peers. Second, not only is it important *who* tells the story but it is also important to understand *how* the story is told. Fisher outlines two major criteria for judgment: narrative probability and narrative fidelity (1984, p. 7). Narrative probability is "what constitutes a coherent story," while narrative fidelity is "whether the stories [we] experience ring true with the stories [we] know to be true in [our] lives" (1984, p. 8). Stories with high narrative probability and fidelity will be ones that persuade and that evoke, whereas stories low in narrative probability and fidelity will be lost in the noise and quickly forgotten. As such, narratives are very culturally particular in most instances because the way a story hangs together and holds true to our experience is different in the United States than it is in Syria. The Narrator must interpret, frame, and connect stories in a way that resonates with the culture of the listener or viewer for the story to have impact. In this sense, we would anticipate women Narrators to hew more closely to cultural narrative standards and practices and to have strong narrative rationality in order to win acceptance, given that women have long been regarded as less rational (and, therefore, less competent as public agents) than men (Campbell, 1989).

ANYTHING YOU CAN DO, I CAN DO (BETTER?)

Contemporarily, men comprise almost the entire list of active, well-known public intellectuals across virtually all fields. Women public intellectuals are clustered, to a great degree, in the fields of journalism and media. While male public intellectuals can certainly be Narrators (Nicholas Kristoff and Charlie Rose are prime examples) and women public intellectuals may inhabit other styles than the Narrator, this chapter is very deliberately woman-focused to open a conversation on the intersections of the academy, expertise, style, and gender. What I do not want to imply is that women who aspire to be public intellectuals must become journalists; rather, I do wish to note that women public intellectuals seem to be well-received and efficacious in these career fields while they are less so in others. The stylistic qualities of The Narrator—a public intellectual who is connective and relational, who operates outside traditional rationalities, who spends just as much (if not more) time listening than talking, who weaves together personal experiences rather than syllogisms—begin to unpack this phenomenon and reinforce style's impact not only on rhetoric and rhetorical theory but also on the materiality of the body politic.

In examining Narrator style, we should also be keenly aware that the roles of narrative and of narration is in flux. Moments of crisis, our era being a striking case in point, engender stories that are often strongly dialectical and polemical. Concurrently, we hear narratives buttressing American political liberalism and economic capitalism alongside narratives challenging the relevance and ethics of those systems for today's political and economic climates. In public discourse, accusations fly about fealty to narratives like Ayn Rand's *Atlas Shrugged* substituting for cultural, economic, and political literacy and leadership. Also in flux is the role of the journalist—outsized, sensationalized, and overdramatized stories serve political masters and corporations rather than the broader public interest—the democratic function of journalism is highly suspect in today's media ecology (Thomas, 2007). Finally, the role of women in public life is evolving. Dubbed the Year of the Woman, 1992 saw four new Democratic female Senators elected—notably, Senator Patty Murray of Washington decided to run after watching the way the all-male Senate Judiciary Committee treated Anita Hill. In more recent days, Hillary Rodham Clinton and Sarah Palin dominate headlines. Fifty-nine percent of women work outside the home, 73 percent of women are registered voters, and women hold a larger share of high school, bachelor's, and master's degrees than men (U.S. Census Bureau, 2010). In writing this chapter, I uncovered more questions than I did answers, but in the context of the flux and evolution of our contemporary moment, I believe The Narrator serves as an intriguing place to begin a conversation on nonmale public intellectuals.

CHRISTIANE AMANPOUR: JOURNALIST AND BADASS

Christiane Amanpour is arguably the most respected woman in television journalism today. Born in London in 1958 to a British mother and Iranian father, Amanpour was raised in England and Iran. Following the deposition of Iran's shah, Amanpour's family remained in Britain. She received a degree in journalism from the University of Rhode Island, went into radio broadcasting in 1981 for WBRU, and stepped in front of the cameras in 1983 at the then-fledgling network CNN. By 1985, Amanpour was on everyone's radar following her DuPont Award–winning report on Iran. Her career was cemented through her work covering the atrocities in Bosnia in the 1980s and 1990s and her journalistic efforts during the first Gulf War. She has interviewed world leaders like France's Jacques Chirac and England's Tony Blair and secured the first television interview with Jordan's King Abdullah. She has four honorary doctorates in humane letters from Emory University (1997), the University of Michigan (2006), Northwestern University (2010), and Georgia State University (2010). An honorary member of the 2010 graduating class of Harvard University and a fellow of the American Academy of Arts and Sciences, Amanpour has won every journalistic prize out there. After twenty-seven years on CNN, Amanpour left the network in 2010 to anchor *This Week* on ABC News (Biography, 2011).

Outside of her compelling credentials, Amanpour's phronesis is also tied to her ethnic, religious, and geographic background. Amanpour's family was among the small Christian minority in Muslim-dominated Iran, and she has lived and received education in the Middle East, Europe, and the United States. She speaks with a slight accent, and she appears as if she could be from a variety of places in the world. Simultaneously cosmopolitan and of the people, Amanpour can stand in a variety of vantage points, making her an ideal Narrator, or viewpoint character. In this role, she does not create the events of the day, but she places the events of the day in a meaningful context.

Physiological Style

Christiane Amanpour is known for her "uniform"—because her work requires her to pack in fifteen minutes, to fly to the other side of the world at a moment's notice and to live in conditions that are often scorching hot, she began wearing a similar look again and again: trousers, white shirt with the collar up, safari jackets. As she explains in an interview with *Harper's Bazaar*, "I don't look good in frou-frou. I'd love to, and I've tried, but I just don't look good in excessive volume. No puff and no plunge" (Davis, 2009). She is often required to wear a bulletproof vest and even a military helmet because she is so frequently assigned to cover conflict and to live in combat zones. Amanpour's fashion, such as it is, has been born of necessity. In fact, she asserts that she will "never turn into some anchor babe" even with fewer field assignments at ABC because clothing "mustn't detract from what [I am] saying" (Davis, 2009). In other words, Amanpour's clothing choices imply that she is only sitting behind a desk for an hour at night but otherwise is ready to be on location in Baghdad by tomorrow. Amanpour's uniform distinguishes her from other female anchors like Diane Sawyer because it conveys a focus not on the trendy but on the utilitarian. Because viewers see the same uniform on Amanpour on location in Beirut as they do behind a desk in New York, they can connect the purpose of her wardrobe to a dangerous, politically involved life and take her seriously on matters on which Sawyer might be dismissed. An important meso-level comment here—I did not find a single interview in which a male public intellectual commented about his own clothing that may be anomalous, but it certainly is relevant to a woman-focused chapter.

Because The Narrator is relational, trustworthiness is central to this style—we must believe, without question, that she knows what she is talking about, that she is telling us the truth, that she is someone we can tune into not only to find out about the events of the world but to understand what those events mean to the individual viewer in terms of the values involved. In 2009, *Harper's Bazaar* magazine challenged Amanpour to a high-fashion makeover, a challenge she accepted. Alongside the photo spread that appeared in the article were Amanpour's views on her fashion code: "Well, no one has ever accused me of being stylish. . . . I have always been concerned, particularly in my job, with being as practical and presentable with as little effort as possible" (Davis, 2009). There are at least two reasons Amanpour appears trustworthy in her physiological style. The first is that she does not seem to be hiding behind makeup, frilly clothes, or bold jewelry. Rather, what we see is what we get—Amanpour's stripped-down appearance communicates a level of honesty that is remarkably refreshing in today's media ecology, where glossy clobbers genuine in a nightly cage match. The second is that Amanpour is always interviewing power players, demonstrating a level of access to the "real" story that others lack. For instance, when Moammar Gaddafi granted a single interview to a US press operative to tell his version of the brewing Libyan revolution, he asked for Christiane Amanpour (Amanpour, 2011, February 28). The visibility of Amanpour's access leads to a stronger sense of trustworthiness among viewers.

As the viewpoint voice, The Narrator must also embody a lived experience that resonates with the story she is telling. Amanpour has a commanding intellect, but that intellect is equally matched by a lifetime of experience living in and talking about some of the world's most conflict-ridden places. Amanpour's coloring and accent are part of her experiential physiological style. She is not white, she is of Iranian descent, and she speaks with a British accent. After this many years in television news, should Amanpour wish to speak English with an American accent, surely she has the funds to hire a diction coach. She has maintained her accent, and it provides her with worldliness she might lack without it. As Rosina Lippi-Green notes in her book *English with an Accent: Language, Ideology, and Discrimination in the United States*, "For most Americans, there's no distinction between British accents. For us, there's just one sort of British accent and it's better than the American accent—more educated more genteel. It's a way of speaking that is all tied up with the

Old Country, the Queen" (qtd. in Lane, 2007). Amanpour's viewpoint, then, is distinct because her vantage point is from three continents and from different cultures. Also, we often see Amanpour reporting on the ground in the Middle East and North Africa, desert topographies where the American psyche envisions enormous conflict and suffering. Most recently, the uprisings in Tunisia, Egypt, Iran, Syria, and Libya, collectively known as the Arab Spring, highlight the impact of Amanpour's viewpoint. Through her decades on television news, viewers have come to associate Amanpour with these regions and, therefore, conclude that her viewpoint rises from her experience of living and reporting from places like Iran and Egypt. Her very physicality from her looks to her locale reiterate that Amanpour has a perspective on these stories that few others have.

Finally, The Narrator needs to be familiar with multiple sides of the story in order to better contextualize and frame the broader narrative for his or her audience. The Narrator is connective, placing people and situations in relation to one another and in relation to the audience. In doing so, The Narrator must communicate a sense of curiosity and openness through her physiological style. In her televised interviews, Amanpour makes consistent eye contact, listens attentively, and always leans forward toward the interviewee when she asks questions, establishing a feeling of intimacy despite the intrusion of cameras. Indeed, she works in her interviews as if the cameras are not there, as if she is having a private conversation with someone like Gaddafi or Blair. That ability to establish intimacy despite being on television is a skill that enables Amanpour to ask questions other journalists would not ask and to get answers other journalists would not be able to solicit. Giving voice to these many characters central to the world's news, Amanpour is able to weave other viewpoints into her own, grounded in an ethic of care for others, enriching her audience's understanding of the event as not isolated but situated in politics, religion, conflict, or the economy.

Psychological Style

In order for The Narrator to achieve psychological style, people's experience with him or her must consistently demonstrate trustworthiness, a wealth of lived experience, and an openness to different aspects of a narrative. As Barry Brummett (2004) contends, consistency "tugs on us." Christiane Amanpour is incredibly consistent. Part of the reason viewers and newsmakers alike trust Amanpour is that she is unafraid to be in immensely dangerous situations in order to bring the story to life. Probably very few people think of Amanpour the way they think of Brian Williams of NBC or Scott Pelley of CBS, dressed in navy suits, looking very manicured, and quite happy to be at a desk in an air-conditioned studio in New York, popping in occasionally at *30 Rock*. The picture in viewers' minds is Amanpour on the ground somewhere far away. As anchor Sawyer described on her February 3, 2011, newscast, Amanpour and her team were in Cairo to interview former Egyptian President Hosni Mubarak, but to get to the interview, "Christiane had to move through those rioting thugs, out again today in the streets, threatening death to journalists" (Amanpour, 2011, February 3). Unlike most prominent news personalities, who rely exclusively on field reporters or other press operations local to the story, Amanpour often goes where the story is, conducts interviews there, and reports on camera from these locations. Her decisions to be physically located at the site of conflict or political contention bring her actions in line with her words.

Amanpour's willingness to risk her own safety to be in dangerous places also reinforces a value of care for others that is often central to women's public rhetoric. For example, Amanpour did more reporting from the Balkans than any foreign correspondent during the Balkans' civil war. In an interview at the US Holocaust Memorial Museum, Amanpour describes the horror of that war and her intense concern for its victims.

> The stories that haunt me are, when we finally went to Srebrenica, and saw these people. I mean, these civilians, who were part of Europe, where there was once the Olympic Games, living like animals, trapped in their little village with the most primitive conditions, as the world looked on. (United States Holocaust Memorial Museum, n.d.)

Later in the same interview, her eyes wet, she recounts,

> So we waited outside and they brought out truckloads of people. . . . And we weren't prepared for what we saw when they took the tarpaulin off, and they were children. All of them were children, desperately injured children with dirty bandages and blood all over themselves and crying and afraid. And I'll never forget that. (United States Holocaust Memorial Museum, n.d.)

Her interview is part of a series for the Holocaust Memorial Museum called "Preventing Genocide: Eyewitness Testimony," and it highlights Amanpour's alignment of rhetoric and action through an ethic of nurturance and care, particularly for the most marginalized and the most vulnerable. She says at the end of the segment, "I do actually think that when journalists do their duty and tell the story, and report the truth, that it does eventually make a difference." Not only was Amanpour determined to be in the Balkans in the early 1990s but she also continues to speak out publicly about the atrocities of that war—that she is still haunted by what she saw, enough that she recognizes the importance of telling the story again and again across different media, which reinforces the consistency of her values.

Another key part of the way Amanpour demonstrates stylistic consistency is in her chosen neutrality—she has tried to make her physiology so neutral that what viewers attend to, instead, is the story. This neutrality carries through her reporting. In her exclusive interview with Mubarak, Amanpour asked challenging and direct questions, such as, "Do you feel betrayed by Americans putting pressure on you to resign?" and "How do you feel about your supporters attacking anti-government protesters in Liberation Square" (Amanpour, 2011, February 3). When she recounts her conversation, she also says the interview was an "extraordinary experience" and that she wanted to understand "how he was doing" in the midst of the political crisis in Egypt. She wrote in her piece on the conversation that he looked "tired but well" (Amanpour, 2011, February 3). She does not demonize Mubarak as so many other journalists have done but tries to provide a balanced picture of an embattled leader in crisis. Even getting to the Mubarak interview required the kind of calm that Amanpour exudes physiologically and psychologically. She describes the journey to the Egyptian presidential palace.

> We had been granted an exclusive interview with the new Vice President of Egypt, Omar Suleiman. We had to take a route that ran through a neighborhood where there were pro-Mubarak supporters in the streets who were setting up their own check points.
>
> When we got stuck in a crush of traffic, we were surrounded by an angry mob.
>
> For about an hour, we worked on negotiating our way out of the situation by talking and staying extremely calm. At one point a solider came up to us. We explained what we were doing and showed him papers that were an official invitation to the interview.
>
> Very, very, slowly the crowd started to fall back and our car was able to move. The other two cars in our convoy were taken to a nearby police station for safety. Nobody was hurt, nobody was attacked, but it was clearly an uncertain and unsettling hour. (2011, February 3)

In an era where so much of journalism is sensationalized, Amanpour's narration stands out for its neutrality and mirrors the kind of neutrality she has developed in her physiological style.

Another element of consistency between Amanpour's physiological and psychological style highlighted by her account of the dangerous trip between her hotel and the presidential palace is the completeness of the experience and the attention to different angles of the narrative. This story is but one example of Amanpour's decision to be physically copresent with a story, but her commitment to "living" the story to the degree she can as a journalist reinforces the kind of trust placed in her and in her narrative recounting of the events of the world. In this way, she bears witness to the narrative, giving voice to aspects of a story we may not recognize as instructive until Amanpour contextualizes them. Always, she finds a variety of voices to tell a story from different perspectives such that she can weave these voices into her own narrative of the issue or event. In writing about her interview with Mubarak, she notes that her scheduled interview was actually with Egypt's new vice president Omar Suleiman, but as the crew was setting up, she asked if she could see President Mubarak. It is my contention that Amanpour is given access when and where others are denied it because of her consistency, her trustworthiness, her willingness to be on the scene, and her ability to bring together sometimes starkly divergent voices into one coherent narrative. In other words, people know they will be treated fairly because of the level of experience and good faith Amanpour has earned through her decades-long career.

Finally, Amanpour demonstrates consistency between rhetoric and behavior across mediated platforms. The clearest example of this is her Facebook page. The picture that greets her "friends" is Amanpour in her previously described "uniform." Many posts are about conflict, violence, and politics in locations like Syria and Somalia, while another great many cover political and economic stories in the United States. More than half of these posts feature a link to a video or transcript of an interview or story Amanpour has done on an issue or event. The remaining posts are Amanpour's own writing as it relates to current topics in the news. On July 23, 2011, she wrote about the terrorist attack on a children's camp in Norway:

> Norwegian friends tell me they worry for their children. How to ex-
> plain this nightmare, and help them emerge from the trauma? They
> are seeking help for those who lived through 9/11. Proportionate to
> population, the Norway massacre was nearly twice as big as 9/11
> was in the United States. Norway is so small, and Oslo like "a little

village," so when the victims' names emerge, everyone will know someone effected. (2011, July 23)

On July 29, 2011, Amanpour posted a video with her interviews with world leaders regarding America's debt ceiling "debate." Above the video, she wrote, "Talking to world watchers and diplomats in DC: they are stunned and bewildered, calling debt ceiling debacle in the world's most advanced democracy 'ludicrous.' See more international reaction from friends and foes alike here" (2011, July 29). Her psychological stylistic consistency from magazine articles to television appearances to interview situations to Facebook add to her perceived credibility and expertise.

In addition, many of her posts have upward of one hundred comments under them from Facebook friends, and given the content of some of the comments, it seems Amanpour is not interested in moderating or judging but in allowing for voices to be heard around a topic. For example, on July 24, 2011, Amanpour posted the link to her interview with New York City Mayor Michael Bloomberg on the topic of same-sex marriage, legalized on that day in New York. The first three comments essentially set the tone for the majority of comments to follow (quotes are re-created as they appear on Facebook):

> Oseloka Ekwuno: "Where are we heading to . . . sodom or gormora. or both?" (2011, July 24)

> Davies Friday Egili Ekpo: "Celebrating immorality all in name of freedom, sidesteping God's way of marriage 4 the pleasure of sinful human." (2011, July 24)

> Mary Lincoln: "Just because Man kind says it alright! does not make it so in the sight of God! and who is gonna challange him on his word, if God say's this life style is an ambomination in his sight! who gone chanllange him on his truth!" (2011, July 24)

Amanpour's decision not to critique or to delete these comments suggests her rhetorical professions of openness, of living the experience, and of bringing together voices play out on her Facebook page.

Beyond consistency between rhetoric and behavior, psychological style is also about identity. Amanpour's identity as a skilled journalist means we are not to know where she falls on the political spectrum or how she feels about a particular issue, but that does not mean she has not cultivated a recognizable identity. Indeed, her identity is as an exceptional journalist:

fair, open, curious, worldly, a traveler, and most of all, a storyteller. Because of her ethnic, religious and geographic history, her identity is also cosmopolitan but "local"—she has lived in the United States for more than thirty years, is married to an American, and has an American son. But she also appears "local" in other locales, in part because her background and her experience as a journalist and traveler have made her into a global-local or "glocal": she wears the appropriate dress for the customs, weather, and politics of an area, she speaks several languages, she is nonwhite but Western, she has a British accent, she has connections to important people all over the world. She stands out by fitting in.

Sociological Style

Amanpour's expertise is received exceedingly well by the public, cementing her sociological style as The Narrator. In 1996, *Newsweek* magazine published an article "The Wooing of Amanpour" that describes the fight networks were having to get Amanpour on their roster: "The object of the major networks' desire is Christiane Amanpour, the CNN correspondent who has parachuted into conflicts from the gulf war to Bosnia and helped establish the cable network as must-see TV for world leaders" (Wooing, 1996). She has a "passionate brand of reporting . . . [and the] networks also crave her ready access to world leaders" (Wooing, 1996). On March 12, 2002, Amanpour was given the Goldsmith Award by Harvard's Kennedy School of Government. The Goldsmith Award recognizes journalists whose work has "enriched our political discourse and our society" (Kennedy School, 2002, March 8). Amanpour was one of the women invited to then California First Lady Maria Shriver's 2010 Women's Conference. The program section on Amanpour reads:

> Amanpour has received many prestigious awards in recognition of her reporting on major world stories. Most recently, she earned her fourth George Foster Peabody award for God's Warriors. For her reporting from the Balkans, Amanpour received a News and Documentary Emmy, two Peabody awards, two George Polk Awards, a Courage in Journalism Award, a Worldfest-Houston International Film Festival Gold Award and the Livingston Award for Young Journalists. She was also named 1994 Woman of the Year by the New York Chapter of Women in Cable and Telecommunications, and she helped the CNN news network win an Alfred I. duPont Award for its coverage of Bosnia and a Golden CableACE for its Gulf War coverage.

Amanpour's 1991 Gulf War reporting also received the Breakthrough Award from Women, Men and Media. Her contribution to the 1985 four-week series, *Iran: In the Name of God*, helped CNN earn its first duPont award. Her international reporting for both CNN and CBS's *60 Minutes* earned her an individual Peabody award in 1998.

Amanpour has won nine Emmy awards, including one for her documentary Struggle for Islam; the 2002 Edward R. Murrow Award for Distinguished Achievement in Broadcast Journalism; the Sigma Delta Chi Award for her reports from Goma, Zaire; a George Polk Award for her work on the CNN International special Battle for Afghanistan in 1997; and the Nymphe d'Honneur at the Monte Carlo Television Festival in 1997, to name but a few.

Her documentary, *In the Footsteps of bin Laden*, won the Sigma Delta Chi award given by the Society of Professional Journalists while *Where Have All the Parents Gone?* has been recognized with a POP Award from Cable Positive for HIV/AIDS coverage. Amanpour was also recently named a Fellow of the Society of Professional Journalists, an honor which recognizes significant contributions to journalism. She has also been bestowed with a number of honorary degrees from America's prestigious universities.

In 2007, she was recognized in the birthday honors list of Her Majesty Queen Elizabeth II with a highly prestigious Commander of the Order of the British Empire. (California First Lady, 2010)

Her professional acclaim is well known, but her Facebook page reveals how admired she is by the viewing public. A friend named Christopher C. Gagliardi writes about Amanpour's coverage of the S&P downgrade of the US credit rating, "Christiane is truly a reporter who isn't afraid to get the inside in-depth story behind the story" (2011, August 8). Another friend, Ramzan Chandio, echoes that sentiment: "Christiane Amanpour we regularly watch your programme regularly, well done" (2011, August 8). Other notes include pep talks like "Great report!" or "Keep up the great work, Christiane!" In addition, more than 192,000 people have "liked" her page on Facebook. In the photos section, the professional photographs of Amanpour elicit quite positive feedback. Queen Esther Kalu noted, "Christiane u r wonderful" (2010, February 17), and Fikru Hambisa wrote, "I always admaire your determination. i do" (2010, June 22). Facebook friend Douglas McTaggart put it best: "Amanpour's 'voice' is unparalleled in the world of news. No matter where she figures in the distribution channels, we will follow her for the information she brings to light. Our thanks for the great body of work that has been created to date and our very best wishes for all that is ahead" (2010, April 29).

"GENDERED" STYLE

Women's physiological style matters far more than men's, as women's appearances are routinely scrutinized, categorized, and judged in ways that rarely would happen to their male counterparts. In the 2008 presidential campaign, much was made of "Wardrobe Gate," the decision by John McCain's handlers to spend $150,000 on a wardrobe for vice-presidential candidate Sarah Palin and her family (Morrison, 2008, October 27). Shocking to many in America was the decision to outfit Palin in an unattainably expensive wardrobe immediately following the worst financial crisis in seventy years—the subsequent PR spin was that the clothes were always intended to be donated to charity (Morrison, 2008, October 27). Very rarely asked, though, was why Palin would need to look so good, to have so many outfits, to be so well coiffed when McCain could wear the same suit every day and hardly a soul would notice. Physiological style, in particular, is highly gendered. High-profile women must think constantly about their physiological style.

In Maria Elizabeth Grabe and Lelia Samson's (2011) study on television newswomen, attractiveness, and professionalism, they note that male viewers were more likely to interpret a sexualized female anchor as *more* professional than an unsexualized one. And yet, when more "masculine" topics headline television news (e.g., war, the economy, and so on), sexualized female anchors are seen as significantly less competent. The Grabe and Samson study also demonstrates the changes in dress for women in television news from the 1980s through the present. In the 1980s, television executives advised women anchors and reporters to have "an androgynous presence" because "trappings associated with female sexual attractiveness would distract from the news messages that reporters deliver" (Grabe & Samson, 2011, p. 472). Today, however, executives (predominantly men) advise women in television to wear their hair at shoulder length or longer, to wear bold makeup (particularly a bold lip color), to wear V-neck or low-cut tops, and to wear oversized jewelry in order to highlight their "femininity" (in Grabe & Samson, 2011; see also Rouvalis, 2006). One need watch only five minutes of Fox News and its hypersexualized female anchors with nonexistent skirt hemlines (notice they do not wear pants) to understand this gem of "professional advice" given to women in television (I Hate the Media, 2009, March 30). Aman-pour's decision to don a neutral and somewhat nondescript "uniform" with minimal makeup and jewelry could be linked to a stronger push toward androgyny thirty years ago when she was first starting her career. It could be that Amanpour is not interested in competing with the Fox "anchor babes." Whatever her reasons, her physiological style gives her command over the story, even stories centered on traditionally masculine topics like war and conflict or politics.

But what does the Grabe and Samson study portend for other women public intellectuals should they want to be taken seriously as experts? Are there fields of expertise that are off limits to women public intellectuals because they are seen as less competent than their male counterparts? What about women who do not wish to embrace androgyny or eschew fashion trends—will they be embraced as public intellectuals or shunned for being insufficiently rigorous because of a more traditionally feminine or trendy aesthetic? Certainly, I do not pretend to have an easy, or even complex, answer to these questions. I ask them, in part, to push a dia-logue on the very gendered nature of expertise. I ask them also because intellectuals in the academy are a significant part of the problem rather than the solution. The academy is supposed to be a place where we model the kind of parity and respect we hope to see in the public, but, clearly, that is not the prevailing wind.

There is a central irony for women who wish to engage broader pub-lics—public intellectuals have to think about what they wear and what meanings people draw from appearance if they are to achieve relevance and connect with publics, but if intellectuals pay too much attention to how they look, their peers consider them to be less serious about their work. As the *Chronicle of Higher Education* (2010) reports, "Any idea that you might put any effort into how you look means you are not putting effort into reading the latest journal article" (Wilson, 2010). I have a num-ber of male colleagues and academic friends with extremely question-able fashion sense, and while those choices will challenge their abilities to connect to and be relevant with a broader public, their clothes will not challenge their perceived expertise. Physical appearance for women intellectuals is tied inextricably to professionalism and perceived ex-pertise. This unfortunate reality is no less true in the academy than it is outside, and I ask that we stop pretending that we are immune to these stereotypes. Moving beyond denial is an excellent first step. We are not disembodied intellects floating in the ether—our physiologies commu-nicate, some more than others.

But physiological style is more than clothing choice, it is also about being able to embody expertise. Here, women also face barriers to equality and acceptance. Part of this reality is that women have fewer role models to show them how to navigate intellectual life. Men hold 75 percent of all full professorships in the United States, and if women associates are ever promoted to full, their promotion processes take a one to three and a half years longer (Misra, Lundquist, Holmes, & Agiomavritis, 2011). More worrisome still, doctorate-granting institutions, where we all earn our PhDs, lag furthest behind in promoting women associates to full even controlling for elements such as, research productivity, educational background, type of institution, and race (Misra et al., 2011). It becomes difficult for women intellectuals to hold out hope that their expertise will be read positively in the public sphere if it is not valued or rewarded in their day jobs.

Very few things challenge a woman's perceived seriousness of commitment to her intellectual work than pregnancy. I hesitated even to include this discussion because it is not part of every woman's experience, but there are also few things more physiologically distinguishing than a woman's ability to carry a child. Pregnant women are widely viewed by men and women as less competent, more emotional, more irrational, and less committed to their jobs than their nonpregnant colleagues (Armour, 2005). Certainly, this can of worms opens up a staggering variety of important questions about human resources, organizational structures, hiring and firing, physical conditions (fumes in lab settings, being attached to a breast pump), and emotional concerns (not wanting to be away from children) issues with which we should grapple. But, in terms of style, the pregnant woman's body detracts considerably from her ability to embody expertise or to be received by the public as an expert because of the negative stereotypes associated with professional competence (Cook, 1998–2013). In addition, a woman's entire physicality is altered by pregnancy—the way she walks, the way she stands, whether she can stand for long periods of time, how much air she has and how she uses her voice, what kinds of topics or words seem "appropriate" for a pregnant woman/mother-to-be to use (Can pregnant women swear? Can they talk about abortion or birth control?), and so on. These physiological adjustments can severely limit a woman public intellectual's efficacy, both inside and outside the academy.

Maintaining consistency between a rhetoric of expertise and an enactment of that expertise that shapes identity is a particular challenge for women who want to be public intellectuals. In our society, the line is very faint (some might say invisible) between expert and scary bitch.

Hillary Clinton has tried to walk this line publicly for decades now. When Bill Clinton was running for the presidency in 1992, Hillary Clinton very (in)famously said, "I don't have time to stay home and bake cookies," a reference to her own impressive career. People went nuts and not in a positive way. Women turned on her for "bashing" traditional feminine roles like housewifery and childcare. More recently, California GOP gubernatorial candidate Meg Whitman, former CEO of eBay, had spent months waging a nasty rhetorical war centered on jobs and the economy with Democrat Jerry Brown. She was seen as overly aggressive and spent the final weeks of her campaign trying to bring it back to life by mailing out "softly focused pictures of the [candidate] as a young woman and of her two children when they were young, and quotes such as 'At the end of the day, my family remains my greatest source of pride'" (Mehta & Mishak, 2010, October 28). Republican political strategist Nicolle Wallace notes, "[The Whitman campaign] revealed the unique pressures on women to show voters all sides of themselves, but none too forcefully" (2011, August 5). In other words, seemingly winning character traits like assertiveness, dedication, energy, and accomplishment hamper women while propelling men to victory. Women who tend toward more traditionally masculine styles may seem more competent in some cases but can very easily be perceived as overstepping their boundaries because of their stylistic embodiments.

Add race to the mix, and the problem compounds for women of color. First Lady Michelle Obama is a two-time Ivy League graduate, successful administrator at the University of Chicago Medical Center, and is now running Joining Forces, a campaign to help assist veterans and their families with the challenges endemic to those communities, and Let's Move, a campaign to educate parents and children about obesity and ways to reduce it and prevent it. During the 2008 election season, conservative commentators whispered about a tape on which Michelle Obama says, "Kill whitey!" (Gaiter, 2008, June 10). She is pictured as an Angela Davis–esque "terrorist fist jabber" on the cover of the *New Yorker* (Pitney, 2008, July 17). Yet, the First Lady was heavily praised across a variety of media sources for her appearance on *The View*, where she talked about loving bacon and not wearing pantyhose (Roberts, 2008, June 22). What we might learn from these very public instances is that consistency is important but it is a particular kind of consistency. Women face an uphill battle for broad acceptance as an expert, but women of color are climbing a mountain.

Of course, some would argue Amanpour is a woman of color, yet she is wildly successful in a business that suggests women ought to demean themselves in order not to scare away viewers with their insight or skill. Several implications seem relevant. First, Amanpour is a woman of a particular color, which is to say, not black and not Latina. Given what we know about the correlational relationship between public credibility and skin pigmentation, perhaps we should not be surprised (Dyson, 2011, June 14). Second, Amanpour is not originally from the United States and speaks with an accent. Her unfamiliar-ness may elide traditional racial-ized sentiments as her accent elevates her above the fray (Lippi-Green, 1997). Third, she is one of those darned elites. Certainly, issues of class are very closely intertwined with issues of race in our culture and in others where Amanpour works. She may report on class uprisings, but she is not flaunting her union card for the world to see. It works for Noam Chomsky; it does not work for Christiane Amanpour.

Finally, the role of The Narrator is to tell the story, but it is not to be the protagonist or author of the story. Notably, Amanpour is not a news-maker. She is not an elected official. She is not a diplomat or high-ranking political operative. She does write the story, but she does not create it. In other words, she is not the story. It seems reasonable that one of the reasons Amanpour is successful, and an inference for other would-be female public intellectuals, is that her chosen role is secondary to the power players, the authors, the ones in charge. Yes, these very serious people choose Amanpour to tell their story, but it remains their story, not Amanpour's. Again, I do not raise this issue to demonize Amanpour or storytelling, nor do I raise it to suggest that women public intellectuals must choose to play second fiddle. I raise it because it helps us reconceive of the ways in which we train all intellectuals to engage with the public but particularly women intellectuals.

In theorizing *feminine style*, Karlyn Kohrs Campbell argues that women rhetors honed a style that emphasized personal tone, evidence via personal anecdotes and experience, inductive structure, audience participation, and identification between audience and speaker (1989, p. 13). This style, Campbell contests, is especially suited for women speakers with women audiences, whereas in the broader public sphere, in realms like law and politics, successful women rhetors largely adapt a more masculine style: deductive, linear, and formal (1989, chaps. 6 & 7). Yet, Bonnie Dow and Mary Boor Tonn (1993) argue that feminine style can "elide the boundar-ies between private and public discourse, illustrating how feminine style can function to offer alternative modes of political reasoning" (p. 288). In their excellent study of former Texas Governor Ann Richards, Dow and Tonn make the case that Richards effectively and persuasively combined the tenets of feminine style that Campbell theorizes while adding "an alternative political philosophy reflecting feminine ideals of care, nurturance, and family relationships" that "functions as a critique of traditional political reasoning that offers alternative grounds for political judgment" (1993, p. 289).

Turning back to Amanpour, we note that she emphasizes personal experience and anecdotes from interviews with world leaders and citizens to rationalize claims. Too, in creating a sense of intimacy in her interview settings, Amanpour reflects the importance of speaker/audience identification. Storytelling is relational—there must be someone to whom to narrate, and relationally focused communication is more strongly associated with traditionally feminine styles (Campbell, 1989). And like Dow and Tonn's work recommends, Amanpour's stories, even when they are about "masculine" subject matter like war or politics, stress an ethic of care and nurturance. Consider, for instance, her Facebook posts on the Oslo terrorist attack on the youth camp. She quotes Norway's Prime Minister Jens Stoltenberg, who "rallied his country with these words: 'We must show humanity, warmth towards others. People need each other. It is human contact that we need now. We can all do this'" (qtd. in Amanpour, 2011, July 23). Rather than simply posting a link to the story, Amanpour writes her own post that underscores the importance and relevance of care toward our fellow human beings, particularly in times of crisis. These choices permeate Amanpour's work and make her persuasive using a contemporary feminine style precisely because she offers an alternative frame to a story—the shooting in Norway, while entirely depraved, also shows individuals and communities acting compassionately toward one another. Not all women employ feminine style as rhetors, nor should they feel limited to that choice. Yet, we see in Amanpour that these style considerations can be highly efficacious in the public sphere. Reconsidering and updating feminine style may be a way for women public intellectuals to raise their profiles and, in turn, their voices. The Narrator is one such iteration of that evolution.

DIMENSIONS OF COMPARISON

Christiane Amanpour is a highly fluid, public intellectual, perhaps more fluid than any public intellectuals in this book. She was born in London, raised between Tehran and London, and is a naturalized US citizen. She is Christian, was raised in a Muslim country, and is married to a Jew. She speaks English, Farsi, and French fluently. Known across the globe for her impassioned journalism, Amanpour is part of every community from the most elite to the most marginalized. Because of her role as Narrator, she is comfortable talking to people protesting in the streets of Egypt and twenty minutes later, talking to the president of Egypt, with whom she is on a first-name basis. Because of her dedication to being where the story is unfolding rather than sitting behind a studio desk continuously, she is welcomed the world over. The Narrator's role is to tell the story, and to tell it well, she must move fluidly between, among, and around intellectual and public realms.

Like The Prophet, The Narrator is split evenly between intellectual and public in terms of degree. This more equitable distribution also helps distinguish The Narrator from The Pundit, an almost exclusively public style. It seems almost counterintuitive that The Narrator would not also be entirely public in her orientation, given that she is highly visible to the global public. Yet, the gendered nature of The Narrator demands an evenness because if she is too public, she is superficial, flighty, and an "anchor babe," and she cannot be trusted to do the tough work of professional journalism. In our era of preoccupation with aesthetics, if she is too intellectual, she is less relevant to the key figures in the story and to the viewing public, and people will stop tuning in (remember when comedian Dennis Miller did *Monday Night Football* coverage?). And, of course, if we are attuned as a culture to aesthetics, we are particularly obsessed with women's aesthetics, so this evenness must be heeded to be successful. Amanpour's interviews are deep, rich, and challenging—she does not shy away from demanding answers and speaking truth to power. Yet, she also posts personal photos on her Facebook page, and she did the fashion makeover issue for *Harper's Bazaar*. Amanpour very successfully walks the line in terms of degree.

Location is a fascinating dimension, given The Narrator's schedule. The Narrator is located on screen, online, and on the page. Amanpour does speaking engagements sporadically across the country and around the world, but, generally, her location is mediated. Geographically, Amanpour has been and continues to go places all over the world to tell the story. She spent more time in the Balkans during their civil war than any international journalist, and she is a fixture in journalism in the Middle East. She has shot two award-winning documentary films, *God's Warriors* and *Where Have All the Parents Gone?*; *God's Warriors* traces both fundamentalists and extremists in the three Abrahamic faiths—to do this work, she shot film across Africa, Asia, Europe, and North America. *Where Have All the Parents Gone?* is a film examining the crisis surrounding AIDS orphans in Africa. Her "day job" is in New York. Part of Amanpour's persona and persuasive appeal is her willingness to be located "there," wherever "there" is at any given time.

In terms of media, Amanpour is savvy. She capitalizes on a breadth of mediated channels but is not as ubiquitous as The Pundit—she has downtime. Amanpour's Facebook page is very active, with many of her friends posting regularly to discussion threads, photos, and links. We can follow Amanpour on Twitter. She hosts *Amanpour* on CNN, and she is online at CNN. Still an active correspondent for foreign news, Amanpour can be seen on a variety of news programs on CNN. Thousands of YouTube videos feature Amanpour's work. Finally, she is also available by Podcast should anyone want to listen to *Amanpour* again. It is significant, though, that Amanpour is not constantly available. Her time away from media channels leads to an impression that she takes time to think, to read, to learn, to travel, to talk to people, *before* posting to Facebook or uploading a video to YouTube. Perhaps for women public intellectuals, in particular, omnipresence is not a winning strategy because it implies a vacuousness to the work.

Finally, in terms of resources, Amanpour used her journalism degree from the University of Rhode Island to excellent effect, landing at CNN in 1983. Since then, she has turned opportunity into success in virtually every venture. Her willingness and desire to travel have made the most of the resources available to her—time and people. Indeed, very likely, that willingness to be wherever the story is has made Amanpour the kind of resource that any network would prize because she opens doors politically, socially, and culturally in her brand of journalism. Like The Pundit, The Narrator is the kind of person we invite into our homes, the kind of public intellectual with whom we forge a more intimate connection. This connection is not as deep as the one The Guru has with followers, but it is warm and friendly enough that it enables Amanpour to be a click away from people at any given moment.

The Narrator style is about telling stories. It is about a willingness to be part of the story, to listen to a spectrum of voices, and to weave together a narrative that contextualizes highly complex political, social, economic, and ecological events for the average viewer. I also mean this case study to be highly gendered in order to begin to unpack the distinct challenges faced by women interested in taking their work public. This is not to say that male public intellectuals cannot be The Narrator or that women who wish to be engaged with broader publics must adapt this style or remain isolated. It is to say, though, that there are very few women public intellectuals at work today in this country, and part of dismantling the barriers to women's success is acknowledging this truth. Demographically, it is also a stark reality that women hold a larger number of earned bachelor's and graduate degrees in this country, so the sooner we begin grappling with these issues of expertise, gender, aesthetics, and politics, the better prepared we are to encourage and nurture women to be engaged intellectuals.

Chapter 7 introduces the most atemporal style, the one that feels the long-wave vibrations of our culture and marries expertise with cultural myth: The Scientist.

7
SCIENTIST STYLE: MICHIO KAKU

If you pay attention to fashion magazines, even in passing in the grocery-store checkout line, you know that style comes and goes with the times. Leisure suits. Shoulder pads. Thrift-store flannel shirts. Neon. The previous five public intellectuals styles in this book, The Prophet, The Guru, The Sustainer, The Pundit, and The Narrator, are like those fashion trends: They are called by a particular moment in our culture to speak to an audience, but they will only be in vogue until the next shift in the social landscape, at which time, another style appears and, more significant, appeals. Temporal styles feel the short-wave vibrations and are similarly shorter lived. They have higher frequency and amplification during the times they appear but barely register in other eras. Most rhetorical styles fit this pattern because they are responsive and, therefore, responsible to the particular problems and issues of that era. Science style, though, is like the little black dress of public intellectual rhetorical styles—it is always in fashion. I should reiterate that it is not that atemporality is somehow the province of science alone or that scientists are somehow better equipped to work this angle. It is to say that these styles, all of them, as constituent parts and, as gestalts, offer promising avenues of taking intellectual work public, and we ought pay attention to these possibilities. We have examined rhetorical styles that are integral to our current moment, called by sociopolitical forces to respond to a broad audience on the issues of the day. Now, we move to investigate a style that is less culturally discrete. Rather, Scientist style transcends time and place to such a remarkable degree that it may provide a real avenue for intellectuals in any or all disciplines to engage a broader segment of the public to solve real problems. Concealing his or her intimidating intellectualism from the broader public but showcasing it to get the project funded, The Scientist chooses neutral territory rather than lab settings to engage the public, but like The Prophet, selects media perceived as more intellectual in order to sell his or her dreams in the public domain.

Scientist style is a rhetoric of dreams. Let me go back a few years. As I was writing some early work that would later become parts of this book, I stumbled across an article, "The Renaissance of Anti-Intellectualism," by Todd Gitlin, in the *Chronicle of Higher Education.* Written in 2000, it details the meteoric political rise of the anti-intellectual, tragically unthinking George Walker Bush, a man elected ahead of unapologetically intellectual and, therefore, tragically elite Al Gore. But it is Gitlin's treatment of the hard sciences that caught my attention. Despite the fact that American anti-intellectualism, Gitlin argues, is older than our nation (Puritans espoused the dubious claim that intellect made one an obvious accomplice of Satan), the "technical intellect" of science had turned our American backwater into a world superpower. Science had cured polio and put humans in space. So, while Americans hold visceral disdain for those who espouse social revolutions à la Noam Chomsky, we embrace the geeks who seek the Fountain of Youth because they articulate our nascent desires for the awesome.

MICHIO KAKU: DREAM WEAVER

Dr. Michio Kaku is best known in intellectual circles as a theoretical physicist and pioneer in string field theory, essentially a quantum theory of gravity. Kaku holds the Henry Semat Chair and Professorship in theoretical physics at the City College of New York. He has authored a number of graduate-level textbooks in theoretical physics as well as at least seventy journal articles and is now researching and writing on the theory of everything, a theory that brings together the four fundamental forces of the universe. Additionally, he has written a number of popular science books, including *Hyperspace* and *Einstein's Cosmos.* His latest book, *Physics of the Impossible: A Scientific Exploration into the World of Phasers, Force Fields, Teleportation, and Time Travel,* was on the *New York Times'* best-seller list for five weeks in 2008. Kaku is known in wider circles for his nuclear policy and global-warming advocacy and for his appearances on numerous television shows like *Larry King Live* and *Countdown with Keith Olbermann.* He also hosts the only nationally syndicated science radio program in the United States called *Science Fantastic,* a ninety-minute show that Kaku explains is dedicated to "futurology," or the science of the future.

Physiological Style

Like Cornel West and Deepak Chopra, Kaku does not particularly look
the part. His hair is wavy, to his chin, graying appropriately for someone
in his late fifties. He dresses comfortably but fashionably. In other words,
Kaku appears atypical for our perceptions of the scientist: no lab coat, no
horn-rimmed glasses, no pocket protector. He is casual, not formal; hip,
not stuffy; relaxed, not stiff. Indeed, Kaku looks rather a cross between
California surfer and dot-com executive, certainly not like a person a
university would try to hide in a lab and restrict to research. His dress
reflects his rhetorical style: thoughtful dreamer and future-seer.

In the four-part *Time* series, Kaku examines four elemental issues associated with time: daytime, lifetime, earth time, and cosmic time. The
series has since been rebroadcast across the pond on the Science channel.
Kaku's physiological style in *Time* is representative of his style across media
appearances. Rather than burdening the audience with data and technical
jargon, Kaku discusses scientific topics, research, methodology, or devel-
opments in the context of how amazing, how remarkable they are, like
dreams come true. In the opening lines of the segment "Lifetime," Kaku
says about a young girl playing with bubbles and running in a sunny park,

> It is just possible that this girl will have more time on earth than
> anyone who has ever lived. She might live for a thousand years.
> Immortality, the quest for more time, is a dream that has driven
> humanity for generations. (Kaku, 2008, May 25)

Kaku is both explicit and implicit. He explicitly discusses the collective
desire for immortality, for finding what he calls "the elixir of life." However,
implicit in his observation is the idea that all science is about fulfilling
dreams in some way. He says later in the show, "Now, finally, in the twenty-first century, this search for more time might be over because scientists
are beginning to crack the secrets of how time changes us day by day.
And, as we understand time, eventually there will be no limit on how long
we might live" (Kaku, 2008, May 25). The dream is here, and science has
delivered it to us. Kaku, representative of the science community, conveys
how science brings our dream, in this case, of immortality, to fruition.

Physiological style reflects a personal worldview. For Kaku, his vision
of science's value to do everything from helping people time travel to
ending nuclear proliferation and global warming is reflected in his physiological style. Kaku's worldview is that most in American culture share his
dreams, that dreams are accessible, even democratic. His choice of words

reflects this accessibility. Kaku tackles immeasurably complex points in the language of the everyday to make the obscure comprehensible. In an October 9, 2009, interview on Sirius satellite radio with host Deepak Chopra, Chopra engages Kaku about parallel universes. Chopra asks, "To my mind, the human body is an example or, for that matter, a leaf or any biological entity, of quantum entanglement. Everything is correlated with everything instantly. What would you say to that?" Kaku responds,

> Well, yes, things are entangled so in some sense, messages can travel faster than light. . . . If parallel universes exist, in the quantum realm, Elvis Presley could still be alive. He could still be alive in a parallel universe that is vibrating out of phase with our universe, so that universe has decohered from ours. We can no longer interact with the universe of the dinosaurs and space aliens. (Chopra, 2009, October 9)

Certainly, there are more scientific-sounding choices available to Kaku to explain parallel universes, but he chooses the accessible and somewhat universal examples of Elvis Presley, dinosaurs, and aliens such that a nonscientific audience would not feel alienated by the discussion. Dreams are universal, so are Kaku's rhetorical choices.

Like West, Kaku opts not to limit himself to classroom teaching, despite having been a professor for thirty years at both the undergraduate and graduate levels. Instead, like his work, Kaku is accessible even for those not pursuing physics degrees in New York. Kaku is a syndicated radio show host, appears regularly on network and cable television in mainstream programs, runs the website Welcome to Explorations in Science with Dr. Michio Kaku, writes columns for publications like *Forbes* and the *New York Times,* and has his own television series like the Science channel's *Time.* Indeed, Kaku's media appearances are illustrative of his worldview that humanity shares common dreams and that those dreams should be available to each of us.

Psychological Style

For psychological style to resonate, it marks a high degree of consistency between thought and action—in other words, we believe the person is genuine and "real." If Kaku believes we all share his dreams, he must engage and invite a broad audience to join him in dreaming out loud. Rhetorical scholars Sonja Foss and Cindy Griffin (1995) explain how invitational rhetoric "involves a view of audience members as equal to the rhetor and as experts on their own lives" (p. 2). Kaku believes and acts as if his audience is his equal and should have equal access to our cultural dreams. On the popular science blog The Daily Grail, poster Greg writes about Kaku, "One of the main reasons I was interested in talking to Professor Kaku was his openness to some of the more 'heretical' areas of science," such as, UFO phenomena (Greg, 2008, October 7). Kaku notes that UFOs are "subject to the 'giggle factor' with scientists, because most assume that the distance between possible civilizations is far too great" (Greg, 2008, October 7). But, Kaku suggests,

> Once you imagine a civilization a million years more advanced (which is a blink of an eye compared to the 13.7 billion year age of the universe) then new laws of physics and technologies open up. . . . For such a civilization, travel between stars might not be such a problem. (Greg, 2008, October 7)

Kaku takes "popular" science topics like UFOs seriously rather than laughing them off as baseless science fiction. In doing so, he engages a significant swath of the public who, whether believers or not, are intrigued by the possibility of alien life beyond our universe. And he invites this audience to dream along with him of how this meeting between an advanced alien civilization and human beings might go:

> Imagine walking down a country road, and meeting an ant hill. Do we go down to the ants and say, "I bring you trinkets. I bring you beads. I give you nuclear energy and biotechnology. Take me to your leader?" Or we have the urge to step on a few of them?? (Greg, 2008, October 7)

Even agreeing to the interview with The Daily Grail, a blog featuring articles, such as, "Southpaws Have a More Balanced Body Map" and "Stars May Be Cosmic Road Signs to Intelligent Aliens," reifies his psychological style as the dreamer who invites others to dream with him.

This invitation to dream is woven throughout Kaku's work. On his website www.mkaku.org, Kaku writes a letter to his fans to enable them to contact him to discuss topics of interest. He instructs fans to call into his radio show Science Fantastic, to post a question to the Science Channel website so he might answer it on the Science Channel on Sundays program, or to e-mail him directly at askmichio@mkaku.org. Additionally, he engages visitors to his site by inviting them to join him on Facebook. Finally, his site gives visitors and fans every opportunity to follow him on the radio, on television, in print, and in person by providing his schedule of appearances, and most listings include words like "join me" or "welcome" so that his audience feels like Kaku sincerely wants them to dream with him and believes them capable of such a task.

This dreamy psychological style is indicative of several characteristics: creativity, innovation, and enthusiasm. Without these elements, dreams remain exactly where they began: in the mind of the dreamer. For those displaying Scientist style, these characteristics are crucial to the rhetorical success of The Scientist. We all dream. For most of us, our dreams make little to no sense, even contextually. However, one thing that is universal about dreaming is that we pull, unconsciously in most cases, elements of our immediate and past experiences into some amalgam of a narrative. For instance, watching a crime show on television after dinner with friends may lead to a dream in which you and your friends are responsible for tracking down a drug cartel, or it may be far more disjointed but incorporate similar elements. In other words, our brains create. Of course, we would envision scientists, in general, to be creative, to take legitimate challenges in our world, and to try to research and find solutions for the challenges for social benefit. Kaku is no different. His scholarly pursuits reflect this coming together of disparate but sometimes tangentially related elements to create theory that speaks to some larger issues of human consciousness, health, or future endeavor. For example, Kaku writes in his book *Visions*,

> By 2020, when personalized DNA sequencing is possible, our ancestral family tree should be nearly filled in, including all the branches which have been nearly forgotten for tens of thousands of years. Not only does the map fill in gaps in the linguistic and archaeological theories about the origins of humanity, it even gives the dates in which missing branches in our family tree diverged from other branches thousands of years before the first written record. (1998, p. 154)

He brings together computation, biology, and what he calls "futurism" to this question of DNA sequencing in the Human Genome Project. His style exudes creativity in discussing the dream of total understanding of humanity—we are closer to "[reading] the mind of God," in Kaku's words.

Not only does Kaku display the creativity inherent to Scientist style but he is also innovative in his approaches to problems. As described earlier, Kaku lacks, or at least represses, the "giggle response" common to most scientists when it comes to questions of "pop" science like time travel. In interviews with everyone from Chopra to Stephen Colbert, Kaku discusses how time travel would be physically possible given the parameters we understand today. His own work in string field theory and the theory of everything assists his innovative style—he seems consistently to be thrilled that this is what he does for a living, that he gets to create and innovate in ways unheard of even a decade ago, and that his vision for how the physical world operates allows for others to create technologies and knowledge bases that will propel future generations far beyond where we thought it possible to go. And, do it boldly.

Finally, Kaku is enthusiastic, a critical element in "selling" science to a lay public. He wrote on the Big Think website on March 15, 2010, "Science is not about memorizing facts. . . . It's about innovation and curiosity and imagining internet access in your contact lenses" (Imagination), a statement indicative of his level of interest and joy in his calling. Certainly, he could not do his day job of teaching theoretical physics without enthusiasm, but he approaches his mediated appearances with as much, if not more, zeal. He understands that the job of the scientist, first and foremost, is to sell ideas. This is where science proves different than other disciplines—for decades (actually centuries), scientists have been required to validate their work to larger publics, even lay publics, to get funding for their work because these experiments—time travel, human longevity, space exploration—require extraordinary financial resources that can only be acquired if pitched with great vigor and enthusiasm not only for the technology and know-how that will make the project possible but also for the dreams that will be fulfilled by spending inordinate amounts of money on said projects. For instance, in an interview on the television show *The Circuit*, Kaku discusses time travel:

> Stephen Hawking once said, "Where are the time travelers from the future taking my picture?" Well, you know, we think maybe they're invisible. By then, time travelers will have invisibility. In fact, we may have it in a few decades. (Kaku, 2008, May 25)

His enthusiasm makes the audience want to believe that not only are we going to be able to travel through time but we will also be invisible. Science can make us superheroes.

Sociological Style

Style is not private. Rather, it must be viewed by a larger public and subsequently judged successful by a larger public in order for it to be validated as legitimate, as in vogue. While the perception of the scientist may not be the most alluring or publically accepted, scientific rhetoric is a differ-ent story. Of course, there are challenges to the social acceptance and good will toward science. For instance, there is not one completely safe rhetorical space for experts in the United States. As Americans, we are a deeply conflicted people. While we laud individual excellence, we are profoundly skeptical of intellectuals. In both Christian and wider Western traditions, curiosity, a trait strongly related to intellect, is associated with the ills and evils of the world. We have to look no further than Eve biting into the serpent's apple and bringing about the "fall of man" through worldly wisdom or Pandora opening the box and bringing illness and death to men to understand how, misogyny aside, that mythos still perme-ates our thinking about intellectuals. America's Puritan heritage vilified intellectuals as agents of worldly evil. In 1642, John Cotton wrote, "The more learned and witty you bee, the more fit to act for Satan will you bee" (Hofstader, 1966, p. 42). Two hundred years later, in 1843, pioneer Baynard R. Hall attested that "smartness and wickedness were supposed to be generally coupled, and incompetence and goodness" (Hofstader, 1966, p. 23). An April 2, 2006, *Washington Post* article "The President as Average Joe" describes how American audiences seemed to respond much more favorably to Bush when he would play up his "anti-intellectual, regular guy image" rather than attempting to appear serious, erudite, or presidential. Indeed, the greater the "fratboy towel-snapping humor" (Baker, 2006) Bush displayed, the more positively Americans felt about him.

Science is no exception to the anti-intellectual trend. In an April 23, 2008, report, the Union of Concerned Scientists identified that roughly eight hundred of the sixteen hundred Environmental Protection Agency (EPA) scientists the union surveyed cited instances of political interfer-ence in their work. Many articulated feelings of extreme pressure by superiors to change or skew their findings in order to continue receiving funding (Union of Concerned Scientists, 2008). Of course, the neocon-servative agenda against science is infamous. A very current example is former vice-presidential contender Sarah Palin, who believes that di-nosaurs and humans walked the earth together six thousand years ago because she has seen pictures that "prove" it (Braun, 2008). Another is the creation-science movement that argues because we cannot see evolution in action, its "invisibility" renders it false. Creation "scientists" even won over the state of Kansas for a time, adding the biblical account of creation to traditional-science curriculum (Wilgoren, 2005). And because science maintains such a high degree of relevance to a broader audience in the public sphere, critics keep a close eye on it.

However dangerous the pursuits of scientists, they escape to a great degree the witch hunt led by critics of intellectual life and freedom like David Horowitz and Lynne Cheney. Many are, at least, passingly familiar with Horowitz's 2006 tome, *The ProFessors: The 101 Most Dangerous Academics in America*. I know some scholars on his list of subversives. Horowitz's basic premise is that unlike in his critical- and analytical-thinking college days, today's experts teach students *what* to think rather than *how* to think. Horowitz contends that universities today are far less academic and far more political, leading to his argument that students of these radical experts are only given half of the story. In an address about the book to Ball State University in Muncie, Indiana, Horowitz proclaimed, "You don't go to a doctor expecting to get a speech about the war in Iraq and you shouldn't get one from your teachers" (Spazz, 2006, November 10). In particular, Horowitz took issue with women's studies programs because it is a leftist ideal, feminism is not about equality, and women's studies programs omit the perspective of men, which, he contends, is a detriment to the educational process. This latest effort by Horowitz is directed almost entirely toward faculty in the social sciences, humanities, and arts—hard-science experts are conspicuously absent, a point that warrants further exploration.

In December 2001, Cheney, wife of former Vice President Dick Cheney, in conjunction with US Senator Joe Lieberman, spearheaded a report by the American Council of Trustees and Alumni that many argue is a blacklist of experts in numerous disciplines. The report/blacklist, *Defending Civilization: How Our Universities Are Failing America*, asserts, among other things, "Colleges and university faculty have been the weak link in America's response" to the attack on September 11, 2001, and "when a nation's intellectuals are unwilling to defend its civilization, they give comfort to its adversaries" (Martin & Neal, 2001). The council cites examples of "anti-Americanism" among experts, such as, the president of Wesleyan University, who argues that among the causes of September 11 are economic disparity and the utter hopelessness that condition breeds in a society. These experts argue that terrorists do not become terrorists by genetic predisposition but are filled with such despair that any offer of spiritual riches is met with extraordinary enthusiasm, even if it comes at the expense of life. Again, though, the 40 faculty on the blacklist and the 117 incidents of anti-American behavior by university experts are confined largely to the leftist revolutionaries in nonscience fields.

Undoubtedly, there are a number of reasons scientists get excluded from Horowitz's and Cheney's wrath. One obvious possibility is that hard

science is tied to enormous grant money as well as private-sector financial riches in a way that other disciplines are not (this point is further
discussed later in this chapter). But from a rhetorical perspective, science
feeds into our individual and collective dreams through its rhetoric. Kaku
in his quest to explain the human lifespan says, "Of all of time's effects
on us, the most profound is that one day, it will end. Our time is limited
so our time is precious" (Kaku, 2008, May 25). In other words, we live in
the fierce urgency of now, an urgency that calls scientists to solve this
profound mystery of our lifespan's limits for all humanity. Much like Joseph Campbell's understanding of mythology, science provides a sense of
wonder and awe about our lives and our world. Fortunately for us, Kaku,
representative of scientific expertise, in general, is there for us. He says
of his thesis, "I want to know if our time on earth, our lifespan, has to be
limited" (Kaku, 2008, May 25). Science uses the best of what is known at
the time to give people insight into how they might lead a useful life; in
Kaku's case, how we might use our time wisely. Of course, Kaku, representative of Scientist style, is successful because he taps the right myths
at the right time and, most influentially, traditional American myths: the
Fountain of Youth, freedom, manifest destiny.

A second reason science may get more of a pass in this country is that
the core dream of science aligns with even the most ardent antiscience
conservatives: to discover God. In July 2010, European physicists using
the Large Hadron Collider have come as close as we ever have to isolating
the Higgs Boson, "a theoretical energy particle which many scientists believe helped give mass to the disparate matter spawned by the Big Bang"
(Miller, 2011). The Higgs Boson is referred to as the God particle because
it is believed to have created the universe. So, religion and science, despite
their current spat, are not antithetical to one another. If science can prove
the existence of God, what greater dream exists in American minds?

Of course, if Kaku merely described dreams, even powerful cultural
favorites like the Fountain of Youth, but was not recognized as a legitimate scientist, his rhetoric would fail. Indeed, he must be recognized by
two distinct audiences as legitimate: other scientists and the lay public.
Kaku's pedigree is a step in legitimating his presence in the intellectual
world. As stated previously, Kaku is appropriately credentialed, having
earned a BS from Harvard and PhD from the University of California,
Berkeley, has written graduate-level physics textbooks, including his 1999
text, *The Introduction to Superstrings and M-Theory*, and has published
over seventy peer-reviewed journal articles. He also clearly knows what
he is talking about. While his explanations are tailored, largely, for the

nonscientific audience, his discussions are peppered with language that reifies his street cred with other scientists and intellectuals. In an interview with *Scientific American*, he says about wormholes,

> We would get the wormhole by grabbing it from the vacuum because they're everywhere. We think that at very small distances, 10^{-33} centimeters, spacetime becomes foamy. The dominant structures at those quantum distances are probably wormholes, little bubbles, universes that pop into existence and then pop right back out of existence. Now if you could manipulate [the so-called] quantum foam, then you could go through one of these bubbles. And in Kip Thorne's original proposal for a time machine, he said that maybe we would obtain a wormhole by grabbing one of these bubbles and expanding it, stabilizing it with negative energy. (qtd. in Minkel, 2003, November 24)

Yet, he puts concerted effort toward making his rhetoric accessible to the lay and nonscientific audiences. I have provided a number of examples of this strategy, but in the same *Scientific American* interview, Kaku describes wormholes as time machines, offering,

> These time machines were traversable. Like an elevator connecting parallel universes, these solutions have an up button and a down button. Under certain conditions, you can go through them easily, just like in the movies. You can look through the looking glass and then come back. (Minkel, 2003, November 24)

In interviews with nonscientists, the host often introduces Kaku through his extensive credentials, a choice that sets up, from the beginning, his legitimacy as a scientist. Kaku then works to "disarm" the audience's perception of an erudite, obtuse scientist by weaving scientific topics with popular language and examples. In addition, his methodology is scientific. Kaku explains in the *Time* series, "The only way to study this is to do an experiment"—the rest of the program serves as his comprehensive guide to the universe of time and our place in it (Kaku, 2008, May 25). Science brings our dreams out of our collective subconscious into the reality of our mythic landscape and is recognized by its audiences as valuable, important to our future success, and part of "who we are" as Americans, acknowledging the rhetorical call to American mythos as a distinct reason for this success.

Like all of our public intellectual styles, Kaku works to be highly visible to both intellectual and lay audiences. For intellectual audiences, Kaku is widely known through his extensive publication record, laudatory teaching at the undergraduate and graduate levels, and his impressive pedigree. For lay audiences, the situation becomes trickier. Kaku, like all public intellectuals, must negotiate the line between overly scientific and overly vernacular. This chapter earlier describes Kaku's extensive media exposure, exposure that is one profitable strategy for reaching and convincing the lay public to have and to fund interest in science broadly. Seeing a scientist that does not look like scientist and seeing him on networks and cable shows we watch regularly, we see Kaku as a more ubiquitous, comfortable, and comforting presence in our lives. Our perception of television and radio is that it is available to everyone, making science appear far more democratic in Kaku's capable hands than it is in actuality. Few could achieve what Kaku has, but we can all benefit and begin to dream because of his down-to-earth approach to science through democratized media channels. In this way, Kaku truly engages and invites the majority of Americans to join him in his dreams and his quest for immortality, for a world without nuclear arsenals, for travel through time. And his enthusiasm convinces us it is possible. Where do we send the checks?

DIMENSIONS OF COMPARISON

Kaku is immensely fluid. Frankly, I am convinced that most people who watch Kaku on the Science channel or Discovery channel or CNN have literally no idea what he actually "does" for a living because he is so fluid. Kaku has held a traditional day job as university professor for more than thirty years and is now an endowed chair. His publication record is beyond comprehension for most scholars—more than ten books, over seventy journal publications, and countless hours spent on the university lecture circuit. He is author of six popular-science works and devotes a substantial amount of time and energy to media appearances with nonscientific hosts and audiences such that although not as ubiquitous as The Pundit, Kaku is easily recognizable by nonscientific audiences. Frankly, his shows are, for lack of a more complete word, cool. More than anything, that cool factor translates and makes Kaku highly fluid.

The second dimension of comparison is degree, which refers to a public intellectual's level of "intellectual-ness" versus his or her level of "public-ness." Kaku, like West, is a very balanced style. As degree is so closely correlated with fluidity, it comes as no surprise that Kaku's levels of "intellectual-ness" and "public-ness" are relatively equal. Without a hefty dose of perceived intellect, it is highly unlikely that we would see Kaku so often in mediated and public contexts. However, should he opt to don a lab coat and thick glasses, appear in laboratory settings, and speak in technical lingo, we could imagine his viewership would decline precipitously. Kaku cements his intellectual bona fides when he says about M-theory,

> Superstrings are in some sense not unique: there are other non-string theories which contain "super-symmetry," the key mathematical symmetry underlying superstrings. (Changing light into electrons and then into gravity is one of the rather astonishing tricks performed by supersymmetry, which is the symmetry which can exchange particles with half-integral spin, like electrons and quarks, with particles of integral spin, like photons, gravitons, and W-particles). (2008, August 18, para. 7)

He bolsters his public street cred by taking on topics like life on other planets. In an article "The Physics of Extraterrestrial Civilizations," Kaku describes,

> The SIM, in turn, will pave the way for the Terrestrial Planet Finder, to be launched late in the next decade, which should identify even more earth-like planets. It will scan the brightest 1,000 stars within 50 light years of the earth and will focus on the 50 to 100 brightest planetary systems. All this, in turn, will stimulate an active effort to determine if any of them harbor life, perhaps some with civilizations more advanced than ours. (2013, paras. 7, 8)

The third dimension is location, or where we "find" a public intellectual style. For Kaku, we might change this to *locations*, plural. First, we find Kaku in the classroom in his day job as professor of theoretical physics at the City College of New York. Perhaps, it is not shocking to find a theoretical physicist in the classroom or university laboratory, but for someone as visible as Kaku, it is important to remember that he is anchored in the academy, a strategy that buttresses his legitimacy among traditional intellectuals. Unlike most academic intellectuals, however, his rhetorical style enables him to transcend the ivory tower of academe and go public but retain a public perception of someone with immense intellectual prowess because of his known association with an established academic institution. Second, we find Kaku on the radio broadcasting his nationally syndicated science program, *Explorations in Science*, a show carried on more than 125 radio stations nationwide. Third, Kaku is located on television, largely in contexts where he is outside, among the people rather than in controlled studio conditions. In the *Time* series on the Science channel, Kaku is ubiquitous: He is in the park, he is at the beach, he is having aging tests conducted in a doctor's office, he examines a lab where they are "growing" the next generation of organs to transplant to enable human longevity, he does tai chi. Central to these appearances is that not only is he a-scientific but he is also almost exclusively public. He is literally modeling his worldview that dreams are for everyone and should be accessible to everyone. He is one of that "everyone."

The fourth aspect of comparison is how public intellectuals use media in their communication practices. Because scientists are accustomed to addressing lay audiences in order to achieve monetary support for their research, they should be more comfortable using popular media than most intellectuals. Kaku is certainly comfortable-seeming in most any mediated setting. He maintains the website bearing his name, he posts accessibly written scientific work as well as personal messages and links to useful sites. Television, though, is where Kaku really shines in Scientist style. Most people, let alone most intellectuals, are camera shy, but Kaku is natural in front of the camera, as if he simply is having a conversation with some friends about the future of the earth or time or the universe. He is featured on his own television programs on Science and Discovery and on other people's programs on CNN, MSNBC, NBC, ABC, PBS, Fox, Al Jazeera, and CBS. More than any intellectual in this study, Kaku is the most likely to be found televised. Radio has long been the people's medium, and Kaku makes excellent use of it, appearing weekly in *Science Fantastic*. Perhaps more significant, Kaku is on Facebook with links to highlights of both his televised and radio broadcasts. In other words, Kaku is interactive. We might imagine this level of interaction with audiences is seminal to Scientist style precisely because The Scientist is accustomed to making a public case for his or her work. The Scientist's media choices reflect the same strategy of his or her rhetoric—accessibility and an openness to the possibility of dreams. Being interactive allows The Scientist more personal access to achieve audience buy-in to those dreams. Of course, Kaku long ago mastered more "intellectual" media like journal articles and books. As mentioned, Kaku has written scholarly topical books, for instance, *Quantum Field Theory: A Modern Introduction* and *Introduction to Superstring and M-Theory*, as well as popular science books, such as, *Parallel Worlds* and *Physics of the Impossible*. As well, he has authored over seventy scholarly articles in journals, such as, *Physical Review* and *Nuclear Physics.* Intuitively Kaku comprehends the necessity of active publishing in his field while pursuing media appearances on a much-broader range of scientific topics via media that are more accessible to lay publics.

Resources may encompass finances, training, credentials, media access, and opportunity. One of the largest science organizations in the United States, the National Science Foundation, with a fiscal year 2014 budget of $7.6 billion, "has the latitude to support emerging fields, high-risk ideas, interdisciplinary collaborations and research that," as the foundation's website states, "pushes—and even transforms—the very frontiers of knowledge" (2013, para. 4). Indeed, NSF's budget page has a press-release section dedicated to publicizing the dreamy projects the foundation funds, such as, cybersecurity and maintaining clean and healthy oceans. Of course, Kaku is not the National Science Foundation, but no other public intellectual of study has access to resources that even come close to those provided by this one organization. The Scientist is eligible for enormous financial resources. We might imagine that Kaku's personal take is higher than most, given his high-profile media presence. And because he is so exceptionally gifted at popularizing science, he has access to opportunities that others may lack. Finally, his training and credentials are impeccable: BS summa cum laude from Harvard and PhD from the University of California, Berkeley; lectureship at Princeton; endowed chair and full professor at the City College of New York and the Graduate Center of the City University of New York.

As President Barack Obama noted on November 23, 2009, in an address to the National Academy of Sciences, "The key to meeting these challenges—to improving our health and well-being, to harnessing clean energy, to protecting our security, and succeeding in the global economy—will be reaffirming and strengthening America's role as the world's engine of scientific discovery and technological innovation" (2009, November 23). In sum, The Scientist employs a rhetoric of dreams to drive a culture-centered, rather than time- or era-centered, audience to dream along with him and support his work trajectory. In the American case of Michio Kaku, he speaks to our cultural mythology of democracy, determination, destiny, leadership, and being the first and the best to win financial and mediated resources to further exploration and research. And we buy it because it sounds very cool, and it speaks to us on a personal level because we are individually invested in larger cultural dreams. The Scientist's style takes us all on a ride toward the awesome, and we will pay big bucks to stay on.

CONCLUSION: STYLE, THE PUBLIC SPHERE, AND A CALL TO ACTION

This book is dedicated to investigating the potential of style as a rhetorical frame for intellectual engagement in the public sphere. As such, the six public intellectual rhetorical styles presented here represent "point[s] of connection between intention and effect, an aspect of social action" (Miller, 1984, p. 153). And at different times and in different cultural milieus, different rhetorical styles emerge as particularly relevant, powerful, and persuasive. Such is the case with the first five styles I have detailed here: The Prophet, The Guru, The Sustainer, The Pundit, and The Narrator. The Prophet is called by a higher power at a time of crisis to judge sinners in the community and outline a path to redemption. The Guru is the teacher who gains a following of disciples and leads them to enlightenment. The Sustainer innovates products and processes that sustain natural, social, and political environments. The Pundit is a subject expert who discusses the issues of the day in a more superficial way via the mass media. The Narrator weaves experience with context, creating relationships between event and communities and offering a form of evidence that flies below the radar in order to provide access to information.

The sixth style is distinct in that it is not constrained by the same boundaries of time that limit the future efficacy of The Prophet, The Guru, The Sustainer, The Pundit, and The Narrator. Instead, The Scientist harnesses the American mythic landscape to secure buy-in to bring dreams to life through scientific experimentation and engineering. It is the difference between focusing on the disease du jour and articulating a path to the eradication of disease forever. The strength of Scientist style is that it eschews the particular in favor of the general—in other words, instead of getting bogged down in time-specific problem solving, The

Scientist rhetorically constructs his or her project as one that answers questions that have plagued humankind since the beginning: a quest for more time; a desire to know what is "out there" whether on land, in the water, or in space; a cure for physical illness; a way to be superhuman; a chance to read God's mind. In this final chapter, I compare the styles using the five dimensions outlined for each style: fluidity, degree, location, media, and resources. More critical, I try to begin to address issues of particular concern for this stylistic intervention.

A STYLISTIC COMPARISON OF THE PUBLIC INTELLECTUAL

A larger comparison across all six public intellectual styles provides sev eral important benefits. First, it offers a lexicon for those of us interested in rhetorical style to use in grappling with issues where style is central or peripheral to understanding other constructs. Second, while style has been studied in fields from fashion to literature, the concept of rhetorical style as applied to social and political issues is relatively young (Hariman, 1995). Because we are in the early stages of discerning how style "fits" into contemporary rhetorical studies, the comparison is particularly valuable as a basis for theoretical development. Finally, the categories of public intellectual rhetorical style remain extendable. New sociopolitical situations will call forth different styles yet undetermined, and styles that transcend those boundaries may be discovered and articulated in future studies. As mentioned at the start of this book and as readers have, no doubt, already discerned, this is an inductive project. Because each of these styles is embodied by a single individual, I invite others to help think through, bolster, extend, challenge, reframe, hybridize, and/or amend the specific styles highlighted. I hope this book begins that conversation.

Fluidity

Fluidity accounts for a public intellectual's ability to move between the "worlds" of intellectual and public. What fluidity really gets at is a public intellectual's rhetorical style and its capacity to appeal to both intellectual and public "worlds." It highlights adaptability. Recall that the history of the prophetic tradition requires the prophet to live a somewhat lonely existence in order to be perceived as authentically called when offering judgment on a nation. Thus, the traditional prophet's fluidity is limited by his or her social isolation. The prophetic public intellectual, though, cannot be isolated; otherwise, he or she would not qualify as a *public* in-tellectual. In other words, the public intellectual Prophet is less isolated than exotic—he or she does not "descend from the mountain" regularly, but when he or she does, we should expect tremendous news. So although Cornel West's prophetic style is highly fluid, he is less of an anomaly for the contemporary iteration of the style than we might assume. I would categorize The Prophet's fluidity as high for public intellectuals.

The Sustainer is tremendously fluid as a public intellectual rhetorical style, and William McDonough is an apt example of this level of fluidity. The Sustainer must be accepted as an intellectual in order to be innovative enough to create and maintain the products and processes that sustain the natural, social, and political environments of which The Sustainer is a part. The Sustainer must also be accepted by the public because that is where the ideas of sustainability are played out and where the effects are felt. The Guru, like The Sustainer, is a highly fluid public intellectual style for the same major reason: He or she must appear the "master" of two worlds. As The Guru exemplifies the both/and through his or her teaching or disciples, a high degree of fluidity is required to achieve this style. The Pundit is the least fluid public intellectual rhetorical style. Again, though, this is not to say that Pundits are not intellectuals—they certainly can be. It is to say that because of their absolute reliance on the mass media, particularly television, they are not embraced by the intellectual community to the same degree and, therefore, do not move particularly fluidly between worlds. The Narrator is overtly fluid, moving in public view between experts to those experiencing the event to the broader public. Held in esteem by journalists, experts connected to the issue or event, and the audience to which he or she tells the story, The Narrator moves easily among worlds. The Scientist is decidedly fluid. Working to reveal only as much "intellectual" as he or she must, The Scientist largely conceals credentials to blend more seamlessly with public audiences in order to couch personal, scientific goals in the "we" language of broader cultural aims. Public intellectuals successful in this style must hint at their level of expertise to remain relevant authorities but are sort of rhetorical CIA operatives in that few audience members will actually know their intellectual, secret identities. The Scientist is the Jason Bourne of public intellectual rhetorical styles.

This comparison of fluidity of public intellectual rhetorical styles indicates two main things. First, and not surprising, some level of fluidity is required of a public intellectual. Generally, this level is average to high. Certainly, if an intellectual is to "go public" and, therefore, avoid the failure of rhetoric that keeps most intellectuals out of the public sphere, we should expect that intellectual to be moderately to highly fluid. Second, a higher degree of fluidity is required for the kinds of public intellectual rhetorical styles we should hope to see. The kind of deliberation we should try to instigate and invigorate in the public sphere requires a keen understanding of issues, a body of knowledge, and a willingness to slow down and tease out ideas, grappling with the entailments of political and social problems and their solutions. Certainly, our communities and our society get much-greater proverbial bang for the buck if this deliberation and interaction occurs in public—we must draw people out of the social and political isolation the academy fosters and through a renewed attunement to style, get intellectuals into the collective mix. Intellectuals with higher degrees of fluidity are by definition more adept agents in reclaiming engagement with the public sphere.

Degree

Degree is very closely associated to fluidity and encompasses a public intellectual style's degree of "publicness" and "intellectualness." So, while fluidity explains a public intellectual's *adaptability* between public and intellectual worlds, degree emphasizes how much *time* and *space* the public intellectual occupies in either realm. The Prophet is both highly public and highly intellectual, but the degree of each is larger influenced by the needs The Prophet perceives in a discrete kairotic moment. In other words, Cornel West, like all Prophet public intellectuals, is more "public" than "intellectual" in times of crisis, like the moment in which we find ourselves currently. So, as the moment calls for judgment and a path to redemption, The Prophet goes "public." For The Prophet, degree is related entirely to timing. Sustainers demonstrate a greater degree of "publicness" as part of their job—indeed, their role is to take sustainable philosophies and processes into the mainstream, thus requiring a more public posture than an intellectual one. Again, this is not to say that Sustainers are less intelligent or capable in terms of gray matter; rather, it is to say that Sustainers take their intelligence to the streets.

The Guru, on the other hand, is more intellectual than public. It is true that The Guru must be public to acquire followers or disciples and to teach those individuals the way to enlightenment. However, the more critical aspect to Guru public intellectual style is to be perceived not as *a* teacher but as *the* teacher. It is imperative that the Guru be seen as one having uncommon and somewhat unattainable wisdom—if everyone could do it, we would not need the Guru. Therefore, a higher degree of "intellectualness" is a mark of Guru style. Conversely, The Pundit is one who performs a high degree of "publicness." Like The Sustainer, a high degree of "publicness" does not mean The Pundit is lacking intellectual capacity, but it does mean The Pundit must always be available and easily accessible through the mass media. The Pundit must have enough of a degree of "intellectualness" to make informed commentary on the issues of the day, but predominantly, his or her degree of "publicness" is significantly more obvious. The Narrator, like The Pundit, is more public than intellectual given the demands of the job. The distinction between Narrator and Pundit is critical, though—The Narrator is perceived as more intellectual than The Pundit because he or she takes time away to research, to experience, to think. The Scientist is quite balanced between "intellectualness" and "publicness." Scientists, like Gurus, must have a substantial body of work to reference. Few, limited by available time or aptitude or both, can reach the intellectual heights of Scientists. Yet, successful Scientists know to code their rhetoric such that intellectual audiences recognize "one of their own," whereas public audiences understand they are dealing with an expert but one that seems organic, sharing the public's terroir.

In terms of what we might take from this six-way comparison, the fact that there are relatively equal numbers of "intellectualness" (Prophet, Guru) and "publicness" (Sustainer, Pundit, Narrator) among the styles, as well as one dead center (Scientist), it becomes clear that balance is crucial to public intellectual style. We can see the need for balance both at the individual and aggregate levels. At an individual level, balance must be in place for a rhetorical style to even qualify as belonging to public intellectual genre. At the aggregate level, it is important to note that our contemporary moment calls for a balance of higher-degree "public" rhetorical styles and higher-degree "intellectual" rhetorical styles. This larger picture highlights again the importance of bringing intellectual endeavor into public life and injecting public ideals into intellectual pursuits. Most critical, though, this idea of balance points to rhetorically sensitive styles across the board. Different kairotic moments in the public sphere call for different degrees of "intellectual" and "public" response—it is not an a priori rule that every sociopolitical climate requires a balance of styles, but, overall, a balance is available, and the public intellectuals who rise at any given time are the ones with the right degrees of intellectual and public. More than balanced, though, successful public intellectual rhetorical styles feel natural, organic, even homegrown when public intellectuals ardently believe that they are foremost a member of society more broadly—not a society but the society. In other words, the styles that flourish and thrive are inclusive, not exclusive, inviting, not discriminating, and open, not closed.

Location

Location refers to the physical places and rhetorical spaces we might find certain public intellectual styles. Cornel West as The Prophet can be located in many places. On the "intellectual" side, he is found in the classroom at Princeton University and in print in over twenty books. On the "public" side, he can be seen leading demonstrations, at political campaign events for candidates, such as, the Reverend Al Sharpton, and on mass media like radio and film. The Sustainer, on the other hand, is seen predominantly in the community. Part of The Sustainer's job is to embed him- or herself in the community such that he or she is perceived as something of a local. In turn, The Sustainer can be found in the local community. For instance, McDonough learns the strengths and weaknesses of a community in which he is set to do a project. He then capitalizes on those strengths to create sustainable economic, social, and natural resources, thereby reducing or eradicating the weaknesses. But, he does so on a community-by-community basis such that, each time, he achieves a sense of the local for that community.

The Guru's job is to teach and practice an otherworldly wisdom to a group of followers, fostering and facilitating a relationship of intimacy. Therefore, wherever we find The Guru engaged in either intellectual or public activities, he or she must make that location *feel* intimate, even if it is a television set as Dr. Deepak Chopra sometimes uses. The Pundit is found predominantly on television and sometimes online, but always the Pundit is located somewhere "mass." Although Paul Begala has, and has had, a number of nonmediated day jobs, we see him only in his capacity as commentator in mediated settings. The Pundit is always in view when we turn on our televisions or computers. Like The Pundit, The Narrator is generally in public view, but the backdrop of the story is dynamic rather than static. So, while we see Begala in CNN's studios, we see Christiane Amanpour and her fellow Narrators wherever the story takes them—the street corner in Cairo, the refugee camp in Bosnia, the hospital in Syria, the desk in New York.

The Scientist is located equally in "intellectual" and "public" spaces. Certainly, we expect Michio Kaku to be an expert, and that level of expertise requires research, lab work, and reflection afforded the professional intellectual—after all, Kaku is an academic. Yet, like his rhetoric, Kaku is careful not to be seen by the public in his own office or his own lab. He may interview other scientists, but it is always on their turf, not his. Wisely, Scientists recognize their work is intimidating to most of the public; even intellectuals in other fields are somewhat unsettled by their scientist peers (or maybe it is just that I feel daunted by the magnitude and objects of their work so I assume others are as well). In order to remove the anxiety provoked by Scientists' "intellectual" surroundings, Kaku works hard to be physically present in neutral or friendly places like the beach or the park when he is on camera. He also has an accessibly written website and Facebook pages for social networking, hardly unapproachable spaces for interaction.

I think the most important element to note in this comparison of the location of certain public intellectual styles is that regardless of their level of fluidity or degree, public intellectuals must *always* be located in the public in substantive ways. And style is the avenue for this location. A style that works with different intellectual and mass publics allows for public visibility. So, location is about rhetorical style—we find public intellectuals where they fit in. There is a danger, though, because the more "popular" the person seems, the more credibility that person has lost with intellectual audiences. Take the 2009 article from *The Atlantic*, "Hating on Malcolm Gladwell: Are Reviewers Just Jealous?" In it, Harvard psychology professor Steve Pinker comments that best-selling author, speaker, and journalist Malcolm Gladwell is a "brand" and a "dilettante" who lacks "technical grounding" and we should "watch out" because he is, essentially, full of it (qtd. in Hudson, 2009, para. 2). And, *The Nation*'s Maureen Tkacik is perplexingly angry about Gladwell's "irritating, un-relenting readability" (Tkacik, 2009). Now, it could be that these review-ers are right, that Malcolm Gladwell, prominent public intellectual and best-selling author of such staples as *The Tipping Point*, is untethered to an intellectual base and is only about generating buzz for himself. How-ever, it could also be that establishment intellectuals view landing on the *New York Times*' best-seller list with the disdain afforded a mention by *People.* There is a price for being too public and too popular, and it is one with which would-be and current public intellectuals must contend.

Media

All public intellectuals make use of some forms of media in order to reach a public, achieve further relevance or notoriety, discuss issues, or make connections. This category of comparison examines the differences in different public intellectuals' media usage. The Prophet may certainly use mass media to accuse the guilty and offer a path to redemption, and West does this through his radio, television, and film appearances. However, The Prophet, because of his or her higher degree of "intellectualness," relies more heavily on other media like books and other print or the perceived "high-end" mass media, such as, NPR. The Sustainer also must make calculated use of media to spread the philosophy of sustainability, but because this public intellectual is concerned predominantly with conservation, he or she is more likely to use "green" media. What this means is, we probably will not see a lot of The Sustainer in newspapers but online. Or, at the innovative extreme where McDonough resides, plastic polymer books that are waterproof, fireproof, do not degrade, and do not waste resources.

The Guru must rely on media to some degree because part of the vocation of The Guru is to build a following, and one way to accomplish this in our current moment is to use media. However, because the relationship between The Guru as the teacher and his or her students is one of spiritual intimacy, The Guru's media use must reflect this. Advents like personal weblogs are one way The Guru might accomplish this. The Guru can use mass media, but it has to be in an intimate way—Chopra does this even with a medium as mass as television. Think Ronald Reagan and the televised eulogy for the space shuttle *Challenger*. At the opposite end from intimacy is The Pundit's use of media—any public intellectual Pundit would need to be adroit in terms of media usage and the more "mass" the media, the better. Almost entirely, The Pundit is located on television. The Narrator lies somewhere in between The Guru and The Pundit. Narrators must be mediated in order to get the story out, but the way Amanpour tells a story retains a sense of intimacy—she creates a feeling of warmth in her interviews while asking penetrating questions. The Scientist runs the gamut of media choices. Kaku has to be published in traditional academic media, such as, peer-reviewed journals and books, in order to remain visible, relevant, and authoritative in that community. Yet, he seems profoundly comfortable on camera, on the radio, and online. His televised choices, though, are quite savvy—he appears on network television only in "news" settings; otherwise, we see him on presumably "smarter" channels like Science and Discovery. However, even those smarty-pants channels are available on basic cable.

For those of us who pay attention to a variety of media, it is no stretch to say that different media manage different impressions. Or, said another way, all media are not created (or received) equally. So, while all public intellectuals employ media, some media is perceived as more intellectually oriented than others: Print and "smart" programming, like NPR and PBS, are obvious examples. Other media are viewed as more "popular," and their corollary, more base: magazines, generic evening news, most online sources. Not surprising then, in comparing public intellectual rhetorical styles in terms of media, the more prosocial styles avail themselves of at least a balance of, if not more of, the "intellectual" variety media. And, in turn, the antisocial style draws on less-intellectual media, predominantly the television.

However, public intellectuals are not merely more or less mediated; rather, there are also certain media that are in a public intellectual's wheelhouse, and there are others that feel less natural. Some public intellectuals may be better suited for television, others may be far more proficient through books and other print media. For still others, it does not seem to make a difference what media are used. For instance, West is online, in print, and on radio, television, and even film. Yet, his choices are always seen as more "intellectual" even if he appears on television, and that is because he is careful about what kinds of shows he participates in—he is never going to make a guest appearance on a sitcom, but he might show up in an interview with Charlie Rose on PBS. Again, proficiency with media is important for all public intellectuals, but the choices they make are equally relevant.

Resources

The final category of comparison is the use of resources by our public intellectuals. Resources have traditionally meant money, but for this project, we are considering other kinds of resources: education, opportunities, media, and the like. The reason this category is important is largely definitional—what does it mean to be an intellectual, and what does it mean to go public? Traditional intellectuals may identify others as intellectual only by proper pedigree—that is, they have the requisite letters after their names. However, being a public intellectual is not entirely, or even at all, about pedigree. Traditional intellectuals may believe that writing on topics of relevance to the public "counts" as going public, even if the results are written only for academic peers. We find ourselves in an era where this kind of opting out is no longer desirable, let alone responsible. Intellectuals must engage in a public venue in a public vernacular. Resources are both about actual command of resources, such as, money, education, media, and the like, and public perception of those resources.

The Prophet certainly makes use of opportunities and media in order to do the job of judging and shining a light to redemption. Yet, we know a Prophet who looks like the elite that he or she judges would be treated as less authentic than a prophet who looks as if he or she is somewhat marginalized and on the level of those he or she judges as sinners. Thus, although The Prophet exercises resources, he or she cannot appear as if that is true.

The Sustainer is an interesting case in resource mobilization because the underlying philosophy of this style is to *put back* rather than take, and this applies to resources. Anything The Sustainer makes use of, he or she puts back into the cycle. So, when McDonough takes money for a job contract, he finds a way to apply the skills of the local community to a sustainable business or industry that puts money back into the community. Resources, for The Sustainer, are created, shared, and maintained indefinitely.

The Guru, as the master of two worlds, is also a master of resources. This teacher has twice the education most have—in Chopra's case, a traditional pedigree in the "logic" of the West and a spiritual pedigree in the philosophy of the East. By bringing two sets of resources together, The Guru acquires a following and teaches his or her brand of wisdom to the next generation.

The Pundit is also one to capitalize on resources, especially media and financial ones. This ability to employ (or exploit, in some people's opinion) resources for mass audiences is both the reason The Pundit is in business and the reason for traditional intellectuals' concern and possible sour grapes about The Pundit's fame. The Narrator, too, marshals resources intelligently—human resources in the form of interviewees and witnesses help The Narrator tell the story while financial and media resources get The Narrator to the story and to the audience.

The Scientist merits special attention in terms of resource utilization. For centuries, almost millennia, scientists have sought patrons to finance and trumpet their work. Even Galileo Galilei, poster person for science's martyrdom at the hands of the Church, found a trove of riches in patrons like the powerful Medici family (Hibbert, 1999). Today, the pot is much grander—the National Science Foundation alone operated with a budget of $7.6 billion in fiscal year 2014, and it is only one of many fund-granting agencies dedicated to scientific pursuits in the United States. However, it is not just financial resources The Scientist masters but opportunity and media publicity, as well. For instance, Kaku uses the most diverse set of media outlets of any public intellectual in this study, and as visibility begets opportunity, his ubiquity indicates seizing upon as many opportunities as possible to bring dreams to bear in real life.

Regardless of rhetorical style, all public intellectuals master and capitalize on resources, financial and otherwise. This ability is perhaps the greatest rift between traditional and public intellectuals and among styles of public intellectuals because ushering resources and applying them to public use relies entirely on one's ability to natively master a public rhetoric. Because traditional intellectuals tend toward the pedantic, specialized jargon of the expert or scholar, they are stylistically unable to manage resources to public advantage. This inability is a failure of rhetoric. Public intellectuals, though, have a successful rhetoric for just this kind of work and because of this physiological, psychological and sociological style, are able to make use of resources to their and, one hopes, the public's advantage. They understand the advantages that a rhetorical approach to style offers: "a consistent emphasis on the role that style plays in specific political situations as a more general mode of persuasion, publicity, controversy, advocacy, and the like" (Vivian, 2011, p. xiv).

THE ENTAILMENTS OF STYLE AS ENGAGEMENT

I wish turning would-be public intellectuals into actual ones were as simple as suggesting a shopping spree or becoming proficient with Facebook. But, this topic would not be getting a book-length treatment if it were an easy switch to flip. As Richard Reeves (2006) reminds us of Collini's work:

> [B]eing an intellectual has always meant having to shuttle between the "two poles" of specialised scholarly work ("the sea-wall of scholarly reputation") and public engagement ("confidently offloading opinions on those topics which the editors of features-pages deem to be the issues of the hour"). But with the former becoming more specialised and the latter more polemicised, the distance between them has become greater. Succeeding in both—necessary to fulfil the role of the intellectual7—has therefore become harder. (para. 17)

In essence, those of us who believe intellectuals should reclaim the critical project of engagement must grapple with the realities of the world we are trying to engage. Specifically, we need to attend to issues of temporality, political scrutiny, public relevance, moneyed interests, and tactics of public relations.

I have discussed how temporality relates to epoch, how historical, social, and political forces compel and constrain the elements and genres of style that can be most efficacious. And, I have located The Scientist not in terms of time but in terms of culture. This first sense of temporality demands further reflection. Many, if not all, of the situated public intellectual rhetorical styles I have identified have been around as far back as memory goes. Most obvious, the prophetic has a rich and storied tradition dating back well before Christ. Human beings have always been storytellers or *homo narrans*. Likely, we can trace The Guru back centuries if not millennia. In other words, we can see both long and short wavelengths at work. What situates the first five styles in the contemporary era, though, is frequency and amplitude. In the last several decades, our sense of crisis has become almost perpetual, or at least so frequent that it seems unending. In large part, this sense can be traced to a media system that escalates the minor to the catastrophic by giving equal voice to fringe theories in a bastardization of journalistic objectivity: Barack Obama eats spicy mustard on his burger, and anyone who eats spicy mustard on a burger is a communist! Teach for America is like the Hitler Youth! Equal marriage signals the End Times! So, frequency is accelerated. Simultaneously, the magnitude of crises we are experiencing today is extreme: a major recession and a slow recovery, a world economic crisis, corruption and scandal in trusted institutions, massive fractures in the health care system, serious problems in elementary, secondary, and higher education, seismic demography shifts, and so on. So, amplitude is greater. To respond to these interrelated changes, certain styles are called on because they *best* function to give perspective, to provide balance, and to frame proportion. As designer Coco Chanel said, "A style does not go out of style as long as it adapts itself to its period. When there is an incompatibility between the style and a certain state of mind, it is never the style that triumphs" (ThinkExist). In other eras less burdened by the kind of frequency and amplitude we are living now, these styles would still exist but would be less rhetorically powerful than they are in our current milieu. More simply, we will always have Prophets and Narrators and Gurus, but those logoi will do public intellectuals less good in the public domain.

In calling The Scientist atemporal, I also should note that atemporality is not necessarily always the province of science and certainly not the property of science exclusively. For instance, The Narrator is the latest iteration in the tradition of the wise person, the keeper of community and social wisdom and lore. Although women have always held this role within their communities or homes, the notion of women as public intellectuals operating in elite circles and commanding audiences of millions is new. Also, The Sustainer speaks of long-term solutions to problems, solutions that ought to transcend time and era. However, given how long scientists have operated in an intellectual-work-for-funding model, however, the rhetoric scientists have developed is immensely powerful and could be valuable in response to some exigencies. Science's stories about itself feature transcendence, the "universal" nature of science, and its timelessness (Lyne, 2001, 2005). I am not advocating abandoning the humanist project or that I do not recognize science as a rhetoric; rather, I am advocating seizing upon the stylistic authority and broad cultural relevance of The Scientist to respond to certain exigencies.

Temporality is not only about timing, it is also about time. And it is about how we spend our time and to what end. In the modern academe, particularly at research institutions, junior faculty members spend much of their time and energy on research and publication in order to meet the ever-more-daunting demands of tenure and promotion. At the same time, most young faculty pursue questions central to the health of their communities and their cultures (Cheney, 2008). However, if these same scholars pursued these identical questions outside of peer-reviewed journals and books, say on television or in their local newspapers, their work suddenly goes from exciting to insufficiently rigorous (Daniels, 1996). In turn, no one is tenured and promoted for being seen as unserious. So, an attitude of dismissal or even hostility to public vernaculars and popular outlets begets generations of intellectuals trained to isolate themselves and preach to their own choirs. In turn, isolation accelerates irrelevance to broader communities that need intellectual engagement to flourish. But, as a fellow traveler down the road to tenure and promotion, I cannot advise that junior faculty pretend the reality is not exactly what it is: hostile to the kind of project I am advocating. What can we do but play along?

First, let us not throw up our hands and walk away. There are spaces where a kind of reimagining is occurring, where time spent engaging the public on scholarly issues in an accessible way is being reframed not only as useful but as revolutionary. One such program is Intellectual Entrepreneurship (IE) at the University of Texas at Austin. Pioneered by Richard A. Cherwitz, professor of communication and of rhetoric and writing at the University of Texas, IE exists in response to the question: "How can we best harness and integrate the enormous intellectual assets of the university as a lever for social good?" (Cherwitz, 2010). Betty Sue Flowers, director of the Lyndon B. Johnson Presidential Library, notes of this guiding question, "It is always a question to be answered in the long term, with the benefit of hindsight, by thoughtful observers, from a high vantage point—something like a tower" (2004, para. 6). As James K. Galbraith, Lloyd M. Bentsen Chair in Government/Business Relations and professor of government, answers, "Ideas are not a scholar's property. They are not a commodity or a brand. They are, instead, the common understandings of a community. Ideas exist only to the extent that they are shared" (2004, p. 3).

The good news is, a number of prominent senior scholars are grappling with reframing what "counts" in terms of how we spend our time as intellectuals. The less good news is that changing our conception of temporality really means changing our culture. As IE founder Cherwitz explains, part of this is reframing service as a legitimate third pillar of tenure and promotion:

> As I see it, IE addresses this issue by making engagement a serious intellectual enterprise—by eliminating (not buying into) the traditional bifurcation of research and service—which by def [*sic*] makes engagement less serious. IE, if you will, collapses the service/teaching/research model. Engagement becomes an inherent part of being a scholar. This is a rhetorical move. (personal communication, December 3, 2010)

Part of the job for those of us in my home discipline, rhetoric, and for other scholars serious about legitimating engagement is to start making this move in our own disciplinary and institutional circles. Galbraith is encouraged by online publishing as a democratizing trend that will, eventually, "cause the breakdown of our ossified system" (2004). But stasis is not an easy thing to break down—change is difficult, and it is painful. Opening a dialogue through my own writing is the beginning of my personal response, but a movement is necessary to challenge the monopoly on intellectual thought by journals and books—they are important, critically important, but they cannot be the entirety of our contribution to society.

A different model is in use at Pacific Lutheran University in the School of Arts and Communication (SOAC). Because SOAC covers a variance of disciplines—art, theater, music, and communication—the division created a document to accompany tenure and promotion files that contextualizes and legitimates scholarly and intellectual endeavors outside of traditional spaces like peer-reviewed journals. It opens with the following rationale:

> This Professional Standards Committee addendum is intended to speak to the creative works and public scholarship routinely performed and presented by faculty members appointed to teach in the School of Arts and Communication at Pacific Lutheran University. Furthermore, this document is intended to explain how and why such scholarship and research endeavors undertaken by faculty in SOAC must be deemed fully equivalent to more conventional research such as publication of peer reviewed journal articles, presentations at academic conferences, book chapters, books, and other traditional forms of scholarship. Clear and cogent

explication of such validity of scholarship is necessary for purposes of understanding and fairly evaluating faculty performances,
particularly in instances including, but not limited to, cases of
promotion, tenure, and salary review. (School of Arts and Communication, 2008)

The document also articulates the significance of the growing movement
of public scholarship in the United States:

Public scholarship encourages academics to reach out to broader and
more generalized communities, thereby directly engaging scholars
in civic and public affairs. One important goal of public scholarship,
among many, is to reduce the degree to which academics are seen
as detached occupants of the proverbial "Ivory Tower." (School of
Arts and Communication, 2008, p. 2)

One of the best at Pacific Lutheran University in terms of public scholarship is Robert Marshall Wells, an associate professor of communication.
Wells received his PhD in American Studies from American University
and wrote a book based on his dissertation detailing a women's prison in
Washington State that allows incarcerated mothers to live with their children. Wells's work is grounded in Michel Foucault's notion of disciplining
the body and contributes to the broader field of prison studies. Yet, because Wells spent most of his professional life as a journalist and because
Pacific Lutheran recognizes public scholarship as valid toward tenure
and promotion, Wells created a documentary film of the women's prison,
called *A Hard Trade: Rebuilding Broken Lives.* that premiered at the Seat-
tle Public Library in 2009. Wells also helped establish the award-winning
MediaLab, an in-house consultancy in which students take a theoretically grounded approach in working with clients to create press releases,
newspaper articles, event plans, and a series of Emmy-nominated and
award-winning documentary films about issues ranging from nontra-
ditional family structures to compassion fatigue. Each film is screened
publicly and is accompanied by a panel discussion featuring academic
and community experts on the topic. In many institutions, though, the
significant, exciting, and groundbreaking work Wells is doing would be
seen as a waste of institutional time and resources—this connotation of
temporality not only is about how untenured, junior, or contingent faculty spend their time but it is also about how tenured and senior faculty
reward public scholarship, if at all.

Outside of time, political scrutiny can scare the pants off would-be public intellectuals. The 2010 election gave us a majority of freshman Republican congressional members who believe either that climate change is not actually occurring or that if it is occurring, it is not accelerated by human activities like the burning of fossil fuels (Douthut, 2010). Most certain, this political sentiment puts scientists in increasingly difficult rhetorical postures as they have to defend the overwhelming scientific data consensus on anthropogenic global warming (AGW) without resorting to calling sitting members of Congress idiots. Intellectuals are trained to reason, to conclude based on evidence, data, and rationality—but the state of our political environment is such that people believe less in truth and more in what comedian Stephen Colbert calls truthiness: "our human preference to follow our own intuition despite the presence of actual facts or evidence" (Science 2.0, 2008, para. 1).

As well, there are real dangers that accompany the kind of political scrutiny the public intellectual incurs. We do not have to look far. David Horowitz's campaign of censorship in the name of academic freedom targets intellectuals, virtually all politically left academics, who he believes are indoctrinating college students as some sort of militant leftist intelligentsia hell-bent on destroying America (Young, Battaglia, & Cloud, 2010). It does, unfortunately, go beyond campaigns. Material damages ranging from the professional, a denial of tenure, to the personal, death threats, are real (Gunn & Lucaites, 2010; Cloud, 2009). Such entailments cannot be bracketed as "fairly rare" or dismissed out of hand if we are serious about intellectual engagement. There is a reason few are brave enough to be Noam Chomsky or Howard Zinn.

To finesse an argument based on evidence that goes against the tide of political power in this country is once again to attend to style. In particular, the history of public cases made by scientists can provide a strategic model for intellectuals facing heated political scrutiny for their ideas. Like Kaku and others employing Scientist style, we can think about moving arguments up the ladder of abstraction from particular (global warming) to universal (America solves energy problem for the rest of humanity). What this does not mean is abandoning evidence or ethic; what it does mean is rethinking the vernacular and the frame of the argument as it is presented to the public. We also can attend to the power of stories as evidence that we see in Narrator style. Narratives, too, pull on deeply woven threads of cultural mythology and serve to ground arguments in a way more palatable to a culture wary of eggheads.

Related to enduring political scrutiny is seizing upon work that holds public relevance. George Cheney, professor of communication at Kent State University and critical organizational theorist, lauds:

> All of the doctoral students I'm working with these days are focused, first and foremost, on questions of social concern, broadly speaking, therefore allowing theories and methods to come to the service of responding to those often pressing questions about human and environmental well-being, sustainability, rights, conflict and hopes. (2008, p. 282)

Unsurprising, scholars are interested in topics of social and political concern. Yet, choice of topic is only the first parenthetical in the relevance equation. The second half of the equation is delivery. Galbraith explains,

> Communication outside the journal and the classroom is an art form. It obviously doesn't take much to go on some cable TV shout show. But the craft of a good Op-Ed, syndicated column, radio commentary, book review, policy essay or pamphlet must be learned and practiced. (2004, para. 10)

Generally, those of us with academic pedigrees including R1 institutions have never thought about, much less attempted, writing an op-ed, a radio commentary, or a pamphlet, largely because those outlets are perceived as a side show to the center ring of scholarly books and journals. Just as writing for peer-reviewed publication requires practice, writing for or speaking to a public audience demands rigor, research, and a more nuanced understanding of audience. And, again, an attention to style can enable that kind of work if we look to intellectuals who are active in public circles as models.

Being relevant is also about elements we dismiss out of hand as outside the purview of the "real" intellectual: fashion and popular culture. Anecdotally, there is an attitude in the academy that a concern for trends in fashion is the mark of a scholar who spends too much time away from the job of thinking and being serious. While I am not suggesting we all need to pick up the magazines in the grocery-store line in order to dress like Eva Longoria or Denzel Washington, it is imperative that intellectuals begin to pay attention to what they wear and the meanings those choices imply. Looking professorial is fine, so long as it is more Andre 3000 than Mr. Magoo. If you read the previous sentence and thought, "Who is Andre 3000?"

this naivety belies another challenge for intellectuals: Our social obsession with style also implores that intellectuals attend to popular culture. In a faculty book-club meeting I attended, we had a discussion about professors trying to "be cool" and what that might mean to us and to our students. One faculty participant, a math teacher who shall remain nameless, announced proudly, "I don't even own a TV. I have no idea who this Jon Stewart is. I live in the middle of nowhere on a nature preserve, and I heat my house by burning wood." Aside from his strange desire to re-create Henry David Thoreau's Walden years, the pride he takes in opting out of popular culture is the prevailing attitude in traditional intellectual circles. This sort of pride is a political sin because it means embracing irrelevance, even celebrating it. I responded to my colleague that I cannot be an effective guide for my students if I do not pay attention to the broader audience—that means I watch TV, I read grocery-store magazines, I even listen to Top 40 occasionally. If we want to connect with broader audiences, we might remember Kenneth Burke's construct of identification: "In being identified with 'B,' 'A' is substantially one with a person other than himself" (1969, pp. 20–21). If we are to be members of a broader community, we cannot eschew fashion and popular culture, because "identification is affirmed with earnestness precisely because there is division" (Burke, 1969, p. 22). We need to give each other room, and support, to be cool.

In the wake of the US Supreme Court's *Citizens United* ruling, much has been made of the hazardous influence of moneyed interests in our political life and discourse (Court, money, and politics, 2010, para. 10). And, as Cyndi Lauper sings to us, "Money, money changes everything" (Gray, 1984). While few of us are contemplating running for office and so are not spending inordinate amounts of time and energy kissing the proverbial rings of the chamber of commerce, our universities and colleges *are* increasingly corporatized in that proving one's worth has a literal, rather than figurative, price tag (Young, Battaglia, & Cloud, 2010). More and more frequently, hiring and even promotion decisions rely on an intellectual's ability to attract grant money in order to finance scholarly endeavors. Regardless of how dirty it might seem, money is part of the reality of the modern academe.

Part of the consideration of public intellectuals, then, is how to make their intellectual pursuits attractive to moneyed interests without the pressure to sell out to those interests. Even the perception of selling out diminishes the impact of the work. Returning to relevance, part of generating buzz about a topic is thinking about its connection to "hot" topics of social or political concern. Using one of the stylistic models from this book, let us imagine Cornel West wants to secure funding for a book on the role of the contemporary black church in politics. Our academic training encourages us to narrow the scope, narrow the potential, narrow, narrow, narrow (Hartelius & Cherwitz, 2010). The public intellectual knows to do the opposite—expand, expand, expand (Hikins, 2010). And he or she knows to connect to something au currant, such as, subverting legal restrictions and using the church to elect candidates. We need to know what our audience finds relevant, not just what other scholars on race and religion find relevant. In thinking like the broader audience member, we can begin to situate ourselves in that broader context. We gain empathy for that position. And empathy compels us to act.

Finally, would-be public intellectuals must understand and employ tactics of public relations. In a question-and-answer session with Michael Schudson, professor of journalism at Columbia University, I asked him how we could better connect our work to the public sphere, and his response was, "We need to be better at PR." The impetus in the academy is to let the work speak for itself, rather than speaking on behalf of the work. Yet, this tendency is part of what makes academic intellectuals appear profoundly isolated and less relevant to society. In publicizing the Intellectual Entrepreneurship program, Cherwitz started an op-ed series in the *Austin American Statesman*, has a Facebook group, sends out dozens of e-mails for public comment, and simultaneously publishes in prestigious journals like the *Quarterly Journal of Speech*. Wells employs students studying public relations and advertising to manage Pacific Lutheran University's MediaLab in terms of its constituent relations. Both of these effective public-relations strategies marries traditional and engaged scholarship and critique in order to bridge communities that do not see themselves as inherently connected. The work cannot just speak for itself—we must speak on behalf of the work.

A CALL TO ACTION

In summary, public intellectual rhetorical style has tremendous impact on the public sphere. It is also an innovative method for categorizing, comparing, and understanding a number of crucial sociopolitical phenomena. Let us move from a place where our work "suppress[es] our convictions, our enthusiasm, our anger, in the interest of achieving an impersonal, 'expert' distance and tone" (Blair, Brown, & Baxter, 1994, p. 383) to a via media, a middle road along which many citizens could walk.

Much of the scholarship on style is descriptive, and much of this book has been used to describe public intellectual styles at work in the public sphere. But this book is also prescriptive. I have used this real estate to write a tough love letter to my fellow academic intellectuals. I have encouraged all of us to reclaim engagement and even activism as intellectual projects and to go public with our endeavors. And I have tried to articulate fruitful vehicles for a public intellectual project. Ultimately, as David R. Seibold (2005) argues, "engagement is much more than the application of theories to real-world problems. Rather, engagement requires being immersed in the lives of real-world groups and organizations and involved in close work and learning with stakeholders" (p. 42). It means collapsing the dichotomies of us versus them and of style versus substance. And it means thinking about temporality, relevance, political scrutiny, moneyed interests, and public relations as these concerns relate to the viability of our work in the public sphere. I mean this book to start a conversation. I mean this book as a provocation. I mean this book as a call to action.

BIBLIOGRAPHY
INDEX

BIBLIOGRAPHY

Amanpour, C. (2011, February 3). Mubarak: If I resign today there will be chaos. *ABC News.* Retrieved from http://abcnews.go.com/International /egypt-abc-news-christiane-amanpour-exclusive-interview-president /story?id=12833673

Amanpour, C. (2011, February 28). "My people love me": Moammar Gadhafi denies demonstrations against him anywhere in Libya. *ABCNews.* Retrieved from http://abcnews.go.com/International/christiane-amanpour -interviews-libyas-moammar-gadhafi/story?id=13019942

Amanpour, C. (2011, July 23). July 2011. *Facebook.* Retrieved from https:// www.facebook.com/amanpourabc?rf=118487321569320

Amanpour, C. (2011, July 29). July 2011. *Facebook.* Retrieved from https:// www.facebook.com/amanpourabc?rf=118487321569320

Armour, S. (2005, February 17). Pregnant women report growing discrimination. *USA Today.* Retrieved from http://usatoday30.usatoday.com/money /workplace/2005-02-16-pregnancy-bias-usat_x.htm

Asen, R. B., & Brouwer, D. C. (2001). Introduction: Reconfigurations of the public sphere. In R. Asen & D. Brouwer (Eds.), *Counterpublics and the state* (pp. 1–32). Albany: State University of New York Press.

Associated Press. (2002, January 10). Cornel West. Retrieved from http:// archives.cnn.com /2002/fyi/teachers.ednews/01/10/west.harvard.ap/

Baker, P. (2006, April 2). The President as average joe. *The Washington Post.* Retrieved from http://www.washingtonpost.com/wpdyn/content/article /2006/04/01/AR2006040101004.html

Barge, K. J., Simpson, J. L., & Shockley-Zalabak, P. (2008). Introduction: Toward purposeful and practical models of engaged scholarship. *Journal of Applied Communication Research, 36*(3), 243–244.

Barge, K. J., Simpson, J. L., & Shockley-Zalabak, P., Eds. (2008). Special issue on engaged scholarship. *Journal of Applied Communication Research, 36*(3), 243–350.

Bawer, B. (1998). Public intellectuals: An endangered species? *Chronicle of Higher Education, 44,* A72.

Begala, P. (2004, October 8). Paul Begala's debate log: Round 3. Retrieved from http://www.cnn.com/2004/ALLPOLITICS/blog/10/08/begala.blog/

Begala, P. (2004, October 13). Paul Begala's debate log: Round 4. Retrieved from http://www.cnn. com/2004/ALLPOLITICS/blog/10/13/begala.blog/

Begala, P. (2006, February 16). VP Cheney: You're lucky those reporters aren't hunters. *Democratic Underground.* Retrieved from http://www. democraticunderground.com/discuss/duboard.php?az=view_all&address =103x190780

Begala, P. (2013, March 11). A prayer for the Catholic Church. *The Daily Beast.* Retrieved from http://www.thedailybeast.com/newsweek/2013/03/11 /paul-begala-a-prayer-for-the-catholic-church.html

Begala, P. (2013, July 17). This is important: NYTs reports that NYers health insur premiums in individual mkt to fall 50% or more under Obamacare. [Twitter post]. Retrieved from https://twitter.com/PaulBegala

Begala, P. (2013, August 6). Prayers with Pres George W Bush & family after reported heart stent surgery. Politics stops at the pericardium. [Twitter post]. Retrieved from https://twitter.com/PaulBegala

Bendroth, M. L. (1996). *Fundamentalism and gender 1875–present.* New Haven, CT: Yale University Press.

Bérubé, M. (1996). Cultural criticism and the politics of selling out. *The Electronic Book Review.* Retrieved from http://www.altx.com/ebr/ebr2 /2berube.htm

Bérubé, M. (1998). *Employment of English: Theory, jobs and the future of literary studies.* New York: New York University Press.

Biography. (2011). Christiane Amanpour. *A+E Television Networks.* Retrieved from http://www.biography.com/articles/Christiane-Amanpour -212140

Blair, C., Brown, J. R., & Baxter, L. A. (1994). Disciplining the Feminine. *Quarterly Journal of Speech, 80,* 383–409.

Bourdieu, P. (1974/1984). *Distinction: A social critique on the judgment of taste.* Cambridge, MA: Harvard University Press.

Bourdieu, P. (1977). *Outline of a theory of practice.* Cambridge, England: Cambridge University Press.

Bowersock, G. (1969). *Greek sophists in the Roman Empire.* New York, NY: Oxford University Press.

Boydston, J. (Ed.). (1990). *The collected works of John Dewey: The later works, 1925–1953.* Carbondale: Southern Illinois University Press.

Braun, S. (2008, September 28). Palin treads carefully between fundamental beliefs and public policy. *The Los Angeles Times.* Retrieved from http://www.latimes.com/news/politics/la-na-palinreligion28–2008sep28,0,3643718.story?track=rss

Brooks, P. (2006). Book review: Public intellectuals: An endangered species? *The Times Literary Supplement.* Retrieved from http://www.the-tls.co.uk/tls/public/tlssearch.do?querystring=peter+brooks+2006&sectionId=1809&p=tls

Brouwer, D. C., & Squires, C. R. (2003). Public intellectuals, public life, and the university. *Argumentation and Advocacy, 39,* 201–224.

Brummett, B. (2000). *Reading rhetorical theory.* Orlando, FL: Harcourt College.

Brummett, B. (2004). *Rhetorical homologies: Form, culture, experience.* Tuscaloosa: The University of Alabama Press.

Brummett, B. (2008). *A rhetoric of style.* Carbondale: Southern Illinois University Press.

Bruni, F. (2011, August 13). Adrift in Iowa: Tired rituals in tough times. *The New York Times.* Retrieved from http://www.nytimes.com/2011/08/14/opinion/sunday/Bruni-adrift-in-iowa-tired-rituals-in-tough-times.html?pagewanted=1

Burke, K. (1969). *A rhetoric of motives.* Berkeley: University of California Press.

Buroway, M. (2004). To advance sociology must not retreat. *Chronicle of Higher Education, 50*(49), p. B24.

Calhoun, C. (1992). Introduction: Habermas and the public sphere. In C. Calhoun (Ed.), *Habermas and the public sphere* (pp. 1–50). Boston: Massachusetts Institute of Technology Press.

California First Lady Maria Shriver's 2010 Women's Conference. (2010). Christiane Amanpour. Program. Sacramento, California.

Campbell, J. (1972). *The hero with a thousand faces.* Princeton, NJ: Princeton University Press.

Campbell, J. (1972, January 17). Time essay: The need for new myths. *Time,* pp. 1–5. Retrieved from http://www.time.com/time/magazine/article/0,9171,877650,00.html

Campbell, K. K. (1989). *Man cannot speak for her: A critical study of early feminist rhetoric, volume 1.* New York, NY: Greenwood Press.

Cantabridgia. (2009, July 20). Henry Louis Gates' arrest report now online. Retrieved from http://blogs.wickedlocal.com/cambridge/2009/07/20/henry-louis-gates-arrest-report-now-online/

Carter, J. E. (2006). *Our endangered values: America's moral crisis.* New York, NY: Simon & Schuster.

Chandio, R. (2011, August 8). Christiane Amanpour, August 2011 [Online comment]. *Facebook.* Retrieved from https://www.facebook.com/amanpourabc?rf=118487321569320

Checkoway, B. (2001). Renewing the civic mission of the American research university. *Journal of Higher Education, 72*, 125–153.

Cheney, G. (2008). Encountering the ethics of engaged scholarship. *Journal of Applied Communication Research, 36*(3), 281–288.

Cheney, G., Wilhelmsson, M., and Zorn, T. (2002). 10 Strategies for Engaged Scholarship. *Management Communication Quarterly, 16*, 92.

Cherwitz, R. A. (2001, December 3). Learning to be a citizen-scholar. *The Chronicle of Higher Education*. Retrieved from http://chronicle.com /jobs/2001/12/2001120302c.htm

Cherwitz, R. A. (2005). The challenge of creating engaged public universities. *Planning in High Education*. Retrieved from http://www.readbag.com /webspace-utexas-cherwitz-www-articles-challenge

Cherwitz, R. A. (2010, March 3). Creating engaged public research universities. *The Huffington Post*. Retrieved from http://www.huffingtonpost.com

Cherwitz, R. A., & Hartelius, E. J. (2007). Making a great engaged university requires rhetoric. In J. Burke (Ed.), *Fixing the fragmented public university: Decentralization with direction* (pp. 265–88). San Francisco, CA: Jossey-Bass.

Cherwitz, RA., & Hikins, J. W. (2010). The engaged university: Where rhetorical theory matters. *Journal of Applied Communication Research, 38*, 115–126.

Chomsky, N. (2010, December 17). Noam Chomsky. *Figure/Ground Communication*. Retrieved from http://figureground.ca/interviews/noam-chomsky/

Chopra Center for Wellbeing. (n.d.a). *The Chopra Center*. Retrieved from http://www.chopra.com/

Chopra Center for Wellbeing. (n.d.b). Ayurveda. *The Chopra Center*. Retrieved from http://www.chopra.com/our-services/ayurveda

Chopra Center for Wellbeing. (n.d.c). Biography on Deepak Chopra. *The Chopra Center*. Retrieved from http://www.chopra.com/about-us /deepak-chopra-md

Chopra Center for Wellbeing. (n.d.d). Primordial Sound Meditation. *The Chopra Center*. Retrieved from http://www.chopra.com/our-services /meditation/primordial-sound-meditation

Chopra Center for Wellbeing. (n.d.e). Seduction of spirit meditation retreat. *The Chopra Center*. Retrieved from http://www.chopra.com/about-us/ press-releases/tired-snow-sleet-and-stress-join-deepak-chopra-week-long -meditation-retreat

Chopra, D. (2000). *How to know God: The soul's journey into the mystery of mysteries*. New York, NY: Random House.

Chopra, D. (2006, September 25). The mind-body bridge. *The Huffington Post*. Retrieved from http://www.huffingtonpost.com/deepak-chopra /the-mindbody-bridge_b_30185.html

Chopra, D. (2009, October 9). Deepak Chopra and Dr. Michio Kaku discuss the future on Sirius XM satellite radio. *Dr. Michio Kaku.* Retrieved from http://mkaku.org/home/?p=690

Chopra, D. (2013, June 25). An open letter to skeptics. *The Huffington Post.* Retrieved from http://www.huffingtonpost.com/deepak-chopra /open-letter-to-skeptics_b_3493419.html

Chopra, D. (2013, August 12). Thinking outside of the (skull) box part 1. *The Huffington Post.* Retrieved from http://www.huffingtonpost.com /deepak-chopra/thinking-outside-the-skul_b_3743986.html

Chopra Foundation. (n.d.). About. *The Chopra Center.* Retrieved from http:// www.choprafoundation.org /about/about-the-chopra-foundation/

Cicero. (n.d.). De oratore. In B. Brummett (Ed.), *Reading rhetorical theory* (pp. 198–293). Orlando, FL: Harcourt Press.

Cloud, D. L. (2009). Gender, identity framing, and the rhetoric of the kill in conservative hate mail. *Communication and Cultural Critique, 2,* 457–479.

CNN. (n.d.). Paul Begala biography. *CNN.com.* Retrieved from http://www. cnn.com/CNN/anchors_reporters/ begala.paul.html

CNN. (2005, February 28).Transcripts: Hollywood's liberal party. *CNN.com.* Retrieved from http://transcripts.cnn.com/TRANSCRIPTS/0502/28/cf.01.html

Collini, S. (2006). *Absent minds: Intellectuals in Britain.* Oxford, England: Oxford University Press.

Conley, R. (1978). Logical hylomorphism and Aristotle's *konoi-topoi. Central States Speech Journal, 29,* 92–97.

Conrad, C. (2003). Setting the stage: Introduction to the special issue of the corporate meltdown. *Management Communication Quarterly, 17,* 5–19.

Cook, S. G. (1998–2013). Mothers in the faculty pipeline. *Women in Higher Education, 13,* 8. Retrieved from http://www.wihe.com/printArticle .jsp?id=18562

Cornille, C. (1991). *The guru in Indian Catholicism.* New York, NY: Peeters.

Court, money, and politics, The. (2010, April 19). *The New York Times.* Retrieved from http://www.nytimes.com/2010/04/20/opinion/20tue2.html

Dahl, R. A. (1985). *A preface to economic democracy.* Berkeley: University of California Press.

Dahl, R. A. (2007). *On political equality.* New Haven, CT: Yale University Press.

Daniels, J. (1996, April 1). A riposte to Michael Bérubé. *Electronic Book Review.* Retrieved from http://www.electronicbookreview.com/thread /criticalecologies/cyclical

Darsey, J. (1997). *The prophetic tradition and radical rhetoric in America.* New York: New York University Press.

Davies Friday Egili Ekpo. (2011, July 24). Christiane Amanpour, July 2011 [Online comment]. *Facebook.* Retrieved from https://www.facebook.com /amanpourabc?rf=118487321569320

Davis, D. (2009, July 16). Christiane Amanpour gets a high-fashion makeover. *Harper's Bazaar.* Retrieved from http://main.stylelist.com/2009/07/16 /christiane-amanpour-gets-a-high-fashion-makeover/

Dean, J. W. (2003, June 6). Is lying about the reason for a war an impeachable offense? *CNN.com.* Retrieved from http://www.cnn.com/2003 /LAW/06/06/findlaw.analysis.dean.wmd/

Deetz, S. (2008). Engagement as co-generative theorizing. *Journal of Applied Communication Research, 36*(3), 289–297.

Dewey, J. (1929). *Democracy and education.* New York, NY: Macmillan.

Dewey, J. (1935). *Liberalism and social action.* New York, NY: Putnam.

Douglas, M., & Isherwood, B. (1979). *The world of goods: Towards an anthropology of consumption.* London, England: Routledge.

Douthat, R. (2010, October 12). Why don't Republicans believe in climate change? *The New York Times.* Retrieved from http://douthat.blogs.nytimes .com/2010/10/12/why-dont-republicans-believe-in-climate-change/

Dow, B. J. (2004). Fixing feminism: Women's liberation and the rhetoric of televised documentary. *Quarterly Journal of Speech, 90,* 53–80.

Dow, B. J., & Tonn, M. B. (1993). "Feminine Style" and political judgment in the rhetoric of Ann Richards. *Quarterly Journal of Speech, 79*(3), 286–302.

Dowd, M. (2004, November 14). Slapping the other cheek. *The New York Times.* Retrieved from http://www.nytimes.com/2004/11/14/opinion /14dowd.html?_r=0

Duke University. (2006, June 23). Americans have fewer friends outside the family, Duke study shows. Retrieved from http://dukenews.duke .edu/2006/06/socialisolation.html

Durkheim, E. (1947). *The division of labor in society* (G. Simpson, Trans.). New York, NY: Free Press.

Dyson, M. E. (2003). The public obligations of intellectuals. *Chronicle of Higher Education,* pp. B11–12.

Dyson, M. E. (2005). Is Bill Cosby right? Or has the black middle class lost its mind? Retrieved from http://www.michaelericdyson.com/cosby

Dyson, M. E. (2011, June 14). Achievement gap; sentencing disparities; Lizz Wright. Retrieved from http://www.podcast-directory.co.uk/episodes /achievement-gap-sentencing-disparities-lizz-wright-15027837.html

Dzikowski, D. (2009). Style is a rhetoric—perhaps the rhetoric—for the 21st century. *Review of Communication, 9*(3), 293–295.

Eberly, R. A. (2000). *Citizen critics: Literary public spheres.* Urbana: University of Illinois Press.

Etzioni, A., & Bowditch, A. (2006). *Public intellectuals: An endangered species?* Lanham, MD: Rowman & Littlefield.

Ewen, S. (1999). *All consuming images: The politics of style in contemporary culture.* San Francisco, CA: Harper.

Featherstone, M. (1991). *Consumer culture & postmodernism.* Thousand Oaks, CA: Sage.

Fisher, W. (1979). Reaffirmation and subversion of the American dream. *Quarterly Journal of Speech, 59,* 160–67.

Fisher, W. (1984). Narration as a human communication paradigm: The case of public moral argument. *Communication Monographs, 51*(1), 1–22.

Fitzgerald, F. S. (1925). *The Great Gatsby.* New York, NY: Charles Scribner's Sons.

Flowers, B. S. (2004, August 23). Inside the ivory tower, but touching the world. *Austin American Statesman.* Retrieved from https://webspace .utexas.edu/cherwitz/www/ie/touching.html

Flynn, D. (2010, July 26). Scientists inch toward finding God particle. *Reuters.* Retrieved from http://www.reuters.com/article/idUSTRE66P4XP 20100726?feedType=RSS&feedName=scienceNews&utm_source

Foss, S. K., & Griffin, C. L. (1995). Beyond persuasion: A proposal for an invitational rhetoric. *Communication Monographs, 62*(1), 2–18.

Fraser, N. (1992). Rethinking the public sphere: A contribution to the critique of actually existing democracy. In C. Calhoun (Ed.), *Habermas and the public sphere* (pp. 109–142). Boston: MIT Press.

Gagliardi, C. C. (2011, August 8). Christiane Amanpour, August 2011 [Online comment]. *Facebook.* Retrieved from https://www.facebook.com /amanpourabc?rf=118487321569320

Gaiter, L. (2008, June 10). Getting whitey: Michelle Obama's secret negro agenda. *The Huffington Post.* Retrieved from http://www.huffingtonpost .com/leonce-gaiter/getting-whitey-michelle-o_b_106092.html

Galbraith, J. K. (2004, September 13). To be engaged, scholars must share their ideas. *Austin American Statesman.* Retrieved from https://webspace .utexas.edu/erwitz/www/ie/galbraith.html

Gamble, A. (2004). Public intellectuals and the public domain. *New Formations, 53.Lawrence & Wishart.* Retrieved from http://www.lwbooks.co.uk /journals/newformations/articles/53%20gamble.pdf

Georgetown University. (n.d.a). Paul Begala biography. *Georgetown Public Policy Institute.* Retrieved from http://explore.georgetown.edu/people /peb/?PageTemplateID=179

Georgetown University. (n.d.b). Course descriptions: Politics and the media. *Georgetown University.* Retrieved from https://www1.georgetown.edu /explore/courses/index.cfm?Action=View&CourseID=PPOL-564

Gitlin, T. (2000, December 8). The renaissance of anti-intellectualism. *The Chronicle of Higher Education.* http://chronicle.com/free/v47 /i15/15b00701.htm

Glenmary Research Center. (1990). Churches and church membership in the United States. *Glenmary Home Missioners.* Retrieved from http://www. glenmary.org/grc/

Gonzalez, R. (2001, December 13). Lynne Cheney–Joe Lieberman group puts out blacklist. *Common Dreams*. Retrieved from http://www.commondreams.org/views01/1213-05.htm

Goodall, H. L. (1996). *Divine signs: Connecting spirit to community*. Carbondale: Southern Illinois University Press.

Grabe, M. E., & Samson, L. (2011). Sexual cues emanating from the anchorette chair: Implications for perceived professionalism, fitness for beat, and memory for news. *Communication Research, 38*(4), 471–496.

Gramsci, A. (1971). *Selections from the prison notebooks*. New York, NY: International.

Gray, T. (1978). Money changes everything. Recorded by Cyndi Lauper. On *She's so unusual* [Record]. New York, NY: Portrait Records, 1984.

Greenpeace. (n.d.) Nuclear proliferation. *Greenpeace*. Retrieved from http://www.greenpeace.org/international/ campaigns/nuclear

Greg. (2008, October 7). Michio Kaku—impossible science. *Daily Grail*. Retrieved from http://www.dailygrail.com/features/michio-kaku-impossible-science

Griffin, S. M. (2005). Trust in government as a constitutional problem. Paper presented at the annual meeting of the American Political Science Association, Marriott Wardham Park, Omni Shoreham, Washington Hilton, Washington, DC. Retrieved from http://www.allacademic.com/meta/p41136_index.html

Gunn, J. (2004). Refitting fantasy: Psychoanalysis, subjectivity and talking to the dead. *Quarterly Journal of Speech, 90*(1), 1–23.

Gunn, J., & Lucaites, J. L. (2010). The contest of faculties: On discerning the politics of social engagement in the academy. *Quarterly Journal of Speech, 96*(4), 404–412.

Habermas, J. (1989). The public sphere: An encyclopedia article. In S. Bronner & D. Kellner (Eds.), *Critical theory and society: A reader* (pp. 136–144). New York, NY: Routledge.

Habermas, J. (1992). Further reflections on the public sphere. In C. Calhoun (Ed.), *Habermas and the public sphere* (pp. 421–461). Boston: MIT Press.

Habermas, J. (1998). *The structural transformation of the public sphere*. Cambridge, MA: The MIT Press.

Halliburton, D. (1997). John Dewey: A voice that still speaks to us. *Change, 29*, 24–29.

Hambisa, F. (2010, June 22). Christiane Amanpour, June 2010 [Online comment]. *Facebook*. Retrieved from https://www.facebook.com/amanpourabc?rf=118487321569320

Hariman, R. (1995). *Political style: The artistry of power*. Chicago: University of Chicago Press.

Harris-Lacewell, M. (2009, June 5). Commentary: Don't hold Obama to race agenda. *CNN.com*. Retrieved from http://www.cnn.com/2009/POLITICS /06/05/lacewell.race.agenda/

Hart, R. P. (1994). *Seducing America: How television charms the modern voter.* New York, NY: Oxford University Press.

Hartelius, E. J., & Cherwitz, R. A. (2010). The Dorothy doctrine of engaged scholarship: The rhetorical discipline "had it all along." *Quarterly Journal of Speech, 96*(4), 436–442.

Haskins, E. V. (2004). *Logos and power in Isocrates and Aristotle.* Columbia: The University of South Carolina Press.

Hawhee, D. (2004). *Bodily arts: Rhetoric and athletics in ancient Greece.* Austin: The University of Texas Press.

Hebdige, D. (1979). *Subculture: The meaning of style.* London, England: Methuen.

Heller, R., & Martin, D. (2001). Using a theoretical multimedia taxonomy framework. *Journal on Educational Resources in Computing, 1*, 1, article 6.

Hibbert, C. (1999). *The house of Medici: Its rise and fall.* New York, NY: Harper.

Hikins, J. W. (2010, July 8). Rhetoric and the human dimensions of disaster: An overlooked lesson from the gulf oil spill. *The Huffington Post.* Retrieved from http://www.huffingtonpost.com/james-w-hikins-phd/rhetoric-and -the-human-di_b_639958.html

Hofstader, R. (1966). *Anti-intellectualism in American life.* New York, NY: Vintage.

Horowitz, D. (2006). *The professors: The 101 most dangerous academics in America.* Washington, DC: Regnery.

Horowitz, D. (2006, November 8). Speech to Ball State University, Muncie, IN. *Students for Academic Freedom.* Retrieved from http://www.stu-dentsforacademicfreedom.org/news/2300/horowitz-attacked-with-pie -at-ball-state-university

Hudson, J. (2009, November 17). Hating on Malcolm Gladwell: Are reviewers just jealous? *The Atlantic Wire.* Retrieved from http://www. theatlanticwire.com/opinions/view/opinion/Hating-on-Malcolm-Gladwell -Are-Reviewers-Just-Jealous-1632

I Hate the Media. (2009, March 30). Fox News ratings are rising, so are its anchors' skirts. *I Hate the Media.* Retrieved from http://www.ihatethemedia .com/fox-news-anchor-babes-short-skirts-video-photo

Intellectual Entrepreneurship. (n.d.). *University of Texas at Austin.* Retrieved from https://webspace.utexas.edu/cherwitz/www/ie/#none

Jacoby, R. (1987). *The last intellectuals: American culture in the age of academe.* New York, NY: Basic Books.

Jacoby, R. (2001). Colleges and universities as citizens: Book review. *Journal of Higher Education, 72,* 247–252.

Jameson, F. (1982). Interview. *Diacritics, 12,* 75.

Jasinski, J. (2001). *Sourcebook on rhetoric: Key concepts in contemporary rhetorical studies.* New York, NY: Sage.

Kahn, S., and Lee, J. *Activism and Rhetoric: Theories and Contexts for Political Engagement.* New York, NY: Routledge, 2010.

Kaku, M. (1998). *Visions: How Science Will Revolutionize the 21st Century and Beyond.* New York, NY: Oxford University Press.

Kaku, M. (2008, May 25). Michio Kaku: Time travel, parallel universes, and reality. Retrieved from http://www.youtube.com/watch?v=RnkE2yQPw6s

Kaku, M. (2008, August 18). M-Theory: The Mother of all superstrings: An introduction to M-Theory. *Dr. Michio Kaku.* Retrieved from http://mkaku.org/home/?s=some+sense+not+unique&x=0&y=0

Kaku, M. (2010, March 15). Imagination: The rocket fuel of science. *Big Think.* Retrieved from http://bigthink.com/videos/imagination-the-rocket-fuel-of-science

Kaku, M. (2013). The physics of extraterrestrial civilizations: How advanced could they possibly be? *Dr. Michio Kaku.* Retrieved from http://mkaku.org/home/?page_id=246

Kalu, Q. E. (2010, February 17). Christiane Amanpour, February 2010 [Online comment]. *Facebook.* Retrieved from https://www.facebook.com/amanpourabc?rf=118487321569320

Karabell, Z. (1999, September 24). The uncertain value of training public intellectuals. *The Chronicle of Higher Education.* Retrieved from chronicle.com/weekly/v46/i05/05b00801.htm

Karwowski, M. (2006). Do we need intellectuals? *Contemporary Review.* Retrieved from http://findarticles.com/p/articles/mi_m2242/is_1682_288/ai_n16911320/

Kellogg School of Management. (n.d.). Course description: The soul of leadership. *Kellogg.* Retrieved from http://www.kellogg.northwestern.edu/execed/programs/soul.aspx

Kennedy, J. F. (1962, September 12). *We choose to go to the moon.* Speech presented at Rice University, Houston, Texas. Retrieved from http://er.jsc.nasa.gov/seh/ricetalk.htm

Kennedy School of Government, The. (2002, March 12). Christiane Amanpour of CNN wins Goldsmith career award. *Joan Shorenstein Center.* Retrieved from http://shorensteincenter.org/2002/03/christiane-amanpour-of-cnn-wins-goldsmith-career-award/

Kezar, A., & Rhoads, R. A. (2001). The dynamic tensions of service learning in higher education. *The Journal of Higher Education, 72,* 148–171.

Knickerbocker, B. (2011, September 17). Michele Bachmann doubles down on "Perrycare": Will it work? *Christian Science Monitor.* Retrieved from http://www.csmonitor.com/USA/Politics/The-Vote/2011/0917/Michele -Bachmann-doubles-down-on-Perrycare.-Will-it-work

Lacan, J. (1977). The function and field of speech and language in psychoanalysis. *Ecrits: A selection* (A. Sheridan, Trans.). London, England: Tavistock.

Lane, M. (2007, March). A British accent: The route to success in America. *BBC News Magazine.* Retrieved from http://www.speechschool.tv /research5.html

Lippi-Green, R. (1997). *English with an accent: Language, ideology, and discrimination in the United States.* New York, NY: Routledge.

Lister, R. (2010). *Alice Walker and* The Color Purple: *A reader's guide to essential criticism.* London, England: Palgrave Macmillan.

Lyne, J. (2001). Contours of intervention: How rhetoric matters to biomedicine. *Journal of Medical Humanities, 22,* 1, 3–13.

Lyne, J. (2005). Science, common sense, and the third culture. *Argumentation & Advocacy, 42,* 1, 38–42.

Maffesoli, M. (1996). *The time of the tribes: The decline of individualism in mass society.* London, England: Sage.

Martin, J. L., & Neal, A. D. (2001, November 11). *Defending civilization: How our universities are failing America and what can be done. Totse.com.* Retrieved from http://totse2.com/totse/en/politics/political_spew/162419.html

Mary Lincoln. (2011, July 24). Christiane Amanpour, July 2011 [Online comment]. *Facebook.* Retrieved from https://www.facebook.com /amanpourabc?rf=118487321569320

Mauss, M. (1973). Techniques of the body. In J. Crary & S. Kwinter (Eds.), *Incorporations* (pp. 454–476). New York, NY: Urzone.

McChesney, R. (2004). *The problem of the media: U.S. communication politics in the 21st century.* New York, NY: Monthly Review Press.

McDonough Braungart Design Chemistry. (2013). Retrieved from http:// www.mbdc.com

McDonough, W. (2013). Biography. http://www.mcdonough.com/biography/

McDonough, W., & Braungart, M. (2002). *Cradle to cradle: Remaking the way we make things.* New York, NY: North Point Press.

McGee, M. C. (n.d.). Isocrates. Retrieved from http://mcgees.net/fragments /essays/back%20burner/isocrate.htm

McGregor, J. (2006, June 12). William McDonough: Design for living. *Business Week.* Retrieved from http://www.businessweek.com/stories/2006-06-11 /william-mcdonough-design-for-living

McTaggart, D. (2010, April 29). Christiane Amanpour, April 2010 [Online comment]. *Facebook.* Retrieved from https://www.facebook.com/ amanpourabc?rf=118487321569320

Media Bistro. (2005, January 5). Nail in the coffin for Crossfire: Stay tuned. Retrieved from http://www.mediabistro.com/tvnewser/archive/2005_01_05_archive.asp

MediaLab. (n.d.). MediaLab: Connecting creative minds. *Pacific Lutheran University MediaLab.*Retrieved from http://www.plu.edu/~ml/index.html

Mehta, S., & Mishak, M. (2010, October 28). Whitman ends campaign by lashing out at media, Brown. *Los Angeles Times.* Retrieved from http://articles.latimes.com/2010/oct/28/local/la-me-1028-whitman-20101028

Miller, C. (1984). Genre as social action. *Quarterly Journal of Speech, 70,* 151–170.

Miller, J. (2011). Higgs Boson—the "God particle"? *Apologetics Press.* Retrieved from http://www.apologeticspress.org/APContent.aspx?category=12&article=3870&topic=336

Mills, C. W. (1944). On knowledge and power. In I. Horowitz (Ed.), *Power, politics and people: The collected essays of C. Wright Mills* (pp. 599–614). New York, NY: Oxford University Press.

Mills, C. W. (1963).The social role of the intellectual. In I. Horowitz (Ed.), *Power, politics and people: The collected essays of C. Wright Mills* (pp. 292–304). New York, NY: Oxford University Press.

Minkel, J. R. (2003, November 24). Borrowed time: Interview with Michio Kaku. *Scientific American.* Retrieved from http://www.scientificamerican.com/ article.cfm?id=borrowed-time-interview-w

Misra, J., Lundquist, J. H., Holmes, E., & Agiomavritis, S. (2011). The ivory ceiling of service work. *Academe, 97,* 1. Retrieved from http://www.aaup.org/article/ivory-ceiling-service-work#.UdxsQdco6ho

Mongabay. (n.d.). Amazon destruction: Why is the rainforest being destroyed in Brazil? *Mongabay.com.* Retrieved from http://rainforests.mongabay.com/amazon/amazon_destruction.html

Morrison, P. (2008, October 27). Wardrobe-gate: It's not just for the lower 48 anymore. *The Huffington Post.* Retrieved from http://www.huffingtonpost.com/patt-morrison/wardrobe-gate-its-not-jus_b_138236.html

National Oceanic and Atmosphere Administration. (n.d.a). Climate. Retrieved from http://www.ncdc.noaa.gov/oa/climate/globalwarming.html#Q1

National Oceanic and Atmospheric Administration. (n.d.b). United Nations Framework Convention on climate change. Retrieved from http://unfccc.int/essential_background/convention/background/items/1353.php

National Science Foundation. (2013). FY 2014 budget request. Retrieved from http://www.nsf.gov/about/budget/fy2014/

Negt, O., & Kluge, A. (1993). *Public sphere and experience.* Minneapolis: University of Minnesota Press.

Nichols, L. (2001, September 28). War of words: UT professor gets slammed by UT president for view on attacks. *Austin Chronicle*. Retrieved from http://www.austinchronicle.com/news/2001-09-28/83161/

Obama, B. (2009, November 23). Remarks by the President on the "Education To Innovate" campaign. *The White House*. Retrieved from http://www.whitehouse.gov/the-press-office/remarks-president-education-innovate-campaign

Oseloka Ekwuno. (2011, July 24). Christiane Amanpour, July 2011 [Online comment]. *Facebook*. Retrieved from https://www.facebook.com/amanpourabc?rf=118487321569320

Olson, C., & Olson, K. (2004). Beyond strategy: A reader-centered analysis of irony's dual persuasive uses." *Quarterly Journal of Speech, 90, 27*.

Parekh, B. (2000). *Hannah Arendt and the challenge of modernity: A phenomenology of human rights*. New York, NY: Routledge.

Parini, J. (2001, December 21). By their clothes ye shall know them. *The Chronicle of Higher Education*. Retrieved from http://chronicle.com/free/v48/i17/17b02401.htm

Paul Begala Quotes. (n.d.). *BrainyQuote*, 2001–13. Retrieved from http://www.brainyquote.com/quotes/authors/p/paul_begala.html

PBS. (2003). This far by faith. Retrieved from http://www.pbs.org/thisfarbyfaith/witnesses/cornel_west.html

Pearce, A. R., and L. C. Castro. (2004, November). The science of engineering and sustainability: A primer. *Center for Development Research (ZEF)*. Retrieved from www.zef.de/fileadmin/downloads/forum/.../2004_3b_Mensah_Castro.pdf

Pew Research Center. (2001, April 10). Faith-based funding backed but church-state doubts abound. *Pew Center for People and the Press*. Retrieved from http://people-press.org/reports/display.php3?PageID=113

Pew Research Center. (2003, November 5). The 2004 political landscape: Evenly divided and increasingly polarized. *Pew Center for People and the Press*. Retrieved from http://people-press.org/report/196/

Pitney, N. (2008, July 13). Barry Blitt defends his *New Yorker* cover art of Obama. *The Huffington Post*. Retrieved from http://www.huffingtonpost.com/2008/07/13/barry-blitt-addresses-his_n_112432.html

Posner, R. (2002). *Public intellectuals: A study of decline*. Cambridge, MA: Harvard University Press.

Postrel, V. (2003). *The substance of style*. New York, NY: Harper Collins.

Pragmatism Cybrary. (n.d.). Cornel West. *Pragmatism Cybrary*. Retrieved from http://www.pragmatism.org/library/west

Project targets sustainability. (2006, June 13). *China Daily. People's Daily Online*. Retrieved from http://english.people.com.cn/200606/13/eng20060613_273493.html

Putnam, R. (2000). *Bowling alone: The collapse and revival of American community*. New York, NY: Simon & Schuster.

Rahn, W. M., & John E. Transue. (1998). Social trust and value change: The decline of social capital in American youth 1976–1995. *Political Psychology, 19*(3), 545–565.

Reeves, R. (2003, July 7). New statesman. *New Statesman Ltd*, 1.

Reeves, R. (2006, June 1). The new intellectual, RSA Journal, June 2006. *Richard Reeves*. Retrieved from http://www.richard-reeves.com/pages /journalism/journalism_item.asp?journalismID=225

ReProduct. (2007, October 18). ReProduct Cradle to Cradle greeting cards. *ReProduct*. Retrieved from http://www.reproduct.net/index.cfm?fuseaction =trees.pageDetails&p=778-78-1223

Rhode, D. L. (2006). *In pursuit of knowledge: Scholars, status and the academic culture*. Palo Alto, CA: Stanford University Press.

Ringen, S. (2007, November 13). Review of the book *On Political Equality*, by Robert Dahl. *London Times Literary Supplement*, 38.

R. N. Fashion Figment. (n.d.). Retrieved from http://rnfashionfigment.com /rnfashionfigment/httpservices.php?f=what_is_styles&act=list

Roberts, D. (2008). Michelle Obama endures public scrutiny. *NPR*. Retrieved from http://www.npr.org/templates/story/story.php?storyId=91779977

Romano, C. (1999). The dirty little secret about publicity intellectuals. *The Chronicle of Higher Education, 19*, B4.

Rousseau, J. J. (1750). *Discourse on the arts and sciences*. Available from http:// ebooks.adelaide.edu.au/r/rousseau/jean_jacques/arts/

Rouvalis, C. (2006, September 5). Female news broadcasters criticize double standard. *Pittsburgh Post-Gazette*. Retrieved from http://www.post-gazette.com/ stories/ae/tv/female-news-broadcasters-criticize-double-standard-449090/

Schneider, A. (1999). Florida Atlantic U. seeks to mold a different kind of public intellectual. *The Chronicle of Higher Education, 46*, B7.

School of Arts & Communication. (2008). PLU professional standards document: Communication & theatre. *Pacific Lutheran University*. Retrieved from http://www.plu.edu/soac/documents/home.php

Schudson, M. (1992).Was there ever a public sphere? If so, when? Reflections on the American case. In C. Calhoun (Ed.), *Habermas and the public sphere* (pp. 143–163). Boston, MA: MIT Press.

Schudson, M. (1998). *The Good Citizen: A History of American Public Life*. New York, NY: The Free Press.

Schwarz, O. (2008). *Transformative Communication*. Leicester, England: Troubador.

Science 2.0. (2008, January 24). Stephen Colbert's 'truthiness' scientifically validated. *ION Publications*. Retrieved from http://www.science20.com/ news_releases/stephen_colberts_truthiness_scientifically_validated

Scott, J. (1994, August 9). Thinking out loud: The public intellectual is reborn. *The New York Times*, B1.

Seibold, D. R. (2005). Bridging theory and practice in organizational communication. In J. L. Simpson & P. Shockley-Zalabak (Eds.), *Engaging communication, transforming organizations: Scholarship of engagement in action* (pp. 13–44). Cresskill, NJ: Hampton Press.

Seigfried, C. H. (2002). John Dewey's pragmatist feminism. In C. Seigfried (Ed.), *Feminist interpretations of John Dewey* (pp. 47–77). University Park: Pennsylvania State University Press.

Sennett, R. (1977). *The fall of public man.* Berkeley: University of California Press.

Shakespeare. (n.d.). *The tragedy of Hamlet, Prince of Denmark. MIT.* Retrieved from http://shakespeare.mit.edu/hamlet/hamlet.5.1.html

Smith, D. (2006, March 22). The next big thing: Museum is the star of S.C. project. *The Charlotte Observer.* 4D.

Spazz. (2006, November 10). Indiana: Two Horowitz protestors arrested. *Portland Independent Media Center.* Retrieved from http://portland.indymedia.org/en/2006/11/349001.shtml

Steiner-Adair, C. (1988). Developing the voice of the wise woman: College students and bulimia. *Journal of College Student Psychotherapy, 3,* 151–165.

Stille, A. (2002, March 23). Think tank: Advocating tobacco, on the payroll of tobacco. *The New York Times*, p. B9.

Time. (2008). New York: BBC America.

ThinkExist. (n.d.). Coco Chanel quotes. Retrieved from http://thinkexist.com/quotation/a_style_does_not_go_out_of_style_as_long_as_it/326820.html

Third term: Why George Bush hearts John McCain. (n.d.) Reviewer ratings [web]. Retrieved from http://www.amazon.com/Third-Term-George-Hearts-McCain/dp/B008SM1HH2

Thomas, H. (2007).Watchdogs of democracy?: The waning Washington Press Corps and how it has failed the public. New York, NY: Scribner.

Tikkun Community. (n.d.). *Tikkun.* Retrieved from http://www.tikkun.org

Tkacik, M. (2009, November 23). Gladwell for dummies. *The Nation.* Retrieved from http://www.thenation.com/article/gladwell-dummies#

Turner, F. (2001, June 29). Letters to the editor: Public intellectuals of today and yesterday. *The Chronicle Review,* 17.

Union of Concerned Scientists, The. (2008, April 23). Hundreds of EPA scientists report political interference over the last five years. *Union of Concerned Scientists.* Retrieved from http://www.ucsusa.org/news/press_release/hundreds-of-epa-scientists-0112.html

United States Holocaust Memorial Museum. (n.d.). Preventing genocide: Eyewitness testimony. Retrieved from http://www.ushmm.org/genocide/take_action/gallery/portrait/amanpour

U.S. Census Bureau (2010). Women by the numbers. *Pearson Education.*
Retrieved from http://www.infoplease.com/spot/womencensus1.html

U.S. Electoral College. 2004 Presidential election popular vote totals (by
city). *U.S. Electoral College.* Retrieved from http://www.archives.gov
/federal-register/electoral-college/2004/popular_vote.html

Vivian, B. (2002). Style, rhetoric and postmodern culture. *Philosophy and
Rhetoric, 35*(3), 223–243.

Vivian, B. (2011). Preface: The problems and promises of rhetorical style. In
B. Brummett (Ed.), *The politics of style and the style of politics* (ix–xxiii).
Lexington, KY: Lexington Books.

Wallace, N. (2011, August 5). What Michele Bachmann learned from Sarah
Palin and Hillary Clinton. *Washington Post.* Retrieved from http://
articles.washingtonpost.com/2011-08-05/opinions/35270884_1_michele
-bachmann-sarah-palin-first-female-president

Warner, M. (1992). The mass public and the mass subject. In C. Calhoun
(Ed.), *Habermas and the public sphere* (pp. 377–401). Boston: MIT Press.

Warner, M. (2002). Publics and counterpublics. *Public Culture, 14,* 49–90.

Weaver, R. (1953/1985). *The ethics of rhetoric.* Mahwah, NJ: Lawrence Erlbaum
Associates.

West, C. (2004). *Democracy matters: Winning the fight against imperialism.*
New York, NY: Penguin Press.

West, C. (2004, May 26). Cornel West commentary: Cosby's comments. *National Public Radio.* Retrieved from http://www.npr.org/templates/story
/story.php?storyId=1910649

Wilgoren, J. (2005, November 8). Kansas school board approves controversial
science standards. *The New York Times.* Retrieved http://www.nytimes
.com/2005/11/08/national/08cnd-kansas.html?hp&ex=1131512400&en
=85eb4c40222ecd56&ei=5094&partner=homepage

William McDonough + Partners. (2013). Retrieved from http://www.
mcdonoughpartners.com/

Wilson, R. (2010, August 8). Professors: Hot at their own risk. *The Chronicle of Higher Education.* Retrieved from http://chronicle.com/article
/Professors-Hot-at-Their-Own/123822/

Wolfe, A. (2001). The calling of the public intellectual. *Chronicle of Higher
Education, 47,* B20.

Women's Conference, The. (2010). Program. Christiane Amanpour. Retrieved
from http://www.womensconference.org/christiane-amanpour/

Wooing of Amanpour, The. (1996, May 19). *Newsweek.* Retrieved from http://
www.thedailybeast.com/newsweek/1996/05/19/the-wooing-of-amanpour
.html

World Commission on Environment and Development. (1987). Our common future. *United Nations.* Retrieved from http://conspect.nl/pdf/Our_Common_Future-Brundtland_Report_1987.pdf

Wright, E. O., & Rogers, J. (2010). *American society: How it actually works.* New York, NY: W. W. Norton. Retrieved from http://www.ssc.wisc.edu/wright/ContemporaryAmericanSociety.htm

Yamagishi, T., & Yamagishi, M. (1994). Trust and commitment in the United States and Japan. *Motivation and Emotion, 19,* 129–166.

Yang, J. L. (2010, July 15). Companies pile up cash but remain hesitant to add jobs. *Washington Post.* Retrieved from http://www.washingtonpost.com/wp-dyn/content/article/2010/07/14/AR2010071405960.html

Yardley, J. (1987, October 11). Trapped in the ivory tower. *Washington Post,* X3.

Yardley, J. (2000, August 13). American statesman. *Washington Post,* X01.

Young, A. M. (2011). Quaffable, but uh . . . far from transcendent: Wine, style, and politics. In B. Brummett (Ed.), *The politics of style and the style of politics* (pp. 263–278). Lexington, KY: Lexington Books.

Young, A. M., Battaglia, A., & Cloud, D. L. (2010). (UN)Disciplining the scholar activist: Policing the boundaries of political engagement. *Quarterly Journal of Speech, 96*(4), 427–435.

INDEX

Anna M. Young is an associate professor of communication at Pacific Lutheran University. Her essays have appeared in *Quarterly Journal of Speech* and *KB Journal,* among others.